TEACHING in the KINDERGARTEN

With Emphasis on the What and the How to Teach

by

HELEN BARTELT HURD

Sioux Falls, South Dakota

THIRD EDITION

Burgess Publishing Company

426 South Sixth Street • Minneapolis, Minnesota 55415

2nd Printing 1966
3rd Printing 1967
4th Printing 1968

Foreword

Whenever kindergarten teachers get together to discuss their work they are concerned with many problems: How shall we know whether we have had a successful year in the kindergarten? What activities are suitable for children of this age? In what ways can these activities be varied so as to meet the needs of the children during the entire year? What should be included in a program for five-year-olds?

The beginning year in school is the foundation upon which the child builds his future. Guidance, therefore, during this habit-forming age is essential. We know that emotional, mental, and social habits start at an early age, so neglect is costly. These habits established and cultivated at this time will affect the child's whole life. The forming of good habits by the pupils is the aim of every kindergarten teacher.

To help the beginning teacher answer the many questions that arise and to provide the experienced teacher with some suggestions that may be new, this book has been prepared. The longer the author has taught, the more convinced she has become that a need for such a book exists. Contained in it are concrete suggestions for planning the kindergarten program, teaching procedures, sources for games and materials, and solutions of common problems.

The material has been compiled from experience the past twenty-five years in kindergarten work. . . As a student and demonstration teacher at the State College of Iowa, as a supervising teacher in the public schools of Sioux Falls, South Dakota, as an instructor in Kindergarten Education at Augustana College in Sioux Falls, South Dakota and, last but not least, as a mother of two daughters, the author has acquired a sympathetic understanding of children and their needs and of the problems of the teacher.

The author wishes to extend her thanks to the "Sioux Falls Argus Leader", and Hugill, Blatherwick, Fritzel and Kroeger, Sioux Falls, South Dakota, architects, for the photographs taken in and around Cleveland Elementary School, Sioux Falls, South Dakota. She also expresses her appreciation to Community Playthings, Rifton, New York, Creative Playthings, 5 University Place, New York 3, New York, R. H. Stone Products, P. O. Box 414, Detroit 31, Michigan, and Triangle School Service, 1401 "C" Avenue, Sioux Falls, South Dakota, for prints of materials and equipment for kindergarten rooms. Thanks to Scott, Foresman and Company, 433 East Erie Street, Chicago 11, Illinois, for permission to use examples of Gothic lettering.

Through the compilation of this book the author hopes to add her contribution in making the kindergarten a better place in which to live--both for the children and for the teacher.

H. B. H.

Table of Contents

Chapter 1

EQUIPMENT IN MOST KINDERGARTENS

Equipment That May Be Purchased for Kindergarten Rooms

Whether ordering for next year or merely cataloging, making an inventory of the equipment already on hand, or selecting new supplies, you should be aware of what constitutes the standard furnishings, equipment, and supplies for the modern kindergarten room.

A good kindergarten teacher is constantly trying to meet the physical needs of the five-year-old child and for this reason you should ask yourself what does it mean to provide for five and six-year-olds at school? The environment you provide for them is very important and the care with which you choose the equipment for them determines what learning will take place.

Since space is of the essence in most rooms, much of your equipment should be moveable and not fastened down.

KINDERGARTEN TABLES

A <u>Rectangular</u> <u>Table</u>* is used in many kindergarten rooms, as a table of this shape seems to encourage conversation among the children. The tables should be strong and sturdy, without drawers, and so they can be folded for easier storage and shipping. Some have hardwood tops with natural finish, others have plastic tops that can be easily washed and kept clean. These tables can be furnished in heights up to 26".

Wood top -- 24" x 48" ($24.50); (see Footnote)
Plastic top -- 24" x 48" ($29.95)

It is possible to provide for mobility in the kindergarten by using <u>Trolley</u> <u>Tables</u>*. These are especially nice if your floor space is limited. One table is always in use with the second one waiting to be pulled out when needed. The top table is one inch higher than the other and provides several sizes for different height children. These may be obtained in maple veneer plywood or birch grain plastic tops.

Wood top -- top table 30" x 60" ($35.50); bottom table 24" x 48" ($24.50)
Plastic top -- top table 30" x 60" ($45.95); bottom table 24" x 48" ($29.95)

---

*PRICE QUOTATIONS: Prices here in quoted were in effect at the time the manuscript was written. They are included here only to show relative value of the equipment mentioned.
**Creative playthings Inc., 5 University Place, New York 3, New York.

Vari-Shaped* stacking tables can be grouped together to form hexagonals, circles, horseshoes, squares and limitless other shapes. Heights of these tables can be changed by replacing different length legs. These light, sturdy tables can be stacked six to seven high. They lend themselves well to room rearrangement and also provide more free space for rhythms and games. They are available in plywood with maple veneer or plastic tops, in two colors, birch or grey-green. 21"x 48" for kindergarten groups.

Wood top -- 21"x 48" ($24.50)
Plastic top -- 21"x 48" ($29.95)

LIBRARY TABLES

Your library table should attract the attention of the children. To accomplish this, make it look different from the other tables in the room. It could be round, oblong, square, or of any irregular shape, and if it is to be an older used table it could be painted a bright color, or the top could be covered with a bright colored oil cloth or doily. The chairs around this table should likewise be attractive and inviting. A Stacking Half-round* table that comes either in maple veneer or birch grain or grey-green plastic top is attractive for use as a library table. A desired height is 22" but they can be purchased up to 26".

Wood top -- ($24.50)
Plastic top -- ($32.50)

For a more permanent reading center, a Round Table* 36", 42", or 48" in diameter meets a felt need. These tables come in any height up to 26". They are obtainable in natural birch finish, and are very attractive with the plastic top.

Wood top -- ($36.00)
Plastic top -- ($50.00)

A very modern version of the library table is the Hexagonal Table*. Six children can look at books without interference. The round tapered legs can be replaced with legs of various heights, allowing for usage in other rooms. It comes in birch grain, scratch proof, non-mar plastic tops or plywood tops with matched maple scratch-resistant veneers. These may be ordered in heights up to 26".

Wood top -- ($36.00)
Plastic top -- ($50.00)

About 40% of the tables should be 21" in height and 60% should be 22" in height.

*Creative Playthings Inc., 5 University Place, New York 3, New York.

KINDERGARTEN CHAIRS

The chair in most common use is one sturdily constructed and not too heavy. This chair is easy to handle and to carry about the room. From six to seven pounds seems to be the average weight. Each child should have a chair. About 40% of the chairs (height of seat) should be 11" with 60% being 12" in height.

If you have old chairs in your room that have to be used, sometimes a fresh coat of paint in bright colors make them seem more attractive and usable.

This <u>Kindergarten</u> <u>Chair</u>* is hygienic, comfortable, and durable with a double back support and a full saddle seat. It is available in seat depths of 12-12". The seat width is 13-1/2". ($6.45)

This sturdy <u>Curved</u> <u>Back</u> <u>Kinder-garten</u> <u>Chair</u>* is less expensive to buy. It is made of hardwood and comes in the natural finish. The seat size is 11 inches by 11 inches, 12 inches high. ($3.35)

<u>Streamlined</u> <u>Chairs</u>* in die-formed steel are modern in design and construction and could be used satisfactorily in the classroom. The scroll seat and back of this chair is of 5 and 7 ply maple or birch veneer. The strong steel frames are electrically fused into one unit making them very durable in the classroom. ($5.40)

4

This <u>Stacking</u> <u>Molded</u> <u>Plywood</u> <u>Chair</u>*
made out of finest maple veneers of-
fers a solution to crowded rooms.
It is light and airy and overcomes
heaviness. Finished in heat-treated
clear plastic with rubber cushion
glides to cut down the noise. Heights:
10"-12" ($7.95)

This <u>Envoy</u> <u>Chair</u>** is a modern
type that perfectly matches body
contours, flexes and settles with
weight distribution for genuine
comfort. Height: 11"-13"
($8.87)

NATURE MATERIAL

Much of your science material is all about you and is yours for the finding it. Many kindergarten teachers have a science table and they display
things that children bring from home such as: shells, stones, seeds, leaves,
cocoons, bird's nests, etc.

As science plays a prominent part in children's everyday life, we must
give them the kinds of play equipment which challenge curiosity and further
their interest in finding out the "why and how" of things about them.

This 30" x 30" x 15" high <u>Pet</u> <u>and</u> <u>Animal</u> <u>Cage</u>** has a hinged cover.
It can be used for cats, rabbits, guinea pigs, or visiting pets. The removable tray can be cleaned without disturbing the animals. ($49.95)

*Creative Playthings Inc.
**Triangle School Service

The <u>Hamster Cage</u>* is all metal and has a revolving treadle wheel, and water bottle feeder. It can be used nicely for housing hamsters, guinea pigs, mice, and other animals that are not too large. ($7.95)

The white plastic <u>One-egg</u> Incu-bator* has tip proof metal legs. Inside is a special bulb for heating. There is a thermometer and water trough for humidity. The entire hatching process can be seen through the plastic window. ($3.95)

Vari-shaped <u>Magnets</u>* are fun to play with and build with. The set includes iron filings. These powerful magnets retain their magnetism indefinitely. ($4.95)

EASELS

The <u>Double Painting Easel</u>* allows two children to paint at one time without tipping or shaking. The 24" x 24" boards are adjustable to the desired heights. The trays hold six jars of paint securely and are removable for easy cleaning. ($15.95)

The <u>Plain</u> <u>Double</u> <u>Birch</u> <u>Easel</u>* encourages free expression by the child. The basswood board 20" x 36" permits the use of large paper. The removable clips at the top of the easel allow the use of various sizes of paper without the use of thumb tacks. The removable pan and trays hold six paint jars. ($14.00)

DRYING RACK

This <u>Aluminum</u> <u>Folding</u> <u>Rack</u>** has 12 plastic lines 4' long. Excellent for drying pictures 18" x 24". It offers 48 feet of drying space. ($3.95)

PAINT TUMBLERS

<u>Unbreakable</u> <u>Tumblers</u>** have snap-on airtight covers for storing paint. 2-1/4" diameter at base, 3-3/4" high they fit snugly in easel trays. The set of six comes in assorted colors. ($1.59)

PHONOGRAPHS

The phonograph may have to be shared with other teachers in your building. If this is the case, try to have your room designated as its headquarters, for the kindergarten teacher is as a rule the one having the greatest use for it.

*Triangle School Service
**Creative Playthings, Inc.

A suggested phonograph to use in the kindergarten is the <u>Califone Premeir</u>*. This three speed easily operated portable plays seven to twelve inch records. It has a wide range tone control. ($64.95)

The <u>Economy 2-Speaker Phonograph</u>* has two 4' extended range speakers. The case is covered with rugged, washable, scuff-proof leatherette. It has a turnover cartridge with 2 separate needles. ($29.95)

The <u>Wire Record Rack</u>** of red vinyl-coated plastic holds sixty 7", 10" or 12" records. ($3.00)

Provision for Play

UTILITY BALLS

These tough inflated <u>Utility Balls</u>** can be used on rough surfaces. They are made of laminated synthetic rubber. Weather and water proof these balls can be easily washed. They can be played with on a wet field, left out-doors, and scrubbed with soap and water. May be selected in several sizes from ten to sixteen inches.
6" ball - ($1.95); 8-1/2" ball - ($3.35); 10" ball - ($3.95)

The <u>Voit Rubber Utility Ball</u>* provides small children with a ball that is softer, more durable, and less expensive than some balls. These rubber balls are often ordered by the physical education department in the schools as standard equipment and may be borrowed from them. This ball may be used on the playground as it is easily washed. It is a utility ball for school playground, gymnasium, and classroom. Weather and water proof, it can be easily washed, kept clean and sanitary. Choose them in several different sizes for use:
7" ball - ($1.95); 8-1/2" ball - ($2.55); 10" ball - ($3.00)

BEAN BAG BOARD

This <u>24"x 24" Board</u>** is made of 1/4" pressboard and has an easel stand. The board has 5 target holes for bags to go through. Contains 4 bean bags. ($8.95)

BALANCE BLOCKS AND BOARDS

This <u>Balance Block and Boards</u>** is indispensible for children for development of grace and poise. There are 4 solid wood blocks 2-1/2 5-1/4" x 11" and 3 wood planks 7/8" x 4" x 44". ($15.95)

*Triangle School Service
**Creative Playthings, Inc.

VARI-PLAY SCREEN

Most kinds of dramatic play are encouraged by this versatile Vari-Play Screen*. Two hinged flaps in the center panel can be raised or lowered to give different openings. The largest opening is shown in the food market as pictured below.

For the doll house wall or divider any combination of the flap open or closed can be used.

Opened out the screen measures 80" long and 48" high. It folds up to 32" x 48".

*Creative Playthings, Inc.
**Community Playthings, Rifton, New York

ROOM DIVIDER PEG BOARD SCREEN

This room divider Peg Board Screen** is made of masonite peg board strengthened by a wood frame 32" x 48". Removable feet can be fitted for either vertical or horizontal placement of board. ($11.50)

DOLLS

Include a few dolls that are not too fragile to withstand successive handling. They should have clothes that can be put on and taken off and sent home once in a while to be laundered. Select the most durable dolls, the fewer parts the better. Choose plain dolls with few frills.

Rubber Baby Doll*

This 18" all vinyl baby doll has movable joints. This sturdy doll comes with layette and an unbreakable baby bottle. Movable eyes are tamper and waterproof. 18" with layette ($8.95); 14" without layette ($5.95)

Rubber Drink and Wet Doll*

This doll is preferred by many because they can take vigorous punishment. Plastic non-removable eyes; movable joints; can be submerged in water and scrubbed. Diaper and nursing bottle included. 10" white doll ($2.00); 10" Negro doll ($2.00)

Raggedy Dolls*

Two amusing 20" cloth dolls spark the interest in the doll corner. These cuddly dolls have been favorites for many years. Raggedy Ann Doll ($3.95); Raggedy Andy Doll ($3.95)

Washable Plastic Cloth Dolls*

These washable plastic cloth dolls have their features embroidered, non-removable facial features and wool hair. Shoes and socks are firmly sewed. Large buttons with finished button holes on removable clothing. Negro boy, white boy, Negro girl, white girl ($8.95)

Child Size Dolls*

These cloth dolls are scaled to child-sized furniture. Removable clothing on all dolls. Father 44" ($16.95); Mother 42" ($15.95); Brother 30" ($9.95); Sister 24" ($9.95); Baby 6" ($6.95); Family Set of Six Dolls ($55.00)

Baby Doll Clothes Assortment*

For 10"-12" doll. Includes bunting, diaper, bib, shirt, romper, dress. 10"-12" ($4.95)

*Creative Playthings, Inc.
**Community Playthings, Rifton, New York

Fiber Doll Coach*

Children love to bring old clothes from home to dress up in. Order a fiber body, spoke wheeled, movable hood doll coach for them to use in the doll corner. 24" handle. This economy doll carriage has been found to give long use in the kindergarten. Yellow ($13.95)

Doll Highchair

29" high, it will hold a 27" doll. 14 lbs. ($5.95)

Stationary Ironing Board*

Completely set up. Shelf with backing holds ironing accessories. 8" wide x 20" long x 24" high ($7.95)

Double Stove*

Your housekeeping corner needs this double stove if the group is large. 12" wide by 24" long by 24" high. There are four burners and a large work space in the center. Plastic turning knobs. ($22.95)

Child-Sized Dresser*

With metal mirror ($23.95)

Rush Rocker*

12" seat, 11" from the floor. Light oak stain finish. ($8.95)

*Creative Playthings, Inc.

Child-Sized Doll Cradle*

Rocker runners. Large enough for 4 and 5 year olds to be the baby. ($14.95)

Aluminum Tea Set*

Double-gauge aluminum set of six cups, saucers, plates, one tea pot, a creamer, and a sugar container. ($5.50)

Pots and Pans*

Six piece set of double-gauge rustproof aluminum heavy bakelite handles attached by means of a sturdy 3-prong fixture. ($4.95)

FLANNEL BOARDS**

This sturdy 18" x 28" board is covered with longwearing flannel in soft pastel tones. Handsomely framed in natural oak. Comes with detachable Tilt-Rite stand for use on the teacher's desk, table, or chalk tray. 18" x 28". ($3.25)

FAVORITE STORIES FOR FLANNEL BOARD**

All stories are screen printed in three colors on white felt, and contain all characters and settings necessary to tell the story. Each story - ($0.85)

Community Helpers -- Doctor, Nurse, Policeman, Milkman and Mailman.
Community Workers -- Butcher, Telephone Operator, Baker, Druggist, Trash Collector, Grocer.

Stories**

The Three Pigs, Snow White, Goldilocks and The Three Bears, Ginger Bread Boy, Little Red Riding Hood, The Ugly Duckling, Henny Penny, Cinderella, Three Billy Goats Gruff.

TINKER TOYS

This educational toy is designed primarily to bring out and develop the child's ingenuity. 90 pieces, 8 wind blades, instructions ($1.19)

*Creative Playthings, Inc.
**Triangle School Service

PARQUETRY BLOCKS**

These blocks are large enough
to be handled easily and are
finished in six primary colors.
Six different color designs are
included. Each - ($1. 50)

LANDSCAPE PEG SET**

Encourages coordination, color
distinction, and mental activity in creating designs. Materials include such as trees,
houses, autos, barns, etc. for
building farmyard and village
scenes.
Price - ($2. 00)

PUZZLES*

These can be made as well as purchased. They can be obtained in an
assorted number of pieces. The small child, inexperienced in working puzzles is happy with fewer pieces, perhaps eight or ten; however, older children
and those who have worked previously with puzzles enjoy having more pieces
with which to work. As the year progresses harder and more complicated
puzzles should be put out for children to use.

There are excellent wooden puzzles that are nice to own as they help
develop finger dexterity. They are made of wood, easily washed, simple,
and attractive. It is possible to buy a self-containing wood tray which makes
them easier to store and more accessible for the children. The tray holds
twelve puzzles, size 9 x 12 inches.

Community Helpers are enjoyed in puzzle sets. They help to orient
them to social studies. 9" x 12" 13/8" thick plywood. Each - ($1. 75)

Inside Puzzle

Behind each puzzle on the inside of the board are behind the scenes
activity.

Wood Puzzle Rack -- ($6. 50)

*Creative Playthings, Inc.
**Triangle School Service

BLOCKS

Mor-Pla Blox* are easy for children to build with. Mor-Play Blox encourage smooth, cooperative social play--no frustrating, sliding-apart building mishaps. Children can build without teachers helping them.

The use of these large blocks provide opportunity for creative experiences, and stimulate social play. These hollow blocks are built for ruggedness. They are sat on, stood on, and walked on by many children during the day.

Corrugated Bricks***

These light weight paper blocks are easy for children to build with. Because of the hazards involved when using heavy blocks, many teachers prefer this type of block for use with five-year-olds. Most are painted to resemble a brick and can be used in building a house, store, or any type of construction.

*Creative Playthings, Inc.
**R. H. Stone Products
***Educational Specialties Co.

Barrel*

> This 17" long, 10" in diameter barrel can be used like hollow blocks.
> This sturdy barrel suggests countless play potentials. Barrel ($2.50)

Peg Board Block Storage Shelf and Block Bin on Casters*

> This peg board holds unit blocks of all kinds, and the spacious storage
> bin can be used for carting unit blocks or hollow blocks. Peg Board
> Storage Shelf ($33.95); Block Bin on Casters ($27.95)

Materials listed in this section may be obtained at the following places:

Triangle School Service
1401 "C" Avenue
Sioux Falls, S. D.

R. H. Stone Products
P. O. Box 414
Detroit, Michigan

Community Playthings, Inc.
5 University Place
New York 3, N. Y.

Educational Specialties Co.
Murray, Iowa

Equipment to Make for the Kindergarten Room

CUPBOARDS

> If you ask the children to bring rugs for resting, a place should be fur-
> nished for storing them. Low, open cupboards are desirable. The children
> may use them by themselves for storing rugs, paper, crayons, and art work.
> Include higher cupboards for the teacher's supplies of paper, paste, etc.

> Most children bring a rag rug or large bath towel for resting. They may
> be sent home several times a year to be washed. Some children bring
> a Kinder-mat**. This plastic pad is 20" x 48", and folds to 12" x 20"
> for easy storage. The pad is easily cleaned with warm water and soap.

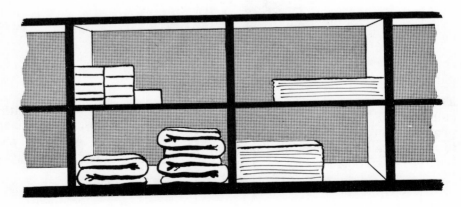

*Creative Playthings, Inc.
**Peerless Maid Plastics, Inc., Farmington, Minnesota

BOOK SHELVES

If there are no shelves in the room or in the cupboard, it is possible to make some. An expensive, satisfactory case for storing books can be made of two apple boxes, painted a bright color and fastened together. A top can be formed by two pieces of wood the width of the apple crate and fastened together at the top in the shape of a triangle. Perhaps you have noticed these racks in your public library. When displayed in this manner, the books with their bright covers are eye-catching, and they tend to encourage children to use books by creating an interest in them. Children achieve independence when they are allowed to choose and handle books for themselves.

EASELS

If you want to make an easel for your room that is easy to make and fun to use, you will need two celotex boards 40" wide by 30" high. This permits the use of larger paper. The easel should stand 50 to 52 inches in height and 28" from the trough to the floor. You will need four legs, 1" by 2" by 52". Nail the celotex boards to the legs so that the top edges are even. Two hinges will hold the board together at the top. Two locking stepladder braces can be used to hold the easel securely in open position. Two wooden cheese boxes 12" in length can be used on each side of the easel for holding paint jars or cartons. A table can be used to set the paint on if you do not care for the holder.

PUZZLES

If it is necessary to make some of your puzzles, you can make them by pasting on a cardboard a picture that children enjoy; shellacking it, and cutting it into the desired number of pieces. Use two pictures exactly alike -- one for the puzzle and the other for the finished picture. As the child puts his puzzle together, he can thus follow the model.

Chapter 2

MATERIALS FOR USE IN KINDERGARTEN ROOMS

PASTE*

Choose paste that will keep over a long period of time, and that will remain in usable condition. Some paste dries out very rapidly, becoming lumpy. About six quarts are usually ordered a year for an average kindergarten class. Firmagrip white paste is of high quality 32 oz. (each $.80); Gallon (each $3.00)

Sanford's School Paste is a white, clean, slow drying paste put up especially for school use. Quart (each $.85); Gallon (each $2.45)

SCISSORS*

When children use scissors in the schoolroom, it is for many the first time. We want to be sure, therefore, that the scissors we give to them are not too stiff. Some teachers prefer the blunt scissors while others like the semi-pointed. 4-1/2" blunt edged scissors ($.39); 5" pointed scissors (each $.49)

CRAYONS*

Order jumbo size colors for kindergarten use. Eight colors in a box. Each child should have a box of colors. Hexagonal, per box ($.40); Anti-roll, pressed ($.40)

PAPER

Construction

Suitable for drawing, watercolors, construction and mounting purposes. Yearly amount ordered for the average kindergarten would include about three dozen packages of 50 sheets each in assorted colors. Package of 50 sheets 9" x 12" ($.36)

Poster Paper

This is very nice to use when light weight colored paper is wanted. Not so heavy as construction paper, it is easier to fold. It is especially adapted for poster work and paper cutting. Price of 100 sheets 9" x 12", Assorted colors. ($.38)

*Creative Playthings, Inc.

Newsprint

This paper is inexpensive. The unprinted paper is good for drawings, cuttings and painting. It should be purchased in large sizes 12" x 18" or 18" x 24" for use on the easel. Six reams is about what the kindergarten teacher orders for a year. 12" x 18" Ream, ($1.90); 18" x 24" Ream, ($3.84)

Manilla Paper

Manilla paper is obtainable in either cream or gray; no smaller size than 12" x 18" should be purchased. This paper is rough and poorly finished but is cheap; for this reason it is suitable for painting and coloring. The paint sticks to it better than to smooth paper. Buff, 12" x 18", 1 Ream, ($3.44)

Finger Paint Paper*

16" x 22" Binney and Smith - Order about two dozen packages. Package of 100 sheets, (each $3.30)

PAINT

Crayola Dry Finger Paint*

Bright clear colors, easy for child to spread. 8 oz. canister with shaker top, (each $1.00)

Bulk Wet Finger Paint*

Crayola quality wet finger paint in eight colors. 8 oz. jar, ($.60)

Liquid Poster Paints*

Preferred by most teachers because of the lovely colors already mixed. 8 oz. jars, (each $.70)

Economy Powder Poster Paint*

Powdered paint is easily mixed, and is used in many kindergartens because of its economy. Order at least two sets of eight colors. Choose striking colors such as red, green, orange, blue, and black. Another shade, flesh, is helpful when painting faces, arms, and legs. Economy Dry Paint comes in an assortment of colors -- per lb. ($.65)

WORK BENCH*

Many kindergartens no longer have this piece of equipment. Boys particularly enjoyed using it. The experience gained at this work bench from using real tools seemed invaluable. The kindergarten teacher recognizes each child's individual effort in relation to his past experi-

*Creative Playthings, Inc.

ence and does not expect finished pieces of work from the five-year-old. This 22" x 42" top is made of 1-3/4" hard maple. It has 15" x 24" x 3-1/2" drawers for storage. This one vise table is 24" high. ($47.95)

A Cross-cut Saw with a medium tooth is better for small children to use. Many saws have a brace for added strength. 16" saw ($1.95); 20" saw ($2.50); Coping Saw ($1.00)

Soft Wood is necessary. If possible, get different sizes--some, one half inch thick and some, one and two inches thick. Pine can often be obtained as scrap from a local lumber company or mill house.

Bit Brace is used to make holes in the wood. ($4.95)

Nails should be selected that are flat headed. Choose different sizes from three-fourths to one inch in length, and in sizes one and two inches. Get them large enough for the child to hold.

Hammers with claws are easier for five-year-olds to handle. The hammer should be heavy enough to help the child drive the nail. About three-fourths to one pound is a good weight. Claw hammer, 13 oz., ($3.95); Claw hammer, 16 oz., ($3.95)

Block Planes help children to shave off unneeded pieces of wood. Block plane, 1 lb. ($3.95)

WASTE PAPER

Wall paper finds many uses in a kindergarten room. Sheets of wallpaper can be used to repaper the doll house or for book covers, flowers, or May baskets. Almost any wallpaper store is glad to give a teacher one of the older books.

Used newspapers may be utilized for table covers and for first cuttings. Children like to make hats from newspapers, and teachers use them in cupboards and drawers.

Old magazines are useful for the children's pictures, charts, books and plain cutting.

Assorted boxes can be made into cradles, drums, trains, beds, wagons, tables, and chairs.

Paper sacks have been very helpful when making hats and masks, also for use in the grocery store and with other projects.

Odds and ends of colored paper are useful. Have children trim off and return useful pieces of colored paper. Many kinds and colors of paper are needed during the work period.

BRUSHES*

For the easel. Order a brush that is soft, that will dry to a point, and that is large enough. You can also buy brushes with handles painted

*Triangle School Service

according to the color of the paint to be used. Total length of handle and brush is about 13 inches. Large size, each ($.29); medium size, each ($.20)

CLAY**

This is an excellent material to use for modeling. It can be obtained in powder form and is quite inexpensive. It is self hardening and can be easily modeled and painted when dry. It is most satisfactory in developing projects. This gray potter's clay can be prepared by the teacher herself. Water is added to the clay in the plastic mixing bag, and the bag kneaded until the clay is smooth and plastic. There is no mess. 5 lb. plastic bag ($.72)

Marblex** is a gray clay in moist form, ready for use. It models like any ordinary clay, but finished pieces harden without firing. Marblex is packed in a plastic bag which maintains the perfect modeling consistency. 1 lb. can, ($.45)

PLASTICINE*

This should not be confused with or substituted for clay. It has more limited use than clay since it is not in a permanent form and cannot be painted. It is available in many different colors. Crayola comes in 1/4 pound pieces and in one pound pieces. Crayola, four - 1/4 lb. pieces ($.54); one 1 lb. piece ($.54)

Permoplast Clay is similar to Crayola. Each piece is separately wrapped in paper and comes in pound packages divided into quarter sections. Permoplast 1 lb. package ($.41)

* Triangle School Service

Chapter 3

THE FIRST DAY OF SCHOOL

The sleek and the combed and the carefully pressed,
The downcast, neglected, and carelessly dressed,
Timid or eager they come to my door,
It's "first day of school," a new world lies before.

And what are the wares that I should display
On this strangely alluring, yet fearsome first day?
Toys and pictures, small flock to beguile,
And for the rough places a quick, ready smile.
The same type of wares I should stock through the year,
Sincerity, sympathy, wisdom, and cheer;
All the spiritual wares of kindness and truth,
And a heart that remembers the foolings of youth.

For here will they live, may they learn how to share,
To be honest and truthful and friendly and fair.
Solemn the thought, the task that I hold,
Casting life patterns and setting the mold.
Will the days they spend here dull the light of their faces
Or make them aware of the stars and the spaces?
The import of "first day" is as wide as the sea,
May they find a true guide in the teacher I'll be.

Author Unknown

ESSENTIALS OF A BEGINNING DAY

A better day usually results if you make sure that the parent says good-bye to the child and does not remain for the school session. This problem can be more easily met the first day of school than several days later. Most teachers encounter this difficulty at one time or another with beginning children. Many teachers say that this situation may go on for several weeks with varying degrees of intensity. For the most part it is usually better to meet it the first day and each succeeding day until the child has become adjusted to his new surroundings.

If the parent expects to meet the child after school for the first few days, suggest that she be on time. This helps the five-year-old feel a sense of security.

Many teachers provide a name tag for each child. Sometimes he wears it on a string around his neck or pinned on his shirt. A hat band can also be made for each child using a three inch strip of oak tag. Fit it to the child's head and staple the band together after putting the child's name on the band with a marking pen. Children learn to recognize their name as well as that of a friend. It helps you get acquainted with the children faster and makes for informality in the room. You may wish to use a different sticker on each hat until the child has learned to recognize his name in print.

Getting acquainted with each child in the kindergarten room as quickly as possible is a big task facing teachers each fall. Below are some suggestions that may help when attempting to do this. Make a head band like the one below out of colored pieces of construction paper. Clip the ends together when you have determined the exact size of each child's head. Decorate the top of each head band by using colored stars; make some with four stars, others with five and some with six. Children who are four, five or six may wear the appropriate head band.

Cowboy hats have an equal appeal for the small child. Below is a suggestion of a cowboy hat that children would enjoy wearing the first few days of school. This enables the teacher to call the child's name correctly whenever she addresses him, and to begin to associate names with the children.

The traditional red apple with each child's name on it can also be used as a means of identification. Pin a large red apple on your door and give each boy and girl one to wear like the one suggested below.

Leaves can also be worn as a means of identification. Use many different colored ones as well as different kinds.

A very simple identification can be made by using pink and blue circles and putting childrens' names on them.

Getting acquainted may take the form of a game. After a day or so of wearing tags, leaves, apples or some form of recognition, play a game with the children telling them you would like to take a turn trying to guess their name.

The majority of children make an easy adjustment to kindergarten. Many of them are older when they start to school for the first time, and others have been to Sunday School, Bible School, or Nursery School and the beginning day is not as frightening to them.

Usually a child is willing to accept the school room, but he is more concerned about his teacher and the group of kindergarteners who will be his friends. This is because boys and girls of this age have no common school background to share with one another. Much depends upon a good start so wear your prettiest dress and your gayest smile.

Begin a fire drill of your own early in the year. You will want to plan it several weeks ahead of any scheduled for the whole school. Make it a game that children play by getting a partner and getting in line to go out-of-doors. The panic that some times accompanies the first all school fire drill will not occur for your children if they are given a chance to play this game ahead of time and participate as they will do when the actual drill does take place.

Your room should be attractively arranged with several different centers of interest. This might mean an enticing library corner with familiar books that children will enjoy. Put out books at this time that are illustrative of the child's immediate experiences, such as trains, animals, and cars.

Flowers in the room, fresh curtains at the windows, and pictures that children like hanging on the walls, help make the room attractive on this beginning day.

It may seem advisable to skip resting on rugs the first few days of school. The shy child may want to rest at a table or not at all. Sometimes he prefers to watch other children for a few days. Try using large newspapers to rest on at first.

A skeleton program made up in large time blocks is advantageous until you have had an opportunity to know your groups better. Kindergarten teachers are usually very conscious of individual differences in children but it is practically impossible to know each child very well the first day and certainly not as well as the last day of school, so, for this reason it seems necessary to help children form certain opinions relative to the beginning days of school:

That the kindergarten is a nice, warm, friendly place.
In my school there are things to do that are lots of fun.
If I am allowed to belong to a group, I must conform to the rules of
    the group.
My teacher is friendly and likes me.

In your effort to make the first day at school as interesting as possible, do not overprepare and have too many materials out in the room at one time. Take time to introduce each new material to the group. Let each child have a chance to handle it and then let the rest of the children watch while the others take their turn.

Break down procedures to the most elementary beginnings. Whole hearted participation comes with freedom from fear of the new situation. Help children understand how to use materials by first demonstrating to them their use and then giving them a chance to try them out so every child knows how to use the materials in the room, and how to do the routine procedures expected of him. This may be best accomplished by working together as a total group for some time. Perhaps a month or more will pass before you will want to break up into smaller groups.

In the beginning, it is wise to give the child something to anticipate the following day. Children respond well to the suggestion that "tomorrow we will paint", or "tomorrow we will hear a story from one of our new books". Something excitingly new is an incentive to return the following day.

Going out onto the playground is very stimulating and frightening to some beginners. Don't try it until the group feels very much at home in their own room. Try marching outside the first few times, it helps keep children together. The first time you take your group outside mark off the part of the play area where they are to be found and play a familiar game so children will feel at home.

It is usually just as well to omit the milk lunch time the first few weeks of school.

First Days in Kindergarten

In many states, children entering kindergarten in September must be five before the first day of November. There definitely is a feeling toward the advisability of raising the entrance age for children. In the past children have been admitted if they were five before January first. The trend now seems to be to require children entering school to be five in September, October, or November. The real advantage in raising the age level seems to be that such a large per cent of the four-year-olds entering school have real difficulty in making school adjustments. In a recent study made by Neith Headly of the

University of Minnesota it was found that 16% of the children who entered kindergarten before they were 4 years and 9 months had real difficulty in making adjustment to kindergarten. Only 4% who had more months of maturity had this difficulty.

The formal registration of the entering child may be set for the opening day of school thus allowing the child to accompany his mother to the kindergarten room while the parent fills out the necessary blanks. No attempt is made to hold school that day and the child is invited to return the following day. Most registrations are not considered complete until a birth certificate or a reasonable facsimile has been presented. Some schools allow children to remain in school only two weeks if they have failed to present their birth certificate.

Some teachers prefer to register children who will be entering kindergarten for the first time during their Spring Tea. Sometime after the first of May, teachers secure the list of five-year-olds who will be entering school in the fall. This may be obtained from the census. In many buildings the P. T. A. help with these teas and send out the invitations to these children to attend a short program at school for them and their mothers. At this time they are given hand-books telling them about school and what is needed in the way of supplies and equipment. This time may also be used for registration. Parents are urged to bring the birth certificate with them, also the health information and record of immunizations. In case a parent is not able to find the birth certificate she will have the entire summer in which to write for one. Many schools have their own booklets that they give to parents. If your school does not have one, an accepted and very usable booklet is "Happy Journey". The price for a single copy is 40¢; for 25 to 99, 30¢; for 100 or more, 25¢.

Chronological age is usually the basis for the division between the morning or afternoon groups, and the parent can be told at the time of registration which session the child will be expected to attend. Usually there is no preference shown if you have one group attend in the morning the first semester and alternate with the other group the second semester. Sometimes it is necessary to ask a few to change from one session to the other because the group is too large. Often preferences can be taken care of in this way.

The formal registration may also be done in the office of the principal, and not in the kindergarten room on this first day of school. If this plan is used, the teacher should be freed from all forms of clerical work. The parents would go directly to the office and the children would remain in the kindergarten room with the teacher.

Many schools limit the first week of school to three fourths of the scheduled time. Many times this proves beneficial to the teacher as well as the children. A short school day in the beginning helps children adjust to the newness of the situation. You have a better chance to know the children as individuals. The children will also know you better and will get to know other children quicker. With smaller groups the first week, it is easier to find equipment and to know where it is kept. You also do not need to be so hurried in your new experiences when the group is kept small.

The number of children attending school the first day of classes could be limited to a half or a third of the group, depending upon the total number enrolled. If this plan is used, letters of greeting could be sent in advance by the teacher telling the children the hours they are to attend the first week of school. One group might be invited from 9:00 to 10:15, and another from 10:30 until 11:45. This plan gives the teacher a better chance to get acquainted with her children, especially if they are in small groups. The following is a suggested letter that might be enclosed:

Dear Grown-up Kindergarten Friend,

I will be anxious to see you next Tuesday, September 2nd. Before you come will you be thinking about something? If you could have one special wish come true, what would it be? Please share it with us in telling time on the first day of school.

We will also play the Rag Doll game and listen to a new story about a kitten called Peppermint (Isn't that a funny name?) and do many other interesting things.

Please come at 9 o'clock until 10:30.

Good wishing!
(Your name)

Program for First Days of School

FIRST DAY

9 - 10 A.M. 1 - 2 P.M.	Everybody sits around the circle or are grouped informally in front of the teacher. They may use rugs or large newspapers. All visit a while together. (Use hat bands or name tags.)

Go for a walk around the room. (Follow the leader) Look at everything in the room. (Lockers, piano, fountain)

When all are seated again get out a toy. (Stuffed dog, cat, pig) Talk about it and have several children tell about it. (Encourage those who have pets to talk) Pass the animal around so children get to see it and feel it.

Go for another walk around the room. Talk about things they notice.

10 - 11 A.M.	When back again show a picture of the stuffed pet. Mount it on a bright colored paper and place it on the easel board. Let a few children touch it if they wish. (Use pictures with the velvet finish.)

Everybody sits informally again and visits. Eat a graham cracker and visit.

Mention the bathroom. Have everyone go who will. While children wait for others they may clap softly.

Rest ten minutes. Use large newspapers for resting. Pretend it is a real bed and smooth it out well. Sing a lullaby to them. Do not use piano at first. Make resting seem very necessary.

11 - 11:30 A.M. 3 - 30 P.M.	Sing a song about the animal or toy you chose for the day.

Talk about the house it lives in.

Mount a second picture about the same subject. Touch it.

Talk about the food the animal eats.

Teach a finger play about the animal. Tell them to tell their mother they learned a finger play.

Get ready to go home. Talk about crossing streets safely. Shake hands with each child, call them by name and tell them you are looking forward to seeing them again tomorrow.

SECOND DAY

Follow approximately the same procedure as the day before; repeat often, make the period of work very short. Avoid much confusion and over-stimulation.

Plasticine could be introduced the second day. Give each child a paper towel to put it on. Use plastic bags to keep their ball of plasticine in, and put each child's name on the back.

Again talk about safety and shake hands to go home.

THIRD DAY

Introduce the library table and chairs. Sit down with a few children at a time and let the others watch. Talk together about how nice it is to have a table of our own to keep books that we like. Look at one picture. Tell about that picture.

Talk about the care of books, and the use of the library table.

FOURTH DAY

Crayons could be used this day. Tell the children where they are to draw; on the paper and not on the tables. Introduce them very carefully being sure to tell the children how to use the bottom, side, and end of the crayon.

Each new medium can be introduced in a group situation, just as the library table, plasticine, etc. were introduced.

Further Orientation of Children and Parents

Since much depends upon a good start, attendance in the kindergarten should be made as important as in any other grade. The five-year-old should form the habit of regular attendance. This is of utmost importance to his school success. When a child must be kept at home, parents are requested to report to the school as promptly as possible giving the reason for the absence. When the child returns to school he should bring a note stating the reason for the absence.

When it becomes necessary to make dental or medical appointments for children during school hours, parents should call the principal and request permission or obtain permission from the teacher. Some schools furnish blanks for this and they must be signed by the dentist or physician.

Every child has the right to good health. For the protection of the other children in your room, those children who do not feel well should be sent home or isolated from the group. The principal may call the parent so that the child will not be alone upon arrival at his home. If the parent of the sick child cannot be reached, it is probably better to isolate him until the end of the session or until the parent can be contacted. For the protection of the child and his schoolmates, suggest to your parents that they keep the child at home when any of the following symptoms appear:

Running nose, coughing, swollen red eyes, sore throat, or swollen glands.
Headache, nausea, vomiting, upset stomach.
Skin rashes, sores, running ears, or ringworm.
Any signs of fever, chills, or loss of color.

It is up to the teacher to help the parent understand what takes place in the schoolroom. In this way parents are more anxious to see that their child attends school regularly. One means of acquainting the parent with the school is the parent-teacher conference. Many times this conference is held in the fall. Some schools schedule the conference just after the holidays and do not issue a second report card. Special conferences may have to be scheduled at other times. Room mothers can be of real value at this time in aiding the teacher with the time allotted for each visit. A room mother waits outside the kindergarten room to greet the next conference appointment and notifies the mother in conference that her time has elapsed by knocking on the door. Several mothers work in shifts on conference days. This frees the kindergarten teacher of the time responsibility involved in interviewing so many parents at one time. Some schools use the bell system to let parents know when their conference time has been used up. The following forms could be used to aid in scheduling the conference. Twenty minute interviews are usually adequate for most conferences.

Form Letter to Send to Parent Telling*
of the Coming Conference

Dear Parent:

Instead of receiving the report card at the end of the second quarter, you will be asked to come to school to talk with the teacher about your child's progress.

You know your child as an individual better than anyone else can. In school he is one of many children and the teacher knows him as a member of the group. This conference is her report on the things she considers most important to share with you.

Parents and teachers everywhere want children to be as happy and as successful as possible. Sharing information with each other about the child helps both parents and teachers to understand him better.

Many of you visit school and attend PTA to find out how the school is teaching your child. That's fine; we are always happy to have you come. But many of you have, no doubt, wished that you could talk to the teacher alone without feeling that you were taking too much of her time.

To provide such an opportunity we are planning to arrange for a visit with the teacher for each kindergarten parent. School will be dismissed several half days to free the teacher for these visits or conferences. We hope you can arrange with a friend or neighbor to care for your child so that you may visit with the teacher undisturbed.

In the near future you will get a note asking you to come to school for such a conference. We hope you will make every effort to come and that you will find the conference an interesting and worthwhile experience.

Since this conference will take the place of the report card, it is important for each mother to come and talk with the teacher.

*Used in the Public Schools of Sioux Falls, S. D.

Daily Schedule

You would want to use three of these forms during the Parent - Teacher conference. One to be given to the Principal for his use, the other to your room mother in charge of greeting the parent, and one for yourself.

SCHEDULE

WEEK OF_____   DAY_____

	CHILD'S NAME	PARENTS
8:30		
8:50		
9:10		
9:30		
9:50		
10:10		
10:30		
10:50		
11:10		
11:30		
1:00		
1:20		
1:40		
2:00		
2:20		
2:40		
3:00		
3:20		
3:40		
4:00		

Invitation to Parent-Teacher Conference

Dear_____,

     Your parent-teacher conference has been scheduled for

_____, January_____ , at_____
         day   time

in the kindergarten room.

_____
                    kindergarten teacher

Please check one of the following, sign, and send this slip back to school.

_____I can come at the time stated above.

_____I would rather come on another day.
            If you checked the second space, we will contact you for another
            conference date.

We will appreciate any effort on your part to keep the above appointment.

_____
                    Parent's Signature

How to Conduct the Conference Interview

Prepare for the interview by reviewing the cumulative folder and by observing the child's behavior in a variety of situations.

Make the parent feel welcome and comfortable. A friendly working relationship is necessary if there are to be positive outcomes.

Be alert to and aware of differences in cultural background. Speak the parents' "language" but do not insult them; avoid talking "down" to them.

Be tactful. Many parents resent inquiry into what they consider their personal affairs. Sometimes parents are on the defensive and are over-critical of what may be innocent comments or questions.

Remember that, typically, parents want to know the facts, though they might not always want to admit them. "Glossing over" the facts probably de-develops very little insight on the part of parents; at the same time, do not be "brutal" in the realism with which facts are presented.

Indicate genuine interest, sincerity and a professional demean at all times.

Keep confidences shared with you by the child or the parents.

Try to place yourself in the parent's position. You then can better appreciate how he feels about what you are discussing.

Avoid comparisons with other children, particularly siblings.

Don't use educational "double talk". Some words, such as immature, aggressive, maladjusted and retarded, which are acceptable educational jargon may have a different meaning for the parent.

Avoid dealing in generalities. Suggestions should be specific and to the point.

Don't lecture! Listen closely and sympathetically. Let the parents talk too!

Be aware of the fact that some parents will tend to be over-defensive of their children. On the other hand, there will be some who will "Identify" with the teacher and will be hypercritical of their child in the hope of demonstrating to the teacher how "cooperative" they are.

Do not cover too many topics in one interview.

Don't extend the conference beyond the point of having covered the topics satisfactorily, even if the time is not all taken.

Prepared by the Staff of
Guidance and Counselor Training
Michigan State University

Parent-Teacher Conference Rating

CHILD'S NAME _____

In making an attempt to put down on paper suggestions gained from the personal interview with the parent, each child is considered as an individual and is not compared to his classmates.

CHILD'S HABITS AND ATTITUDES

SCHOOL ADJUSTMENT

HEALTH STATUS

EMOTIONAL STABILITY

SPECIAL ABILITIES AND INTERESTS

SUGGESTIONS OR QUESTIONS

*Form used by author in her class at Augustana College.

Forming Letters

You may wish to give your parents this sheet showing how children form letters. Since writing is not taught in the kindergarten, and yet many children want to write their name, this sheet could be given to the parent at the time of the parent-teacher conference, and the parent would then know the correct way to help the child write his name at home, if he asks to do so.

From the Basic Language Program by Marion Monroe, A. Sterl Artley, and William S. Gray. Published by Scott, Foresman and Company, Chicago.

Profile of a Kindergarten Child

When a parent visits your room, give this form:

1. Does the child participate in discussion? Is he interested in it? or is he inattentive?
2. Does he interrupt when others are talking? (Both children and adults).
3. Does he listen when other children tell things?
4. Does he use more than his share of time for telling things?
5. Can the child speak so that others can easily understand him?
6. Does the child participate in singing? Games? Activities?
7. Does the child show interest in the story? Can he repeat what happened in the story?
8. How well does the child pay attention?
9. How well does he listen to and follow directions? Does he depend on his own listening to know what to do? Or, does he depend on watching others having their example to follow instead of knowing for himself.
10. How independently does he work, dress himself, etc.?
11. How well can he color?
12. How well can he cut?
13. Which hand does he favor?
14. Does he accomplish things such as washing, drinking milk, coloring, dressing, picking up, etc. in a reasonable amount of time?
15. Does he strive to always be first, regardless of how the job is done? Is he last?
16. Does the child do his best with handwork? Or, does he just do it to get it done?
17. Does he share toys, etc., willingly?
18. Does he keep a new or favorite toy longer than his share of time?
19. Does he pick up and stop playing at the end of playtime? Or does he continue until he is individually reminded to stop?
20. Does he show interest in more than one type of activity?
21. How well does he get along with other children?
22. Is he kind, courteous?
23. Does he like kindergarten, if not, why not?
24. How well does he accept correction?
25. Does he have a sense of right and wrong?
26. Is he overly aggressive? or, is he too shy?
27. Does he appear happy and healthy?
28. Observe his muscular coordination. (Walking, skipping, etc.)
29. Does he take pride in his personal appearance--cleanliness, neatness, etc.?
30. Does he show awareness of numbers and interest in them?
31. Is there anything the teacher should know about your child that would assist her in teaching?
32. Do you have any questions on what you have observed? If so, please discuss it with the teacher?

Chapter 4

KINDERGARTEN
PROGRAMS

Little effort seems to have been made in the schools to standardize kindergarten programs. There may be several reasons for this. Some sessions of kindergarten last all day, others only half a day, and still others of a shortened duration such as two hours. In crowded school rooms this has been true the past few years when trained teachers were hard to find and space limited.

Mary D. Davis reports in an article entitled: "General Practice in Kindergarten in the United States", National Education Association, Washington, D.C., 1925, that roughly 35% of the time in kindergarten was spent in physical education, and under physical education she listed: play on apparatus, out-of-door play, games, rhythms, rest, and lunch. 33% of the time was given to general arts, which included housekeeping, fine and industrial arts, and dramatic art. 16% of the time was spent in general assemblies such as planning the work, evaluations, hygiene, and nature. 9% was given to literature and language, which included stories told and read, conversation, original poems read and repeated, and finger plays. 6% of the time was spent in music, which included singing, music appreciation, and rhythm band.

Most kindergarten programs vary a great deal but they do include many of these periods: A Conversation Period which includes roll call, flag salute, and health inspection; An Activity Period that includes the planning, carrying out of the work children choose to do, cleaning up, and evaluation of the work; Health Activities which include a tone drill, new song, review song, and a music appreciation song; Rhythms that include interpretive rhythms, rhythm band, basic rhythms, and story plays; Stories including pictures, poems, stories told and read, and dramatization; Games including play on the apparatus, and indoor and out-of-door games.

At the beginning of the year it is necessary to start with some kind of a frame work when planning what the program will include. Try using a skeleton program at first until many problems have been determined for you such as: the time of the recess, duties, etc. This also gives you a chance to become better acquainted with your children before you attempt to follow a more rigid routine. On the other hand do not make your schedule so flexible that the children feel the lack of repetition and routine. It is probably better to decide upon a routine to follow so that the children will sense this pattern and will know what they are expected to do, and then at a later date break it down into smaller time limits.

Although it is true that kindergarten programs do vary greatly even in the same school building, there are certain underlying facts that most teachers keep pretty well in mind when making out their program such as: You may have to experiment to find a time schedule for your program. Five-year-olds, not physically able to give attention for too long a time, are noted for their short attention span. For this reason your periods should

38

average between fifteen or twenty minutes in length, with the exception of the work period, which usually runs forty-five minutes to an hour. Of course the planning, clean up, evaluation, and work time are all included in this hour. Children are sometimes asked to sit too long at one time. Make sure you provide activity enough in your program. It seems advisable to schedule an activity period following one of inactivity such as: Songs, rhythms, stories, and games.

Since the child's need and his interest determine what happens next in the kindergarten, sometimes it is impossible to keep to your allotted time for one activity. Some days it may be to your advantage to have a longer work period or a longer rhythm period and you may have to omit some period entirely that day in order to do this. Do not rush children from one activity to another in too short periods of time. It would be better to eliminate one period entirely that day than to do this.

A SAMPLE KINDERGARTEN PROGRAM IN LARGE TIME BLOCKS

9:00- 9:15
1:00- 1:15   Opening, roll call, flag salute, health inspection

9:15-10:00
1:15- 2:00   Work Period--choosing, work, clean up, evaluation

10:00-10:30
2:00- 2:30   Health activities--Toilets, milk lunch, recess

10:30-11:30
2:30- 3:30   Directed activities--Songs, rhythms, stories, games

A SAMPLE KINDERGARTEN PROGRAM FOR A TWO HOUR SESSION

8:30- 8:45
1:30- 1:45   Roll call, flag salute, greeting

8:45- 9:30
1:45- 2:30   Work period

9:30-10:00
2:30- 3:00   Health Activities

10:00-10:10
3:00- 3:10   Rhythms

10:10-10:20
3:10- 3:20   Stories

10:20-10:30
3:20- 3:30   Games

A SAMPLE KINDERGARTEN PROGRAM FOR A
TWO AND A HALF HOUR SESSION

9:00- 9:15 1:00- 1:15	Opening, roll call, conversation
9:15-10:00 1:15- 2:00	Work Period, planning, clean up, evaluation
10:00-10:10 2:00- 2:10	Rhythms
10:10-10:30 2:10- 2:30	Health Activities
10:30-11:30 2:30- 3:30	Varied Activities, Music, games, stories, dramatization

A SAMPLE KINDERGARTEN PROGRAM FOR A
FULL DAY SESSION

9:00- 9:15	Roll call, flag salute, greetings, health inspection
9:15-10:15	Work Period, planning, clean up, evaluation
10:15-10:30	Health Activities
10:30-10:45	Songs
10:45-11:00	Rhythms
11:00-11:15	Stories
11:15-11:30	Preparation for luncheon
11:30-12:15	Lunch
12:15- 1:00	Get ready for resting on cots
1:00- 2:00	Rest on cots
2:00- 2:15	Get dressed, toilet, milk lunch
2:15- 3:00	Stories, out-door play

Chapter 5

PLAY IN THE KINDERGARTEN

Children need a place to play. This may be either inside or outside of the school building. It is better to make use of both of these settings. Boys and girls need to be out-of-doors some time every day if the weather permits. If you have playground equipment at your school, organized games will not have to be planned as frequently. Much of this play is spontaneous. An example of this is running on the playground, moving all the time, with no rules. Often children of this age prefer to play alone.

Kindergarten children require plenty of time to play. Play is one of the best ways they have of learning. All games played should be fun and relaxing for the child, and they should provide for:

Social development through participation in a group activity, in this way children are learning to play together.

Establishment of habits of fair play, taking turns, sharing equipment with others, and being a good sport.

Opportunity to think when it is necessary to follow simple directions, developing mental alertness.

Development in leadership, initiative, and the ability to give simple directions.

Motor co-ordination, and large muscle development.

It makes a great difference what kind of toys children have. If we are going to put money into them here are a few suggestions as to things we should look for when buying toys:

Buy those toys that stimulate activity. The child, not the toy, should be the busy one.

Select for a five-year-old the type of toy that trains the large muscles. Wagons, scooters, and trucks fit into this category.

Choose a few sturdy toys rather than many fragile ones. Toys that can be used hard will bring much more satisfaction to all children than cheap, poorly constructed ones that are easily broken.

Watch out for toys with sharp edges and pointed parts. They become dangerous for the kindergartner to handle.

Consider the age of the children who will be using the toys. If the toy is really meant for a young child, he will like it and will not need to be shown how to use it.

Buy good toys that can be used hard, day after day, in the schoolroom. Although they are not cheap, they will pay in the long run.

Some of the toys you will select will especially appeal to the girls, such as dolls, buggies, slides, paints, blackboards, ironing boards, irons, and other doll house equipment. Girls are more interested than boys in domestic play. Furthermore they differ more in their choice of playthings and they like a wider variety of materials with which to play. A girl's interest in dolls is much greater than a boy's. Around eight or nine, a girl ceases to play very much with dolls; some boys lose interest at four or five. A kindergarten girl likes to play in the doll house or doll corner because it creates imagination and she loves that kind of play. Because boys like mechanical toys, a great variety of toys are necessary. This may be one reason why some teachers feel that in making toy selections, we neglect the boys. Some of the toys that they especially enjoy are building and manipulative blocks, the work bench and tools, wagons, trains, boats, balls, bean bags, and the jungle gym.

Kindergarten children need confidence in singing alone. They are often reluctant to do this in an audience situation, but will perform quite readily in a game. For this reason many kindergarten games will be accompanied by music, adding to the pleasure of singing and helping the child develop rhythm and grace. A singing game such as "Follow the Leader" gives the child an opportunity for originality in choosing the activity for the group to follow and imitate. Other singing games such as "The Farmer in the Dell", or "Looby Loo", require the child to learn the sequence of the action in order to play the game. Many kindergarten song books include several popular singing games for the five-year-old. A card catalogue entitled "Rhythmic Activities"*, Series 1 by Francis R. Stuart and John S. Ludlam, list many old and new games and include the accompanying record and music. The following kindergarten games can be found in this file:

Singing Games

The Thread Follows the Needle (English)
Snail (French)
Skip To My Lou (American)
Shoo Foy (American)
Sally Go Round The Moon (English)
Round And Round The Village (English)
Rig-A-Jig-Jig (American)
Ride A cock Horse (American)
Pussy Cat (English)
Pop Goes The Weasel (American)
Paw Paw Patch (American)
Oats, Peas, Beans (English)
Mulberry Bush (American)

Muffin Man (English)
Merry Go Round
Looby Loo (English)
London Bridge (English)
I See You (Swedish)
How D'ye Do My Partner (American)
Hippity Hop (American)
Hi, Little Lassie (Swedish)
Hickory, Dickory, Dock (English)
Farmer In The Dell (American)
Did You Ever See A Lassie (Scottish)
Clown Dance (American)
Clap Dance (Bohemian)
Bean Porridge Hot (American)
Zoo (American)

Games

The games played in the classroom of the average kindergarten are usually simple ones with few rules and directions. For this reason it is usually possible to explain the whole game to the children, and then give direc-

*Rhythmic Activities, Stuart-Ludlam, Burgess Publishing, Minneapolis, Minnesota

tions for the various parts of the game. As the year progresses, more complicated rules and suggestions can be added to the games they have already learned.

Many games can be accompanied by music. This is an added enjoyment for children. By the end of the year children may also be able to improvise games from stories and rhythms.

When a game is presented, certain teaching situations develop. Many times the game itself does not include enough players. In order to catch the interest of more children, it is possible to start with two players doing the same things, thus offering an opportunity for more to take part.

In order that all children may have a chance to play the game, ask those who have already had a turn to raise their hands and request them to sit down and watch the others play.

To eliminate the possibility that most girls would choose another girl friend, and most boys select boys to take their places, you can suggest that when they choose a new partner each girl choose a boy and vice versa.

Activity Games

THE SQUIRREL AND THE NUT

Formation: Informal

Directions: Squirrels close their eyes and hold out their hands. One child puts the nut in some other child's hand. That child chases the other one back to his place.

FOLLOW THE LEADER

Formation: Children form a line with the leader at the head.

Directions: Children follow the leader about the room doing what the leader does.
Leader makes different movements as he leads the group.
Leader in turn chooses a new leader.

RHYTHMS IN ORDER AROUND THE CIRCLE

Formation: Circle or informal.

Directions: Play any good skip or march.
Children stand in circle, starting with one child and going directly around the circle.
The first child may skip around the circle and back and then sit down.
The second child may run, the third might hop, the fourth skip.
Repeat until every child is seated.

PROMENADE AND SKIP

Formation: Circle or informal.

Directions: Walk to first part of the music as teacher plays a walk.
Skip to last part of the music as teacher plays a skip.
Partners choose two more to walk and skip with them.

BLIND MAN'S BLUFF

Formation: Informal or circle.

Directions: One child, blindfolded, tries to catch another child who evades
his grasp, the game being played within a circle formed by all
the children.
Devices within a group may be used to give a clue as to the
whereabouts of the child who is being sought.
The blindfolded child may call "Jacob", and the other child
must answer, "Rachel". The child who is being sought may
hold a bell which he tinkles at intervals.

KNEEL TAG

Formation: Informal.

Directions: Children may play this game as any other simple game of tag
except that the players are safe if they kneel. One child is
"It". As players are tagged they also become "IT".

WHISTLE BALL

Formation: Children are sitting in a circle.

Directions: The children may sit in a circle. A ball is handed around the
circle. The child who is holding the ball when the instructor
whistles must leave the circle. The game continues until one
player is left.

Bean Bag Games

Bean bags are something small children enjoy using very much. They
can be made in such attractive shapes such as a frog, sun fish, turtle, etc.
They can be made of almost any material such as drapery material, felt,
wool, cotton, chintz, and oil cloth. A bean bag is flexible and it is easy for
the child to catch and to pick up. Beanbags are used very nicely out-of-
doors, also as they do not roll and are easy to throw.

BEAN BAG TOSS

Formation: Circle.

Directions: Toss the bag around the circle from one child to the next.
Change directions. Vary it by using two bean bags or by
throwing across the circle.

BEAN BAG RELAY

Formation: Three groups or lines.

Directions: Beginning at the front of the lines, each child passes the beanbag over his head until the last child in the line receives it.
He immediately goes to the head of the line and again passes
the beanbag back through the line.   The winning line is the
first line in which the child who was at the head when the game
started arrives at the head of the line again after everyone has
had a turn.

BEAN BAG BOARD

Formation: Straight line or a circle drawn on the floor.

Directions: Throw the bean bag into the circle.   Start with one large circle.   Later have two or three circles smaller in size.

HIDE THE BEAN BAG

Formation: Two lines or two teams.

Directions: Several beanbags may be hidden by one group of children.
The second team must look for them until all are found.
The second team then hides the beanbags and the first
team hunts for them.

GETTING ACQUAINTED

Formations: Children seated in circle, teacher standing in the center.

Directions: The teacher says, "I am Mrs. Jones," and tosses the beanbag
to one of the children.   The child catches it and exchanges
positions with the teacher, introducing himself before he
tosses to another child.   After you become better acquainted
the child tossing the beanbag may name the child to whom he
tosses the beanbag.   Those that have had a turn, step to one
side or sit down so that a different child has a turn to play the
game.

Sense Games

Some games played in the kindergarten develop the sense of hearing by
asking children to identify voices or sounds.

Still others encourage the child to name the object that has been removed from a group of articles placed in a basket or on a table.   This re-
quires the child to give strict attention to all articles in order to tell what
has been removed.

By the end of the year children will be able to improvise sense games
of their own and they enjoy doing this.

WHAT COLOR IS GONE?

Formation: Informal circle.

Directions: Several papers of different colors are placed in the center of the circle. (May be cut in various shapes such as balloons, eggs, balls). One child is chosen to close his eyes, another removes one color. He guesses which one.

THE POLICEMAN

Formation: Circle.

Directions: One child is the policeman. Another child walks up to him and says: "Will you help me?" Then the policeman asks him: "What is your name?" The child must tell his name. (Both first and last if he knows them.) Then he asks the child: "Where do you live?" The child must then tell his street address. The policeman asks him. "What is your telephone number?" The child tells him his number. The policeman then takes the child to his place in the circle. (home)

MOTHER CAT AND HER KITTENS

Formation: Informal.

Directions: Teach the verse, and choose one child to be the mother cat. Act out the verse. After the kittens have stolen away, the mother cat calls, "meow", the kittens answer, "meow". The mother cat goes to find her kittens.

Verse: "Mother cat and kittens were fast asleep one day. The mother wanted to sleep, but the kittens wanted to play. So they got up, oh, so softly, and walked away."

RING BELL RING

Formation: Informal.

Directions: One child is chosen to blind his eyes. Another child moves to a distant part of the room and rings a bell. The child in the center points in the direction he thinks he hears the bell.

DOG AND BONE

Formation: Informal or in circle.

Directions: One child is selected to be the dog. He sits in the center and closes his eyes. The dog's bone, which is an eraser, block, book, etc. is placed near him. A child is selected by the teacher and he attempts to sneak up to the dog and touch his bone without the dog hearing him. If the dog hears someone coming, he turns around and says, "Bow! Wow! Then, the player must return. A child who is successful in touching the bone before the dog hears him becomes the dog and the game is repeated.

Variation: The game may be changed into a tag. The dog tries to tag the child attempting to touch his bone. That child is safe only by touching the bone or by reaching his own place before being tagged. If he is tagged he is the dog.

I SAW

Formation: Circle.

Directions: One child is chosen to be in the center. He says, "On my way to school this morning I saw"----dog, pony, car, cat, bird, airplane, postman, etc. He then imitates, in movements or gestures what he saw and the others try to guess what it was. The child who guesses correctly goes into the center and the game starts again.

WHO HAS GONE FROM THE ROOM?

Formation: Informal.

Directions: One child is chosen to be it. He closes his eyes while the teacher indicates which child shall leave the room. After this child has left, the child who is it opens his eyes and guesses who has gone. If he manages to name the child correctly, that child is it the next time. If he fails to name the child, he closes his eyes again, the child returns to the room, and the child who has been it guesses who has returned.

WHAT AM I DOING?

Formation: Circle.

Directions: One child blinds his eyes. Another is chosen to do something: run, hop, clap, walk, or skip. The child who is chosen asks: "What am I doing?" The other child guesses.

I'M BEING VERY TALL

Formation: Informal.

Directions: One child goes to the center and covers his eyes.
Someone is chosen to tell the others what they are to do.
The children sing and follow the music. (Music is in many of the newer song books.)
The child in the center guesses what they are--small or tall.

Verse: "I'm very, very, small,
I'm very, very tall.
Sometimes small, sometimes tall.
Guess which I am now."

LITTLE TOMMY TITTLE MOUSE

Formation: Circle or Informal.

Directions: Teach verse. One child sits in the house and closes his eyes.
Children say the poem. At the right place, one child knocks and says, "It is I".

Verse: "Little Tommy Tittlemouse,
Living in a little house.
Someone's knocking, "Me, Oh, My."
Someone's calling, "It is I".

PIN BALL ON THE BACK

Formation: Informal.

Directions: Children cover their eyes. One child hides the colors.
Others hunt for the colors.

Variations: Teacher pins colors behind the back of one child.
Another child tries to see what color it is. Both must keep their hands behind them.
Teacher may put a color behind her. Children guess which color is gone.

Ball Games

ROLL BALL

Formation: Circle or on the floor.

Directions: Roll ball back and forth across the ring.
Roll back so that in passing, it will cross the circle chalked on the floor, and then, reduce the size of the inner ring to make the game more difficult.
Use the ball to knock over objects such as Indian Clubs, etc.

BOUNCING BALLS

Formation: Children stand in ring, with one in the center.
It may be either teacher or pupil.

Directions: Teacher bounces ball to different children who bounce it back.
Children bounce ball to another child in turn.
Teacher bounces it to child, who then bounces it and catches it himself, and then bounces it back to the teacher.
Teacher throws ball into the air and calls child's name, and the child designated runs up and catches it on the first bounce, if possible.

KICK BALL

Formation: Circle.

Directions: Kick ball across the circle to someone else.
               Use a large ball - basketball or volley ball.

DODGE BALL

Formation: Circle with several children in the center.

Directions: Roll ball trying to hit those in the center.   The child succeed-
               ing in hitting those in the center takes that child's place.

Quiet Games

LOST CHILD:

Formation: Informal.

Directions: One child is chosen to blind his eyes.   The teacher chooses
               one child to leave the room.
                    Everyone left changes places in the circle.
                    The child who has his eyes closed tries to guess who is
               missing.   If he cannot guess he must take his place and choose
               someone else to be it.   When you have played the game several
               times, one child may do the choosing in place of the teacher.

HUCKLE, BUCKLE, BEAN STALK

Formation: Informal.

Directions: Use any small object for hiding.   All the children leave the
               room except one.   This one child hides the object in plain sight.
               The rest of the children are then called back and begin to look
               for the object.   When one sees it he does not say a word but
               goes directly to his place and says, "Huckle, buckle, bean
               stalk!   The game goes on until all the players have found the
               object.   The first one to find the object hides it next time.

WONDER BALL

Formation: Children are seated in a circle.

Directions: A ball is passed around the circle from child to child while the
               following verse is said:

Verse: "The wonder ball goes around and around.
               To pass it quickly you are bound.
               If you're the one to hold it last
               You are OUT!"   (Child holding the ball on the word "Out" is
                              is out of the game.

CALL BALL

Formation: Children are standing in a circle.

Directions: One child is chosen to be it. He must stand in the center of the circle and call out a player's name. The child called must run in and catch the ball before it bounces. If he does he gets to be it.

Games

This is a list of books that could be used by the kindergarten teacher in selecting games to be played. The games recommended for use in this handbook were taken from thist list:

BOOK	AUTHOR	PUBLISHER
Four Hundred Games for School	Acker	Owen Publishing Co., Dansville, N. Y.
Graded Lessons in Fundamentals of Physical Education	Baker, Gertrude Warnock, Florence Christensen, Grace	A. S. Barnes & Co. New York City (1938)
Games for the Playground	Bancroft, Jessie	The Macmillan Co., New York City
Physical Training for the Elementary Schools	Clark, Lydia	Sanborn and Co., Chicago, Ill. (1921)
Fitness for Elementary School Children Through Physical Education	Victor Dauer	Burgess Publishing Co., Minneapolis, Minn.
The Book of Games	Forbush & Allen	John C. Winston Co. Chicago, Ill.
Let's Play	Geister, Edna	G. H. Doran Co., New York City (1923)
What Shall We Play	Geister, Edna	G. H. Doran Co., New York City (1924)
Illustrated Games & Rhythms	Geni	Prentice Hall Inc.
Treasure Bag of Game Songs	Gordon, Dorothy	E. P. Dutton & Co., Inc. New York City (1939)
Games for Boys and Girls	Harbin, E. O.	Abingdon-Cokesbury Press, New York City (1951)

BOOK	AUTHOR	PUBLISHER
Rhythms and Dances for Elementary Schools	LaSalle, Dorothy	A. S. Barnes & Co., New York City
Book of Action Songs for Home and Kindergarten	Malone, K.	G. Schirmer, Inc. New York City
Active Games	Mason-Mitchell	Ronald Press
Play Activities for Elementary Grades	Nagel	C. V. Mosby Co.
Small Songs for Small Singers	Neidlinger, Albertina	G. Schirmer, Inc. New York City (1925)
Physical Education for Elementary Schools	Neilson, N. P. Van Hagen, Winifred	A. S. Barnes & Co. New York City (1931)
Physical Education for Primary Grades	Ocker	A. S. Barnes & Co. New York City
Games for the Elementary Schools Grades	Richardson, Hazel	Burgess Publishing Co., Minneapolis, Minn.
Games and Game Leadership	Smith, Chas. F.	Dodd, Mead & Co. New York City (1934)
Rhythmic Activities I	Stuart, Francis R. Ludlam, John S.	Burgess Publishing Co., Minneapolis, Minn.
Physical Education	Wild and White	Iowa State Teachers College Cedar Falls, Iowa

Chapter 6

CONVERSATION AND
TELLING TIME

Opportunities for developing language experiences occur throughout the entire kindergarten day rather than in one set period. When the children first arrive at school they have many things to tell each other or the teacher. During the work period there will be a great many conversations going on at one time about the work they are doing. All a kindergarten child needs is practice and something to talk about. If he isn't given this chance he doesn't learn to speak well. For this reason there should be many conversations going on in the kindergarten between children.

During the conversation period or "telling and showing" time that is set aside for that purpose the child learns to speak more distinctly, he is helped to increase his vocabulary, and to overcome his shyness.

Most all kindergarten children love to walk up in front of the group and tell about something or show some favorite toy. They seem to enjoy this more than anything else they do in kindergarten. They will talk about things they have done on the way to school, or what they saw on T-V the night before. They will bring a much loved toy to show, or model a new dress. They are very anxious for all present to see what they have brought.

Parents who have visited school at this time cannot help but marvel at the thrill children get at making speeches or giving demonstrations with something they have brought to show to the group. This should be encouraged during this period so children will grow up unafraid of audiences and groups of all kinds and able to speak clearly to them.

It is necessary sometimes to help boys and girls restrict themselves to one specific topic, otherwise they may ramble on and on about several things and take too much time from the other children. Limiting him in this way doesn't dampen his spirits and does give more children a chance to have a turn. It does help him organize his material and to think about the one thing he intends to talk about. If something like this isn't done other children pick up the idea of rambling on and on in order to make their turn seem more important.

If done sparingly and in good faith, you should correct the obvious common grammatical errors such as the wrong use of 'me' and the common mistake of using 'ain't' for isn't. Such correction must come at the time the mistake is made and of course should be held to a minimum. Too many of these suggestions at one time tend only to further confuse the child and may take away some of his eagerness to take part.

Most five-year-olds have a vocabulary of over two thousand words, and they like to be given a chance to use them. They enjoy 'trying on' new words they hear adults use. As teachers, we must be careful in our use of words, in order that boys and girls may hear words spoken correctly. We need to speak slowly and simply.

By the time a child enters kindergarten he should no longer be using baby talk. Baby talk is no longer accepted at this age. The five-year-old, therefore, should be encouraged to make a real effort to speak distinctly and clearly. When he finds out he is not easily understood he usually begins to make an effort to speak clearly.

Group planning and talking about the things that children bring to school and about experiences they have had create healthy conversation in the kindergarten.

During telling time help the child see the advantage of taking turns in telling as well as being a good listener while other children are talking. Above all else, the kindergartner learns that if he is going to be able to hold the attention of the group while he is speaking, he will have to speak clearly and loudly enough for all to hear.

Since reporting an experience in words is more difficult than "showing" and describing it, many difficult attempts are eased by using a "showing" time. Almost any sort of article is brought to school at this time. Later on in the year when the children have had many chances to do this, it may be nice to limit the things children are to bring to the particular unit of work you are talking about, or you may wish to set aside one particular day for this purpose. Children enjoy bringing books, records, stories, etc.

Other things to be discussed and included in the conversation period are discussions based on special units of work and on kindergarten activities that relate to the seasons of the year, holiday festivals, and excursions undertaken by the entire group.

This particular period seems to be an ideal time for helping to form habits necessary for happy living together in the kindergarten.

Many teachers feel that they would like to help children with speech defects but they are not quite sure just what they could do in their class room along this line. Many times a group lesson is helpful in which you spend some time with a special sound that is bothering the entire group or some children in it. The following lesson is a suggestion that could be used for this particular reason. Others may be equally as beneficial.

Some Suggestions for Helping
Kindergarten Children in Speech

Sing simple songs, including the favorite nursery rhymes. It will give the children pleasure as well as help them feel the rhythm if all of you clap your hands in time to the music of the songs.

Play with them. The toys you have in your room will give you numerous ideas for helping them in their speech. It is very important to enjoy this playtime period together.

Read to them. Simple stories with large colorful pictures are recommended. Try to make this a quiet, relaxing time for all. If any direct speech work is done, choose only a few simple words for drill.

Dramatize favorite stories, perhaps asking other children to take some of the parts. Use the same stories over and over until all feel acquainted with them.

Play phonograph records on speech sounds to the children. Try to follow the suggestions for using that are recommended.

If it is necessary to isolate difficult speech sounds, use large pictures that represent a particular one. A picture of a teakettle, for instance is helpful in teaching the s sound.

SOME RECOMMENDED MATERIALS FOR
KINDERGARTEN

Speech Is Fun, by Genevieve Arnold. University of Houston, Houston, Texas.
Talking Time, by Louise Scott and J. J. Thompson; Webster Publishing Co.;
       St. Louis, Missouri.
Speech Development Records For Children, by Elaine Mikalson. Pacific
       Records Co., Box 2033, Pasadena 2, California.
What They Say, Audio Visual Kinesthetic Flash Cards For Teaching Phonics
       And Phonetics, by Louise Binder Scott and Morell Kresser.

Many times it is possible to make up a story that children will enjoy and that they will also benefit from. The enclosed story is one that has been used with success with five-year-olds.

RICKY, THE BABY RABBIT

Once there was a baby rabbit named, Ricky. He had not learned how to say his name right. He called himself, "Wicky."

Ricky's father was a very proper sort of rabbit. He always dressed up every day and was so proud of himself. And how disappointed he was that his son, Ricky, couldn't say his name right. One day he said to Ricky:

"You must start with the er sound when you say your name, Ricky. Listen: R-icky."

Ricky tried to make the er sound, but he just couldn't say it right. He was so anxious to please his father, however, that he decided to ask some of his friends for help.

Mother Hen was in the barn yard and Ricky asked her: "Hen, will you tell me how to say my name?"

But Mother Hen just answered: "cluck-cluck," and that didn't help Ricky.

Ricky saw Mother Robin looking for worms and asked her the same question. Mother Robin just answered: "cheap-cheap," and that didn't help Ricky.

A Raggedy Ann doll was sitting near a tree and Ricky was very disappointed when she didn't answer his question.

Then Ricky heard a sound from a proud rooster: "R-r-r-r-r-r-!" the rooster crowed at the top of his voice.

Ricky ran to the rooster and cried: "Say it again! Say it again!"

The rooster crowed once more.

Ricky had found someone who could help him make the er sound. Every day he practiced crowing the way the rooster crowed and it wasn't long before he learned how to say his name, Ricky.

Posture: Stand very tall and flap your arms the way a rooster does.

Breathing: Crow like a rooster.

Relaxation: Be Raggedy Ann:

Raggedy Ann is my best friend.
She's so relaxed; just see her bend.
First at the waist, then at the knee.
Her arms are swinging, oh, so free.
Her head rolls around like a rubber ball.
She hasn't any bones at all.
Raggedy Ann is stuffed with rags;
That's why her body wigs and wags.

-- Scott-Thompson

CAT AND RATS

Games: Cat is under table. Rats come on tip toe near cat.
Cat comes out to see if it is raining. (Holds up paws.)
If she says, rain, rats come nearer; if she says:
"rats", rats run and cat runs after them.

RING AROUND THE ROSEY

Courtesy of Mrs. Tjumslands,
Speech Teacher Sioux Falls Public
Schools

Group Lesson For S Sound

Materials: Pictures--snake--swing--slide--sun--see saw

HAVE YOU SEEN SI?

Teacher: (Holding picture of snake toward herself.) I wonder who can guess what this picture is. It is long and green. It can curl up, crawl on the ground and up the trunks of trees. It doesn't have any legs. (Children guess.)

Teacher: Does any one know what a snake says? (Answer should be s . . .

Teacher: (Spots a child who is making s sound correctly.)_____, won't you come up and show everyone how you are making the snake sound? (Child comes and makes the sound.)

Teacher: Let's make the sound together now. Remember, your teeth must be closed in the way you chew your food and your tongue should be on the roof of your mouth. It helps to smile a little when you say it: s . . . .

Teacher: (Picks up other pictures.) I have some other pictures. I shall show you them one at a time and you tell me what you see.

Children: Swing, etc.

Teacher: Do you hear the snake sound when you say swing? Let's say it again and see if you feel teeth coming together when you say it. (Proceed in same manner with other pictures.)

Teacher: (Picks up game, Have You Seen Si.) Now I shall tell you a story about a boy named, Sam. (Shows Sam.) Sam had a little cat, named Si. (Shows Si.) Si ran away every day and always hid under a house. (Show pictures of blue, pink, yellow and green houses.)

Then Sam would have to knock at every door and say: "Miss Blue, have you seen Si?" Miss Yellow, etc. until he found Si. Then Sam said:

"There you are, Si. Shame on you for running away from home."

(Children play game. One child is chosen to be Sam and Si, the cat, is hidden behind one of the houses.)

Chapter 7

THE RHYTHM PERIOD

The five-year-old is happy when given a chance to respond to music. He enjoys it even more if there are not too many exacting movements required.

Many kindergarten songs are followed by rhythms and are to be used for free rhythmic expression. Each song is at first sung for the children several times in order that they may feel the rhythm before any attempt is made to express it. Children enjoy interpreting the music in a free way, just as it appeals to them.

As the songs are learned discussions about them by the five-year-old himself furthers the interpretation of them.

Pictures, stories, poems, and finger plays all help to encourage the children to develop a variety in expression. Boys and girls are naturally rhythmic and it would be nice if all primary grades could find time to include some time for rhythm. In this way more children would be helped to develop better muscle coordination, and it would also help to assure us that kindergarteners would not be sitting still for too long a time without activity being provided.

As the year progresses encourage original interpretations of the music. Many beginning children are fairly good at basic rhythms, and we should help them learn new things about rhythms, such as associating the name of the rhythm with the response, executing rhythm in a desired way, and improvising variations to the rhythms.

Rhythms in the kindergarten should always be fun and related to a child's interests and activities. He needs opportunity to try out different things to music and to participate in many kinds of musical experiences. Rhythms come into our daily program in many ways other than the regular time set aside for them. Entering a kindergarten room during a schedules work period one might find skipping or hopping or jumping going on as part of that activity, or vocalizing in the doll house. Rhythmic activities grow naturally out of the things boys and girls do all day long in the classroom as well as on the way to school.

Being frogs, elephants, giants, high stepping horses, or airplanes give the child opportunities to express his originality. These responses are most valuable when the five-year-old himself suggests them and executes them, rather than the teacher showing him how to do them. Some music does suggest a more or less definite response as the march, skip, or run, while other types may mean very different things to different children.

If boys and girls are allowed to talk about and discuss the characteristics of the things they are trying to interpret they are much better able to carry them out in action. For instance, it helps to discuss how the rag doll is made and how it is stuffed. The body is very limp and very relaxed. If the child knows these things he is much better able to carry out an interpretation of them. Many times the teacher asks thought provoking questions to arrive at some of this information and other times she shows pictures, movies, or slides to motivate the rhythm period. When several children do an interpretation well she asks them to demonstrate to the entire group rather than doing it herself.

Rhythmic Activities in 4/4 Time

CLAPPING

Variations: It is often possible to improve rhythmic responses by playing contrasts and showing them sharply.

Simple clapping.
Clapping with hands above head.
Clapping with hands behind back.
Clapping loud and soft, slow and fast.
Clapping loud and slow, soft and slow.
Clapping with partner.

WALKING OR MARCHING

General
Instructions: Body should be erect.
Child should keep time to the music.
Music should be clear, with correct accent.

Variations:

TIPTOE
Walk lightly on toes.
Follow the light, soft music.

GIANTS
Take long heavy strides.
Follow the slow and ponderous music.
Place arms above head, close to the ears, to give a feeling of height.

HIGH STEPPING
HORSES
Lift knees high, on level with hips.
Point toes downward.
Step lightly, first toe and then heel.

TRAMP
Put feet down flat and hard.
Walk heavily.
Follow slower and more ponderous music.

TRIANGLE
ACTIVITIES
Use the triangle to tell the child when to change the activity:
Walk (triangle) clap.
Walk (triangle) turn in opposite direction.

Rhythmic Activities in 3/4 Time

Variations:

SKATING	Alternate sliding of feet, without either foot leaving the floor.
RAKING LEAVES	Put one foot in advance of the other and sway forward and backward in time.
BOUNCING BALLS	Stand or walk. Push hand down on first beat of the measure.
ROCKING DOLLS	Couple arms as if holding a doll and sway arms from right to left in time to the music.
SHOVELING SNOW	Push hands and arms forward. Throw arms back over shoulders.
SWINGING	Put arms above head as if holding ropes. Stand with one foot forward. Transfer weight from one foot to the other with a backward and forward rhythmical movement. Keep knees from bending. Face each other in pairs and take hold of hands. Let a third child swing his hands forward and back.

Story Plays

As we develop our centers of interest during the year, there are appealing story plays that can be dramatized with the aid of music. The suggestions as to what movements to include in the story play should come from the children themselves, and should be kept very informal. In a story play the activity itself is usually exaggerated. A few suggestions might include:

SNOW FUN

SNOW FLAKES	Children can dance lightly on tip toes. With their arms outstretched, they twirl around. As the music slows down they slow down, and finally fall to the ground.
WALKING IN SNOW	As the snow is heavy, children may walk with big heavy steps. The walking can become slower and harder as the music finishes.
ROLLING SNOW BALLS	Children go through the motions of making the snow ball and shaping it. Start it as small as possible, and roll it. The rolling becomes more difficult as the ball grows larger.

Rhythmic Interpretations

FALLING LEAVES Run and whirl lightly on tiptoes to the music.
Have arms slightly raised. Children can stoop to the floor at the end of the piece.
Give plenty of opportunity for creativeness.

BROWNIES Quickly run on tiptoes with body slightly bent forward.
Child shakes his finger, and light music is played.

SQUIRRELS Stoop slightly and run lightly to rather fast music.
(Children can stoop down and pick up nuts.)

DUCKS Start from a squatting position, hands on hips, elbows flapping like wings.
Sway from side to side, waddle to slow music.

TURKEYS Walk stiff legged.
Stand tall with head high.
(Children can put their hands on hips for wings.)

TOYS Stiff jointed dolls.
Limp dolls, such as a rag doll.
Jointed hopping dolls that jump and land on both feet.
(Music same as for other dolls but an octave higher.)
Soldier dolls that keep knees stiff and mechanical in action.
Dancing dolls that stand on box. (Someone winds doll up and she dances around with short, light steps.)

TOPS Twirl around.
Alternate in directions so as not to get dizzy.
Slow up as top runs down.

JUMPING JACKS Side jump with both hands and arms overhead and legs apart.
Music should be very highly accented.

TEDDY BEARS Walk on tiptoe in time to the music, with knees slightly bent and hands held out as paws.

HOBBY HORSES Gallop in time to the music, with arms raised as if holding the reins.

ROCKING HORSES One foot should be in advance of the other. Both feet should be flat on the floor. The trunk and head are erect.
The body moves forward and back, bringing into play the knee and ankle. Swaying music can be used for this.

TRAINS Place hands on the waist of the one in front of the child.
Shuffle feet on the floor.
Make sounds for the bell and other noises made by a train.

PINOCCHIO	Stiffen the arms and legs, walk like you were made of wood.
AIRPLANES	Run, with light, short steps. Arms should be out-stretched.
	Make a buzzing sound as your motor starts up.
	Crouch down when first starting, and then rise to a standing position.
	After the run, return to the crouching position, for a "landing".
HELICOPTERS	Rise in place, arms outstretched, twirl about the room.
RABBITS	Hopping on hands and knees in time to the music.
	Hopping with paws outstretched.
BUTTERFLIES	Light running steps. Arms move rhythmically up and down, in long sweeps.
FLYING BIRDS	Moderate running steps. Arms are outstretched and moving up and down.
ELEPHANTS	Bend the body with arms hanging down for a trunk.
	Walk with big, wide, heavy ponderous steps.
	Music should be slow so children can take big steps.
GIANTS	A long heavy stride. Should be slow and ponderous music.
	Body should be held erect.

When children are asked to give their individual interpretation of a rhythm, suggest listening to the music to see what the music suggests to them. We may not care to have the same activity all the way through; that is, we may start with a walk, and also play a run. After we have played the music, we should give several children a chance to express their ideas about what the music tells them to do. Let the children interpret it in their own way. After they have done this, discuss the ones they liked the best, and let them tell why they liked them. Make the children feel that this is a time when they do what the music tells them. The teacher will guide the children only as the need arises.

It is surprising how well some five-year-olds are able to respond to basic rhythms. Many are acquainted with them before they enter kindergarten. The ones we include most often are:

WALK	The body should be erect. The child should keep time to the music.
	The music should be clear and strongly accented, so that the children will know when to take a step.
	Music should be varied so that walking will not become monotonous; that is, we shall want to include many marches during the year, rather than always playing the same one; otherwise children become careless in their rhythms.

HOP   Take position for hopping. Bend at the knee.
Hop in time to the music on the other foot.
Alternate feet to avoid fatigue.
(As this is tiring to a beginner, the activity should not
    be too long.)

JUMP   Jump forward on two feet. (This activity should not be
    continued too long.)

SKIP   Alternate feet on the hippety-hop movement.
Bring knees up high. (Music should be light, and not
    too fast.)

Rhythm Band

STEPS IN DEVELOPING A RHYTHM BAND

Children love to experiment with band instruments. These instruments could be left out on the table or on low shelves for them to experiment with before school time. Small groups of children may even enjoy this during regular school time.

In the beginning, when just getting the band started, first give the children the instruments that are easiest to play. Drums are always simple for a five-year-old--also bells and rhythm sticks.

At first play a simple march and give each child an opportunity to play a drum. Acceptable drums can be made from large oat meal boxes.

After each child has had the fun of playing a drum, and responding to the march music, another instrument may be introduced, such as the bells, rhythm sticks, or sand blocks. Let each child have a chance to play the instrument you introduce next. After all have had a turn to play, the boys might play the drums and the girls play the new instrument.

Do not select a director until every child has had an opportunity to think rhythm for himself.

When all the children have had many chances to play sound-producing instruments, let them play imaginary ones such as violins, horns and drums.

Instruments that are usually used in a kindergarten band are tambourines, drums, bells, cymbals, rhythm sticks, sand blocks, and a triangle. Most of these can be made if you do not wish to or can not afford to order them.

Let children learn how to use the instruments. After introducing each instrument, one at a time, add more.

Play one type of instrument and let the other children be the audience and listen. Play loud and soft with the music. Children can play solo parts, after which they can interpret different kinds of music. Boys and girls who have shown ability in playing the different instruments could be chosen first as directors - a reward for being good helpers.

Rhythms and Seasons

These rhythms seem to lend themselves to certain seasons of the year.

FALL

Happy Songs For Happy Children
  Hippity Hop

Our First Music
  I'm Tall, I'm Small
  Hunting
  Galloping

The Kindergarten Book
  Raking Leaves
  Walking to School
  Pushing a Wheelbarrow
  Twirling Leaves
  Birds Flying South
  Squirrels Gathering Nuts

HALLOWEEN

The Kindergarten Book
  The Witch Is On Her Broom Stick

Rhythms For Little Folks
  Halloween Brownies
  Halloween Cats

The Kindergarten Book
  Giants
  Ghosts

Songs Of The Child World
  The Shoemaker
  The Brownies

THANKSGIVING

Singing Time
  The Big Tall Indian

The Kindergarten Book
  Indian Camp

Children Come and Sing
  The Turkey

American Singer
  Ten Little Indians

CHRISTMAS

Rhythm Fun
Prancing Reindeers
Jack in the Box

American Singer
Rocking Dolly in a Crib
Xmas Bells Ringing
Rag Dolls
Marching Tin Soldiers
Ice Skating
Sliding on Sleds
Rocking Horses
Dancing Dolls
Swinging Tops

Music For Early Childhood
Jack In The Box
Round The Xmas Tree
Bells On Santa's Sleigh

Happy Songs For Happy Children
Funny Jumping Jack
Making Snowballs and Throwing at Snowmen
Jack Frost
Snow Flake Dance
Fairy Dance
Xmas Train Of Toys
My Xmas Drum
Walking To The Toy Store
Ringing Santa's Sleighbells

The Kindergarten Book
Toy Shop At Night
Bouncing Balls
Marching Soldiers
Dance Around The Christmas Tree
Santa's Helpers

Rhythms of Childhood
Rock My Dolly
I'm A Funny Jumping Jack

WINTER

The Kindergarten Book
Warming Hands
Running in the Snow With Galoshes On
Rolling Snowballs
A Cat Walking In The Snow
Going To Church
Clapping Hands To Keep Warm

American Singer
Coasting
Skating

Rhythmic Games and Dances
Snowflake Dance

Rhythm Fun
Skating

Singing Time
Snowflakes

VALENTINE'S DAY

Singing Time
The Postman

The Kindergarten Book
Sending A Valentine

Arnold's Rhythm Book
Hippity Hop To The Valentine Shop

SPRING

Rhythm Fun
Birds In The Springtime
Playing Ball
Dancing Raindrops

American Singer
Roller Skating
Jumping Rope
Planting Gardens
Hanging May Baskets
Birds Singing
Swaying Trees Rocking Babies In Their Nests
Seeds Unfolding
Birds Soaring And Dipping

Happy Songs For Happy Children
Merry Wind
April Rain
Picking Flowers
Teeter-Totter
Swinging
The Sun--The Rain

Walk The World Together
March Winds Blowing
A Garden

The Kindergarten Book
    Wading in Water
    Rowing A Boat
    Seeds And Flowers
    Bouncing Balls
    See Sawing
    Roller Skating to School
    Fluttering Like Butterflies
    Bicycle Riding
    Swaying Trees

EASTER

American Singer
    Rabbits Hopping
    Planting Seeds

The Kindergarten Book
    Bunnies Hopping

Records

Included in this list are victrola records suitable for use in the kindergarten. Some of these records may accompany song books or poetry books; others may be used at resting time or during the rhythm period.

RESTING TIME

Lullaby - Sandman - Hush My Babe - Cradle Song - Sweet-Low
    Volume 1, R. C. A. Victor Records, Album E-77
When The Little Children Sleep
    R. C. A. Victor Records, Album E-83
Indian Lullaby
    R. C. A. Victor Record, Album E-83
Sleep, Baby Sleep
    R. C. A. Victor Record, Album E-83

SINGING GAMES

Ten Little Indians
The Snail
Looby Loo
Oats, Peas, Beans
Jolly Is The Miller
Sally Go Round The Moon
The Thread Follows The Needle
London Bridge
Soldier Boy
The Farmer In The Dell
Skip To My Lou
    R. C. A. Victor Records, Album No. E-87

Bounce Around - The Shoemaker - Dancing In A Ring - Jing Jang -
Hey Jim Along - Jim Along Josie - Yankee Doodle
Decca Records, The American Singer Bk. 1, Album A. S. - 1

INTERPRETIVE RHYTHMS

Ducks, Camels, Horses, Elephants, Trains, Soldiers, Tops, Airplanes,
Swings, Seesaws, Rowboats, Bicycles, Fairies.
Run, Walk, Skip, Jump, Gallop, and March.
Childhood Rhythms, Series 1, Ruth Evans, 326 Forest Park Ave.,
Springfield, Mass.

Gnomes, Dwarfs, Fairies, Clowns, Skipping, Flying Birds
Rhythmic Activities
Vol. 1 & 2, R. C. A. Victor, Album No. E-71-72.

The Waltzing Elephant - Young Peoples Record
The Dance Of The Candy Dolls - Columbia Record

The Farm - Rhythm Time Records Vol. 1
Night Time - Rhythm Time Records Vol. 2
Play Activities - Rhythm Time Records Vol. 3
Train - Rhythm Time Records Vol. 4
P. O. Box 1106, Santa Barbara, California.

Estamae's "Toy Shop" and Other Rhythms For Little Folk.

Album 1

Trombones, Trucks, Balls, Toy Soldiers, Trains, Jumping Jacks,
Rocking Horse, Dancing Dolls, Tops, Drums, Wind-up Dogs,
Donkeys, Jack-in-the-box, Cowboy Hat, Toy Piano, Roller Skates,
Baby Dolls, Tricycles, Airplanes, Rhythms--Skip, Tip-Toe, Walk,
Run, Jump, Heel-toe, Gallop, Clap Your Hands To The Music,
So--My Little Broom, My Toes, My Knees, Teddy Bear, One,
Two, Buckle My Shoe

The music is delightful and fits the action very nicely. The voice right
along with the music tells you what to do.

Album 2 - "Let's Have Fun Dancing" ($6.50)

Shoo Fly	Swap and Dive
Ti-Dee-O	Skip To M'Lou
A Hunting We Will Go	The Grapevine
Clap Happy	Polish Kapers

Album 4 - "Circus Fun" ($6.50)

Ten Little Indians	Hot-Cha
The Merry Farmer	Hokey Pokey
Did You Ever See A Lassie	Little Brown Jug
Three Blind Mice	Patty Cake Polka
Jolly Miller	Bingo
Gingersnaps	March-Skip

<u>Single Records</u>
>Clap Your Hands To The Music So
>My Little Broom, My Toes, My Knees
>Teddy Bear; One, Two, Buckle My Shoe
>Hickory Dickory, Two Little Blackbirds, How D'ye Do, My Partner
>Merrie Mac March; Pixie Polka
>Shoo Fly, Ti-Dee-O

These records must be ordered directly by mail from
Estamae Mac Farlane
2820 7th Avenue
Pueblo, Colorado

STORIES TOLD AND SUNG	AUTHOR	RECORDS
Ginger Bread Boy	Allen	Columbia Record
Goldilocks	Allen	Columbia
Two Little Trains	Brown	Columbia
My Chocolate Rabbit	Clooney	Columbia
Dandy, Handy, Candy	Clooney	Columbia
The Circus Day Parade	Faith	Columbia
The Little Engine That Could	Ives	Columbia
Peter Rabbit	Kelly	Columbia
Goldilocks	Luther, Frank	Decca
Little Red Riding Hood	Riggs	R. C. A. Victor
Billy Goats Gruff		Childcraft
Sambo And The Twins		R. C. A. Victor
Little Firemen		Young People's

POEMS

Record Album For "Time For Poetry"	Arbuthnot	Scott Foresman
Songs From "When We Were Very Young"	Milne	Columbia
Singing Album Vol. 1 "Now We Are Six"		Decca

SONGS

Songs From The Kindergarten Book	Album K	Ginn & Co.
Singing Program	Album No. E-83	R. C. A. Victor
Mother Goose	Luther, Frank	Decca
Nursery Rhymes	Luther, Frank	Decca
Songs of Safety	Luther, Frank	Decca

HABITS

The Nagger	Lewis	Capitol
The Noisy Eater	Lewis	Capitol
Cleanliness	Snooks	Capitol
Crossing Streets	Snooks	Capitol
Table Manners--Truthfulness	Snooks	Capitol

FAIRY TALES	AUTHOR	RECORDS
Peter Pan	Arthur	Columbia
Hansel and Gretel	Rathbone	Columbia

MUSICAL STORIES

Jimmy Cricket And The Sandman	Edwards	Columbia
Peter And The Wolf	Godfrey	Columbia
Tubby The Tuba	Jory	Columbia

RECORDS THAT INSPIRE ACTION

Train To The Farm	Children's Record Guild
Train To The Zoo	Children's Record Guild
Guess Who I Am	Columbia
Let's Have A Rhythm Band	Columbia
Lead A Little Orchestra	Columbia
Toy Town Parade	Columbia
Two Little Trains	Columbia
Ten Little Indians	The Record Guild of America
The Waltzing Elephant	Young Peoples Records
The Circus Comes To Town	Young Peoples Records
Little Brass Band	Young Peoples Records
Little Indian Drum	Young Peoples Records
Building A City	Young Peoples Records
Rainy Day	Young Peoples Records
When The Sun Shines	Young Peoples Records

CHRISTMAS RECORDS

Frosty The Snowman	Columbia
Here Comes Santa Claus	Columbia
Rudolph The Red Nosed Reindeer	Columbia
Story Of The Nativity	Columbia
Little Engine That Could	Columbia
Night Before Christmas	Peter Pan Records
Jolly Old St. Nicholas	Peter Pan Records
Grandfather Kringle	Columbia

EASTER RECORDS

Peter Cottontail	Columbia
Eggbert The Easter Egg	Columbia
Mr. Bunny	The Record Guild of America
Easter Parade	Peter Pan Records

SING 'N DO ALBUMS, #1, 2, 3, 4, 5

School Price Per Album $5.95 Postage Paid

Order from: Sing 'n Do Company, Inc.
P. O. Box 279
Ridgewood, New Jersey

Album #1   (Grades K-3)

I'm A Ding Dong Ding Dong Choo Choo
Maybe I'll Find A Kitty Under The Christmas Tree
An Indian Song
I'm A Little Puppet
My Little Puppy
Here Comes The Circus Parade

Album #2   (Grades K-3)

The Lazy Little Hen
I Am The Wind
The Clock Song
The Tiptoe Elf
Johnny Jump-Up
At The Rodeo

Album #3   (Grades 1-6)

Holiday Songs
The George Washington Song
Strolling Down The Street Easter Morning
When The Flag Is Passing By
I'm A Sailorman
If You Ask Me Why I'm Thankful
Caroling

Album #4   (Grades K-3)

In The Toy Shop
If I Could Have A Pony
The Little Rag Dolls
I'm A Little Chinese Doll
The Snapdragon Song
When The Little Dutch Shoes Parade

Album #5   (Grades K-3)

Down On The Farm
Little Ducky Daddle
You'll Never Catch Me
Little Scarecrow
Pumpkins On Parade
Needle In A Haystack

Rhythm Books

This list includes a group of rhythm books which were used in making the suggestions in this book. Others are included that would be usable in the schoolroom.

BOOK	AUTHOR	PUBLISHER
Arnold's Collection of Rhythms for the Kindergarten	Arnold, Francis	Willis Music Co. Cincinnati, Ohio
The American Singer	Beattie, Wolverton Wilson, Hinga	American Book Co. Chicago, Ill. (1944)
Play A Tune	The World of Music	Ginn and Co. Chicago, Ill.
Follow The Music	Goit and Bompton Watters	C. C. Birchard & Co. Chicago, Ill.
Time, Rhythm, and Song	Martin & Burnett	Hall and McCreary Chicago, Ill. (1942)
Rhythm Fun	Renstrom	Pioneer Music Press Salt Lake City, Utah
Happy Songs For Happy Children	Siebold, Meta	G. Schirmer, Inc. New York, N. Y.
Rhythms For Children	Luckhardt and Belder	Taylor & Co., Inc. New York, N. Y.
Rhythms of Childhood	Crawford and Fogg	A. S. Barnes & Co. New York, N. Y.
Rhythms For The Kindergarten	Hyde	Summy Co. Chicago, Illinois
Twenty Marches	Concord Series No. 5	G. Schirmer, Inc. Boston, Mass.
Music For The Child World Vol. 1-2	Hofer	Summy Co. Chicago, Ill.
Rhythm and Action	Ditson, Oliver	W. W. Norton Co. New York, N. Y.
Skips and Rhythmical Activities	Buckingham	Summy Co. Chicago, Ill.
Rota Pieces For Rhythm Band	Diller and Page	G. Schirmer, Inc. New York, N. Y.
Kindergarten Band Directions	Volow	Ludwig, Chicago, Ill.
Music Rhythms and Games	Weiland	Follet Publ. Co. Chicago, Ill.

BOOK	AUTHOR	PUBLISHER
Music in Playtime	Bentley-Matthewson	Summy Co. Chicago, Ill.
Singing Games For Children	Hamlin-Guessford	Welles Music Co. Cincinnati, Ohio
Rhythm Fun	Renstrom	Deseret Book Co. Salt Lake City, Utah
27 Songs, Rhythms & Story Plays	Stein	743 E. Lexington Blvd. Milwaukee, Wis.
16 Rhythms & Story Plays	Stein	743 E. Lexington Blvd. Milwaukee, Wis.
Interpretive Rhythms For Kindergarten	Culbertson	Box 1736 Milwaukee, Wis.
Handbook For Rhythm Band		C. G. Conn Elkhart, Indiana

Chapter 8

LESSON PLANS FOR A YEAR IN KINDERGARTEN

(SEPTEMBER THROUGH MAY)

Home and Family Life

Since kindergarten children do not share a common school background, many kindergarten teachers begin their year with this unit, knowing (1) that all children are familiar with home living, and (2) that the equipment needed, such as the doll house, furniture, and dolls, is part of the room equipment, and (3) that boys and girls will have an opportunity to use it.

SUBJECT MATTER

The Family

Members of the family:
Father, mother, sister, brother, grandmother, uncle, etc.
Ways to help the family:
Wipe dishes, sweep, run errands, dust, iron, watch the baby, etc.
Place of employment of members of the family:
Bank, store, school, office, garage, packing plant, etc.
Duties of each member of the family:
Keep house, make a living, etc.

Our Homes

Kinds:
Bungalow, apartment, duplex, basement, rambler, colonial, trailers, etc.
Material used in building homes:
Brick, wood, cement, stucco, stone, glass, steel.
Color of homes:
Red, blue, green, combination of colors.
Size:
Split level, basement, one floor, rambler, two story, etc.
Location of homes:
Stress learning street address and telephone number.

Food Served in the Home

Kinds of food:
Vegetables: kinds and where grown
Fruits: kinds and where grown
Breads: where made, and of what
Cereals: kinds, where grown, and how obtained

Meats: kinds, how kept and where obtained
Milk: how it gets to us; how it is kept sweet.
Source:
Markets, gardens

DEVELOPMENT

Telling Time

Engage in formal conversation about our homes, the people in
them, as well as the food we eat.
When talking about home life, use pictures taken from magazines
and mounted. (Very good ones can be found on family life,
types of homes and various kinds of food.)

Activity Period

Use these materials:
Color and paint pictures of the members of the family, where
they work, and where they live.
Make charts showing fruit and vegetables that are good for
us.
Make a bulletin board showing foods that make up a good
breakfast, lunch and dinner.

Model fruits, vegetables, and other food from play dough,
plasticine, or clay. If clay is used, it can be painted and
shellacked when dry.

Cut a picture of a home. Make a bulletin board using address
of child. If he knows his telephone number, use string and
connect with other childrens' homes.

Cut out furniture found in homes. Make charts, or booklets
of rooms in our homes using the furniture.

Make booklets depicting family life. Use old magazines and
colored pictures to make them. Make into one large booklet
on the family.

Individual scrap books can be made of family life, either use
magazine pictures or let children paint or color their own.

Build a play house. Use large building blocks. If none are
available, use playhouse screens.

This is also a good time to remodel an old play house that
might be in the room. Do such things as paper the walls,
hang up new pictures, paint the furniture, etc.

SONGS

Kindergarten Book   Pitts, Glen, Watters   Ginn & Co.

My Bed, p. 7; Everybody Says, p. 6; Pinky Winky Baby, p. 47;
What Are Babies Made Of? p. 47; Pat-A-Cake, p. 49; Bed Time,
p. 55; Lullaby, p. 61; I Always Want My Teddy Bear, p. 60;

Don't Drop Your Shoes, p. 60; Sleep, Baby, Sleep, p. 59; To Baby Land, p. 58; Hippity Hop to Bed, p. 55; Shoes, p. 126; Doll's Lullaby, p. 129.

Singing Time   Coleman   The John Day Co.

Baking Apples, p. 9; Go To Sleep, p. 19; The Canary, p. 20; Market Man, p. 40; Telling Time, p. 18.

My Picture Book of Songs   Dalton, Ashton, Young   Donohue & Co.

My Grandma, p. 25; Helping Mother, p. 25; Dolly's Lullaby, p. 33; Grandpa's Farm, p. 57.

The American Singer   Beattie, Wolverton, Wilson, Hinga   American Book Co.

Lullaby, p. 4; Calling, p. 6; Dolly's Lullaby, p. 6; Sleepy Time, p. 7; Baby's Song, p. 7; The Telephone, p. 9; Washing Dishes, p. 9; Washing Dishes, p. 10; A Song To Mother, p. 11; Rockaby Baby, p. 12.

Music For Young Americans   American Book Co.

Time to Rise, p. 13; Wake me, p. 14; What Time Is It, p. 15; Telephone, p. 16; The Washing Machine, p. 17; Be Polite, p. 17; Lady, Lady, p. 18; Mocking Bird Lullaby, p. 19; My Kitten, p. 19; My Tree House, p. 20; Mammy Loves, p. 20; Helping Mother, p. 21; My Prayer, p. 21.

Music For Early Childhood   Silver Burdett Co.

Counting Song, p. 8; Dance To Your Daddy, p. 10; Dolly's Lullaby, p. 12; Housecleaning Song, p. 12; Oh, Daddy Be Gay, p. 13; Setting The Table, p. 10; Who's That Knocking at My Door?, p. 14.

Singing Fun   Wood   Webster Publ. Co.

How Many People Live At Your House?, p. 49; The Old Clock, p. 63.

Happy Songs For Happy Children   Siebold   G. Schirmer, Inc.

Peek-A-Boo, p. 24; Our Piano, p. 23; Mama Dolly, p. 22; My Dolly, p. 21; The Rag Doll, p. 21; My Kitty, p. 20; My Doggie, p. 20; Daddy's Fiddle, p. 12; New Shoes, p. 32; My Parasol, p. 5; Daddy, p. 27.

POETRY

Childcraft   Field Enterprises

Song For A Little House, p. 128; The Shiny Little House, p. 129; Moving, p. 130; A New Friend, p. 130; Mix A Pancake, p. 132; Saturday Shopping, p. 132; Shelling Peas, p. 132; When Young

Melissa Sweeps, p. 133; Food, p. 135; The Cupboard, p. 135; Animal Crackers, p. 136; Shoes, p. 138; Galoshes, p. 138; Choosing Shoes, p. 139; Time To Rise, p. 143; Breakfast Time, p. 143; After A Bath, p. 145; Joys, p. 146; Mumps, 147; My Bed, p. 148; Everybody Says, p. 184; Daddy, p. 185; Dresses, p. 185; Uncle Frank, p. 187; Greaty-Great Grannie, p. 187; Doorbells, p. 187; Only One Mother, p. 194.

Time For Poetry   Scott, Foresman
                                                   & Co.

My Brother, p. 163; Fun In A Garret, p. 99; New Shoes, p. 97; The Cupboard, p. 7; Bunches of Grapes, p. 7; Smells, p. 3; Neighborly, p. 2; "SH", p. 3; Walking, p. 3.

Now We Are Six   E. P. Dutton Co.

Solitude, p. 1; Binker, p. 15; The Good Little Girl, p. 66; A Thought, p. 69; Cradle Song, p. 87; In The Dark, p. 99; The End, p. 102.

Let's Say Poetry Together   Rasmussen   Burgess Publ. Co.

Bedtime, p. 74; The Clock, p. 69; Mitten Song, p. 71; My Hands, p. 76; Nursery, p. 76; One Thing At A Time, p. 75; Only One Mother, p. 74; Politeness, p. 70; Prayer, p. 70; Song For A Little House, p. 73; What Shall I Buy, p. 75.

Choral Speaking   Educational Publ. Co.

Carolyn Goes Shopping, p. 26; Whistle, p. 55; A Present For Mother, p. 56; Hush-A-Bye Baby, p. 63; Grandpa's Farm, p. 86.

Everything And Anything   Aldis   Minton, Balch & Co.

The Sprinkler, p. 93; Naughty Soap Song, p. 91; Everybody Says, p. 89; Mouths, p. 87; Friends, p. 71; Night and Morning, p. 69; Dresses, p. 65; Feet, p. 49; The Goldfish, p. 27; Grown Up, p. 17; Hiding, p. 5.

The Sound of Poetry   Austin   Allyn & Bacon

Song For A Child, p. 30; Cats, p. 31; Bedtime, p. 92; The Critic, p. 92; Good Night, p. 93; I See The Moon, p. 94; Now I Lay Me, p. 94; My Bed, p. 94; Two In Bed, p. 95; Counting Sheep, p. 96; Snoring, p. 96; The Clock, p. 96; Softly, Drowsily, p. 98; Good Night, p. 99; The Big Clock, p. 99; The Toaster, p. 100; The Package, p. 100; In My New Clothing, p. 102; Newspaper, p. 102; Sneezing, p. 105; Mumps, p. 106; The Mitten Song, p. 107; Tummy Ache, p. 107; Walking, p. 108; Shoes, p. 109; Galoshes, p. 110; New Shoes, p. 110; Choosing Shoes, p. 111.

FINGERPLAYS

<u>Rhymes</u> <u>For</u> <u>Fingers</u>
<u>And</u> <u>Flannelboards</u>   Scott & Thompson   Webster Publ. Co.

My Family, p. 78; See My Family, p. 78; This Is The Father, p. 78; Here Is Baby's Tousled Head, p. 79; Five Little Babies, p. 79; This Little Boy, p. 80; Here Are Mother's Knives and Forks, p. 80; Thee Thee That, p. 81; These Are Grandmother's Glasses, p. 81; Indian Finger Game, p. 82; Here's A Little Washboard, p. 82; Ten Little Clothespins, p. 83; This Is The Way, p. 84; This Is A Fence, p. 85; Here's A Cup Of Tea, p. 85; Two Little Houses, p. 85; Someone Is Knocking, p. 86.

BOOKS

TITLE	AUTHOR	PUBLISHER
A House For Everyone	Miles and Lowrey	Knopf
10 In A Family	Steiner	Knopf
The Biggest Family In The Town	Sterling	E. M. Hale
Peek-A-Boo	Kessler	Doubleday & Co.
Kiki Goes To Camp	Steiner	Doubleday & Co.
Family Helpers	Hefflefinger	Melmont Publ.
Joel Gets A Haircut	Corcos	Abelard Press
The Very Little Girl	Krasilovsky	Doubleday & Co.
The Listening Walk	Showers	Thomas Crowell Co.
Everybody Has A House	Green	Wm. R. Scott
Kiki Dances	Steiner	Doubleday & Co.
Hello Peter	Gipson	Doubleday & Co.
Good Times At Home	Bauer	Melmont Publ.
The New Pet	Flack	Doubleday & Co.
Mommies	Carton	Random House
Goodnight Moon	Brown	E. M. Hale
Grandfather And I	Buckley	Lothrop, Lee & Shepard
The Quiet Mother	Zolotow	Lothrop, Lee & Shepard
The Lonely Doll	Wright	Doubleday & Co.

TITLE	AUTHOR	PUBLISHER
To Church We Go	Trent	Follett
Here Comes Daddy	Parks	E. M. Hale
Saturday Walk	Wright	Cadmus
A Day With Daddy	Tresselt	Lothrop, Lee & Shepard
Mommies At Work	Merriam	Knopf
My Own Little House	Kaune	Follett
Miss Frances' Story Book Of Manners	Horwich	Rand & McNally
Bubble Baths & Hair Bows	DeSantis	Doubleday & Co.
Everybody Eats & Everybody Has A House	Green	Cadmus
I Want To Be A Homemaker	Greene	Childrens Press
I Want To Be A Musician	Greene	Childrens Press
Hide And Seek Day	Zion-Graham	Harper & Bros.
Moving Day	Marino	The Dial Press
Find Out By Touching	Showers	Thomas Crowell Co.
I Wish I Had Another Name	Williams-Lubell	Atheneum
The Great Big Noise	Weir	Wilcox & Follett
The Water That Jack Drank	Scott	E. M. Hale

GAMES

Rhythmic Activities	Stuart-Ludlam	Burgess Publ. Co.

Bean Porridge Hot, p. 3; Broom Dance, p. 11; Dance of Greeting, p. 23; Did You Ever See A Lassie, p. 25; Farmer In The Dell, p. 27; Hickory, Dickory, Dock, p. 30; Looby Loo, p. 52, Muffin Man, p. 61; Rig-A-Jig-Jig. p. 82; Round And Round The Village, p. 84; The Thread Follows The Needle, p. 101; Tippy Toe Dance, p. 103.

Preparation for Winter

There are many sources for unit development in the kindergarten. The units and centers of interest that are easily developed and highly enjoyed are the ones most closely related to the child's experience. As children have watched their family, as well as the birds, and other animals get ready for winter this unit has a special appeal.

SUBJECT MATTER

How Our Parents Prepare For Winter

How does father prepare for winter?
He takes off the screens, puts on storm windows, check the heating plant, brings in bulbs from the garden, winterizes the car.
How does mother prepare for winter?
She cans fruit and vegetables, stores the food, and preserves jellies and jams and pickles.

How Nature Prepares For Winter

Animals and Birds
Change their coats, change their form, build different homes. Some burrow underground, others hibernate, some store their food. Some migrate in the fall, others stay all winter. Learn the names of birds migrating because of cold weather.
Plants
Leaves change color and fall to the ground. Some plants are seed plants such as beans, peas, oats. Collect seeds. See how they differ in size, shape, and color. Make a seed collection or chart. Some plants produce fruit, such as apples, pears, plums, and cherries. (Ask children to bring seeds from fruit. Discuss what we know about them.
Trees
Talk about different kinds of trees and their habits. Collect leaves, notice their size, shapes, and colors.

DEVELOPMENT

Telling Time

Take an excursion to see signs of fall.
Discuss signs of fall seen on the walk. (Relate discussion to subject matter above.)
Talk about the seeds children bring and make charts of them or arrange a seed collection.
Talk about developing a science corner and have children bring seeds, leaves, grains, etc.
Talk about the different kinds of trees seen on the excursion.
Collect leaves and mount them or press them.

Activity Period

Crayons and Paint
Draw and paint fall flowers, fall leaves, trees and plants, and animals. Use color wash on some when completed.
Make pictures of children picking fall flowers, raking and burning leaves.

Paint pictures of animals preparing for winter.
Draw and paint pictures of things seen on our walk.
Clay and Plasticine
Model a squirrel, and other animals children have been dis-
cussing.
Model fall fruits and vegetables.
Make trees and leaves.
Paper Tearing And Cutting
Cut and tear fall flowers and leaves, mount on colored paper.
Also cut trees and leaves, as well as fall fruit.
Cooking
Make apple or plum or grape jelly at school with fruit chil-
dren decide upon.   Store it away for use at a room party.

SONGS	BOOK
"Harvest"	Days Of Make Believe
"Apple Tree"	Singing Time
"Falling Leaves"	Singing Time
"October"	Singing Time
"The Leaves"	The Kindergarten Book
"Down! Down!"	The Kindergarten Book
"Wind Is Singing"	The Kindergarten Book
"The Caterpillar"	Days of Make Believe
"The Busy Squirrels"	Days of Make Believe
"November Winds"	American Singer
"The Empty Nest"	American Singer
"The Golden Leaves"	American Singer
"Whirley Twirley"	My Picture Book of Songs
"Crunch Leaves"	My Picture Book of Songs

RHYTHMS

Children will enjoy individual interpretation of various rhythmic movements about fall activities: raking leaves, pushing the wheel barrow,
tramping through the leaves, falling and twirling leaves, and shuffling
through the leaves.   They will also take part in gathering nuts and fruit
as we do in the fall.   Birds leaving for the winter is another interpretation that can be used along with hunting.

STORIES	AUTHOR
"All Ready For Winter:	Adelson
"From Crocus to Snowman"	Bascom
"Hurry, Scurry, and Flurry"	Buff
"Now It's Fall"	Lenski
"All Around Us"	Bendick
"Fall Is Here"	Parker
"Autumn Harvest"	Tressett
"Gray Squirrel"	Witty
"Come Summer, Come Winter"	Shannon
"The Four Seasons"	Gottlieb

GAMES

"Animal Chase"	Games For The Playground
"Oats, Peas, Beans"	Games For The Playground
"Squirrel In The Trees"	Games For The Playground
"Rabbit In The Hollow"	Rhythms and Dances
"Did You Ever See A Lassie"	The Kindergarten Book

Halloween

GENERAL AIMS

To interpret holidays in a simple way understandable to children.
To provide a rich experience in the arts.

SUBJECT MATTER

Discuss things to do on Halloween Night. Such things as:
Show our lanterns, ring door bells for "tricks or treats", have
fun!
Talk about dressing warmly; crossing streets carefully, watching
for cars.

Talk about how we can plan for Halloween at school:
Plan a party (keep it simple), choose committees such as decorating, entertaining, table setting, games, clean-up.

DEVELOPMENT

Telling Time

Let children tell how they plan to spend Halloween. Let them tell
how they are going to dress and what they are going to do.

Activity Period

Masks
Use large brown grocery sacks and let children create their
own faces for the masks.
Or use soap boxes and create a face and stuff them and put
them on a broom stick to ride.
Jack-O-Lanterns
Each section could make its own real Jack-O-Lantern. Together the group could plan what kind of expression they
want the face to have. Each child could help scoop out
the insides, while the teacher does all the cutting.
Each child can have his own Jack-O-Lantern by using small
brown or white grocery sacks and painting them completely orange. Then put in the face, and tie the bottom
of the sack with yarn after putting newspaper inside the
sack. Paint the bottom of the sack green to represent
the stem.

Owls
> Use a regular brown paper towel. Double it and stuff it with newspaper. Shred the bottom, and tie with yard. Put an owl face on the front. Masking tape may be used to attach the sides. Some prefer to use brown paper bags for this.

Spook Tree
> Use a branch of a lilac bush or any bush and mount it on a square box or plant it in a flower pot and fill with clay. Let the children make anything "spooky" out of white, black, and orange paper such as cats, pumpkins, or witches.

A general discussion about the things you see at Halloween and what they look like often helps them get interested in using other media such as clay, paint, etc.

> Draw a pumpkin and put yarn around the outline, and color the inside.
> Make drawings illustrating a Halloween story.
> Make napkins and doilies for the party and decorate them.
> Paint stories of what the children will wear and do Halloween night.
> Make clay pumpkins, jack-o-lanterns, and cats. Paint the ones made of clay.
> Cut and tear pumpkin faces.

HALLOWEEN PARTY

Planning a simple party gives excellent chance to stress many basic fundamentals, such as planning a group activity, sharing and giving.
Discuss party preparations such as what to do at the party which might include:

> Frost graham crackers with colored powdered sugar icing. Use raisins to make the pumpkin faces.
> Pop corn during the time the children are in the room and let them listen to it pop and then eat some of it.
> Some children enjoy bringing a vegetable from home, cutting it up and putting them all together to make vegetable soup.

SONGS

The Kindergarten Book   Ginn & Co.

> Halloween Is Coming, p. 73; See My Big Eyes, p. 73; Boo!, p. 73; I'm A Jack-O-Lantern, p. 75; Halloween Has Come, p. 75.

Music For Early Childhood

> Halloween Mask, p. 97; The Witch Rides, p. 97; Halloween Fun, p. 98.

Singing Time   Coleman & Thorn   The John Day Co.

    Halloween, p. 46.

Music For Young Americans   American Book Co.

    Witches, p. 111; False Face, p. 112; Halloween Pumpkin, p. 113;
Goblin In The Dark, p. 113; Halloween Night, p. 114.

The American Singer   American Book Co.

    Funny Witches, p. 55; Brownies and Witches, p. 55.

Happy Songs For Happy
    Children   Siebold   G. Schirmer

    Halloween, p. 31; The Brownies, p. 10.

More Singing Fun   Wood   Webster Publ. Co.

    Three Green Goblins, p. 15; I'm Not Scared, p. 16; Tonight Is
Halloween, p. 18; Witches' Dance, p. 19; Smallest Witch, p. 20.

My Picture Book of Songs   Dalton, Ashton,
                      Young   M. A. Donohue

    Boo!, p. 21; Mr. Jack O'Lantern, p. 21.

Singing Fun   Wood   Webster Publ. Co.

    Three Little Pumpkins, p. 6; Halloween's Coming, p. 7;
I Made A Jack-O-Lantern, p. 8; In A Pumpkin Patch, p. 9.

Songs And Stories About
    Animals   Crowinshield   Boston Music Co.

    Black Cat, p. 27.

RHYTHMS

The Kindergarten Book   Ginn & Co.

    Jack-O-Lantern Parade; Halloween Spooks And Witches Creeping
About On Tiptoe, Trying To Scare People, p. 20; Pretend To Be
Gnomes With Short Bodies, Large Heads, And Big Feet, p. 74.
Skipping To The Field To Pick Pumpkins, p. 73; "Gigue", Corelli
Jack-O-Lantern Parade, "Tiptoe March", p. 20; Children Pretend
To Steal From House To House And Scare People, "Gnomes,
Reinhold, p. 74 (Victor Rhythm Album One).

Children can be ghosts trying to glide about softly and quietly. Boys
and girls love to be witches riding on a broom stick and they can make
up their own songs to well known tunes such as:
    Tune: The Mulberry Bush
          "I'm going to ride the witch's broom.
          The witch's broom, the witch's broom.
          I'm going to ride the witch's broom
          High up to the moon. "

Happy Songs For Happy   Siebold   G. Schirmer, Inc.
  Children

  The Brownies, p. 10 (Song And Dance).

Romp In Rhythm   Seatter, Minnis,   The Willis
                                 Wallace   Music Co.

  Brownies Cavort--Tip Toe, p. 8; Brownies Side Skip, p. 9;
  Ringing The Bell, p. 10; Scampering, p. 12; Jack-O-Lantern
  March, p. 13.

Games-Rhythms-Dances   Barnett   George Stanley Co.

  Pumpkin Man and Brownie, p. 32.

RECORDINGS

Phoebe James Records, Box 134, Pacific Palisades, California,
  "Halloween Rhythms"

Bowmar Records, Inc., 10515 Burbank Blvd., North Hollywood,
  California, "Holiday Rhythms", also Rhythm Time No. 2
  (Scarecrow Walk)

GAMES

Pin The Tail On The Black Cat
  Draw a picture of a large black cat, omit the tail. Cut many tails
and give to the children. One child is blindfolded at a time. He tries
to see how close he can come to pinning the tail on the cat. The one
coming closest to the correct spot, wins.

Poor Pussy
  The group form a circle, sitting on chairs. The one who is "It"
goes to different ones in the circle, kneels down and "Me-ows" in a
mournful tone. The child in front of whom Pussy is kneeling, pats
Pussy on the head three times, each time saying, "Poor Pussy." The
trick is not to smile or laugh as he pets her and says: "Poor Pussy".
If he does, he must be Pussy.

Pumpkin Chase
  Children are seated in a circle, one child in the center. When
the music starts, pass a pumpkin around the circle. (Can use a ball
with a face colored on it). When the music stops, the child with the
pumpkin must go in the center.

Musical Chairs
  Tape a paper pumpkin on the back of one chair. When the music
starts the children proceed around the circle until the music stops.
When the music stops, the child in the 'Pumpkin' chair is out. The
game continues until all are out.

A Jack-O-Lantern For You
  Children stand in a circle, one child is in the center. He places
a small jack-o-lantern in one hand and calls on a child from the cir-

cle to guess which hand it is in. (You may use a song with it, from the Kindergarten Book, p. 86.

Goblin In The Dark

  Tune: The Farmer In The Dell

The children may sit around a circle. One child is chosen to be the Goblin in the dark. The children sing:
 "The Goblin in the dark, the Goblin in the dark
 Hi! Ho!, on Halloween, the Goblin in the dark.

  The Goblin takes a witch.
  The Witch takes a ghost.
  The ghost takes a cat.
  The cat takes a brownie.

  They all screech and scream, they all screech and scream
  Hi! Ho! on Halloween they all screech and scream. Boo!"

STORIES

TITLE	AUTHOR	PUBLISHER
Georgie To The Rescue	Bright	Doubleday & Co.
Gus Was A Friendly Ghost	Thayer	William Morrow & Co.
A Tiger Called Thomas	Zolotow	Lothrop, Lee & Shepard
Over And Over	Williams	Harper & Bros.
Wobble, The Witch Cat	Calhoun	Morrow & Co.
Georgie	Bright	Doubleday & Co.
Georgie's Halloween	Bright	Doubleday & Co.
Danny's Luck	Davis	Doubleday & Co.
Punkin's First Halloween	Reinecke	T. S. Denison
Scat, The Witch's Cat	Ross-Werth	Whittlesey House
Mousekin's Golden House	Miller	A Guild Book
Tell Me Mr. Owl	Foster	Lothrop, Lee & Shepard
The Witch of Hissing Hill	McCaffery	Morrow
The Witch Who Wasn't	Roth	MacMillan
Story Telling With The Flannel Board	Anderson	T. S. Denison & Co.

  Queer Company, p. 21; The Teeny Tiny Woman, p. 28; Halloween Subtraction, p. 32.

Peter Pumpkin	Ott	Doubleday & Co.

FINGER PLAYS

<u>Rhymes</u> <u>For</u> <u>Fingers</u>   Scott and   Webster Publ. Co.
<u>and</u> <u>Flannelboards</u>   Thompson

Halloween, p. 39; Ten Little Pumpkins, p. 60; Three Little
Witches, p. 61; Five Little Goblins, p. 61.

Christmas

No day in the whole year so stirs the child's imagination as Christmas.
It is a stimulating time to children.   There is so much to do and to see at this
time of the year.   The stores are full of toys that each child hopes he will re-
ceive.   There are other programs, many times very elaborately planned and
many times rehearsed.   Because of all these outside activities, it seems
much better if we keep our school plan simple.

SUBJECT MATTER

<u>Why do we have Christmas</u>?

Talk about the real meaning of Christmas.   (To celebrate the
birthday of a King.)

<u>Why do we give gifts</u>?

To show our love and affection to our family and friends.

<u>To whom do we give gifts</u>?

To our families and friends.

<u>How do we celebrate</u>?

Hang up our stockings, decorate trees, sing carols, exchange
gifts, etc.

<u>How could we decorate our room</u>?

Make paper chains, bells, wreaths, candles, etc.

<u>Talk about buying a tree</u>

How large should it be? What kind?
Who shall buy it? (All of the children.)
How shall we decorate it? (Make the ornaments.)

<u>Plan a Christmas Party</u>

Plan the games and songs.
Make doilies, napkins.
Divide up into committees.

DEVELOPMENT

Telling Time

Many of the children will want to tell of things they have seen in the windows and stores.

Talk over what they would like to make as gifts for mother and father. Decide what will be needed to make these gifts.

Discuss ways of decorating the kindergarten and the tree.

Activity Period

Crayons and Paint

Draw and paint pictures of people going Christmas shopping.
Color pictures of toys children have asked Santa to bring.
Decorate tags and wrapping paper.
Make a gift for mother and father, and wrap them.
Make doilies and napkins, and decorate plates for the party.
Draw and paint snowmen.
Make a Christmas Frieze.
Paint Christmas trees.
Decorate cones.

Clay and Plasticine

Model trees, santas, sleighs, and bells.
Fashion of clay some of the toys you would like to have under your tree.

Paper Tearing and Cutting

Cut and tear Christmas trees.
Make tree decorations and window decorations.

SONGS

The Kindergarten Book   Ginn & Co.

Bells of Christmas, p. 78; Christmas Song, p. 78; The Angels, p. 79; O Little Town of Bethlehem, p. 79; Away In A Manger, p. 80; Chimes of Christmas, p. 80; Kitten's Christmas Song, p. 81; Silent Night, p. 81; Greeting Song, p. 82; Jingle Bells, p. 82; Santa's Helpers, p. 83.

Music For Early Childhood   Silver Burdett Co.

Mary Has A Baby, Yes, Lord, p. 103; Round The Christmas Tree, p. 104; I Saw Three Ships, p. 105; Santa's Sleigh, p. 105; In A Manger, p. 106.

Music For Young Americans   American Book Co.

Santa Claus Is Coming, p. 116; Christmas Is Coming, p. 116; O Christmas Tree, p. 117; We Wish You A Merry Christmas Day, p. 118; Christmas Day, p. 118; Merry Christmas, p. 119.

The <u>American</u> <u>Singer</u>   American Book Co.

> Christmas Bells, p. 58; The Christmas Tree, p. 60; Christmas Holidays, p. 61; Jingle, Jingle, p. 60; I'll Hang My Stocking, p. 62.

<u>Singing</u> <u>Time</u>   Coleman-Thorn   The John Day Co.

> Happy New Year, p. 1; Snow Flakes, p. 3; Santa Claus, p. 4; The Snowman, p. 5; Christmas Bells, p. 6.

<u>More</u> <u>Singing</u> <u>Fun</u>   Wood   Webster Publ. Co.

> Christmas Lullaby, p. 26; Sing On Christmas Morn, p. 27; Christmas Candles, p. 28; Mister Santa Claus, p. 29; Santa's Sleigh, p. 30; Christmas Tree Lights, p. 31; Christmas Counting Song, p. 32; On The Hay, p. 33.

<u>Happy</u> <u>Songs</u> <u>For</u> <u>Happy</u> <u>Children</u>   Siebold   G. Schirmer

> Out Walking, p. 30; Santa's Sleighbells, p. 30;

<u>Singing</u> <u>Fun</u>   Wood   Webster Publ. Co.

> Ten Little Jingle Bells, p. 24; Magic Time, p. 25; Christmas Tree Angel, p. 26; On A Christmas Night, p. 27; Santa's Reindeer, p. 28.

<u>My</u> <u>Picture</u> <u>Book</u> <u>of</u> <u>Songs</u>   Dalton, Ashton,   M. A. Donohue
                                        Young   & Co.

> Santa Claus, p. 29; Bein' Good, p. 29; My Christmas Stocking, p. 31; Decorating The Tree, p. 31; Dolly's Lullaby, p. 33; Christmas Toys, p. 33.

STORIES

TITLE	AUTHOR	PUBLISHER
Where's Prancer	Hoff	Harper & Bros.
The Night Before Christmas	Moore	E. M. Hale & Co.
The Animals' Merry Christmas	Jackson	Simon & Schuster
How The Grunch Stole Christmas	Dr. Seuss	Random House
Christmas Eve	Hurd	Harper & Row
The Christmas Forest	Fatio	American Book Co.
The Glorious Christmas Soup Party	Hale	Viking Press
The Faraway Christmas	Hurd	Lothrop, Lee & Shepard

TITLE	AUTHOR	PUBLISHER
The Animals' Christmas Tree	Peters	Walck
The Year Santa Went Modern	Armour	McGraw-Hill
The Christmas Kitten	Konkle	Childrens Press
Santa's Toy Shop	Disney	Simon & Schuster
The Christmas Bunny	Will & Nicholas	Harcourt, Brace & Co.
Christmas Eve At The Mellops	Ungerer	Harper & Bros.
Christmas Is A Time Of Giving	Anglund	Harcourt, Brace & World
Rudolph, The Red-Nose Reindeer	May	Maxton Publ.
Christmas In The Stable	Lindgren	Coward-McCann
A Pussycat's Christmas	Brown	Thomas & Crowell
How Mrs. Santa Claus Saved Christmas	McGinley	J. B. Lippincot
Story Telling With The Flannel Board	Anderson	T. S. Denison & Co.
Little Janie's Christmas	Virginia Smith	Wilcox & Follet Co.

Wee Ann, p. 137; The Runaway Coolies, p. 68; Pedro's Christmas Flower, p. 185; A Jolly Fellow, p. 190; The Smith's Christmas, p. 252; The Jingle Bells, p. 247;

RECORDINGS

Decca Album A & DA 290	A Christmas Carol	
Decca Album DA 399	The Littlest Angel	
Decca Album DA 533	The Small One	
A Firefly In A Fir Tree	Knight	Harper & Row
A Christmas Stocking Story	Knight	Harper & Row
Angels & Berries (Candy Canes)	Knight	Harper & Row

CHRISTMAS GAMES

Rhymes For Fingers and Flannelboards	Scott & Thompson	Webster Publ. Co.

Dreams, p. 64; The Angel On My Christmas Tree, p. 65; Five Bright Stars, p. 65; The Toy Shop, p. 66; This Baby Piggie, p. 66; In Santa's Workshop, p. 67; Eight Tiny Reindeer, p. 68; Santa's Reindeer, p. 69; Christmas Presents, p. 69; This Little Present, p. 70.

CHRISTMAS GAMES

Christmas Shopper
 The children are seated in a circle or at their tables, and the "shopper" stands in front of the group. Each child is given the name of a toy, such as doll, train, sled, or skates. The child who is "It" may say: "I want to buy a teddy bear and a ball." Whoever is a teddy bear and a ball try to change places before the shopper gets one of them. If he does, he remains the shopper for a second time. If he fails, a new shopper is chosen.

Going To The North Pole
 One child is the leader. Eight children representing the reindeer, form in couples, hands joined behind them. Another child, the driver, is placed at the end of the line. The reindeer march around the room chanting: "We are Santa's reindeer, we are Santa's reindeer. Prancing from the North Pole at forty miles an hour." When the driver calls, "Giddap", the leader turns and tries to catch a reindeer, who now run about the room. He may chase them until the driver calls, "Whoa". The last one caught becomes the leader. The leader takes the driver's place. If no one is caught, both keep their places a second time, when a new driver and leader are chosen.

Chimney Corner
 A child is chosen to be Santa Claus and takes his place in the center of the room. The others line up on two sides of the room. Santa turns around several times saying, "Which chimney shall I enter?" Suddenly he points to one child and exclaims, "I think I shall climb down that one." Immediately the child indicated changes places with the one opposite him. If Santa catches a child, he is allowed to remain Santa a second time; if none is caught, a new Santa is chosen.

Lost Reindeer
 All the players but two form a circle. Of the two, one is Santa Claus, the other, Santa's reindeer. The reindeer, with some bells in his hand, and Santa, who is blindfolded each time, stand inside the circle. The circle begins to move, singing: "Jingle Bells." Then the singing ceases and all players stand quietly as Santa calls out, "I've lost a reindeer. I must find him." The reindeer tiptoes up to Santa, rings the bell, and quickly moves away. Santa tries to catch him. After a few minutes, whether Santa succeeds or not, two other players take their places.

Merry Christmas
 One person is chosen to be Santa. The other players join hands in a circle. Santa touches two of the players joined hands and those players run in opposite directions. When they meet, they shake hands, say: "Merry Christmas" and continue around the circle. The first player back in place becomes Santa.

Christmas Wreath
 This is a version of "London Bridge is Falling Down". Using an inflated inner tube wound with strips of green crepe paper, two

children hold the wreath high in the air while the others form one line and walk under it. The last line might be: "Christmas time is almost here, and we catch you."

Over The Housetops

Divide the class into teams. Each team has three ten pins spaced at equal distances between the starting line and the goal line thirty feet away. The clubs represent house tops and each player is a Santa. On the signal, the first Santa from each team runs to the first housetop, jumps over it and continues. After the last jump he runs to the first housetop, goal line and returns, jumping each housetop on the way, and touches the next Santa, who then proceed in the same manner. If a housetop is knocked over, the player must reset it and jump successfully before continuing.

Hide The Christmas Bell

This game is played like hide the thimble only use a small bell instead of a thimble.

Christmas Tree Skip

Draw several small Christmas trees around the circle. Have children skip around the circle and when the music stops, children must find a tree to stand on or they are out of the game. Game continues until all are out.

Christmas Chairs

This game is played like musical chairs. Tape a Christmas card on the back of a chair. Children march around the chairs until the music stops. Whoever is on the "Christmas Chair" is out, and he takes a chair from the end of the line and puts it away. Game continues until one child is left.

Pass The Christmas Toy

Make a toy from construction paper. Pass it around the circle as the music plays. When the music stops, the child holding the toy is out of the game. Continue until only one child is left.

Writing A Letter To Santa

Teacher usually starts the game as children are seated around the circle. She says to the child next to her: "I asked Santa to bring me_____." Each child repeats what he heard from the child ahead of him. This is said only once by each child. The last person in the line stands and tells what he has heard.

Bell Toss

Toss bean bags at cardboard bell with hole in the center. Prop it up on the floor a few feet from the line for the children to stand behind.

Mailman

Children sit in a circle. Each child rolls the ball to some friend in the circle as he says: "I am mailing a Christmas present to_____ _____."

Reindeer and Santa Claus

Formation: Groups of three. Two (reindeer) stand side by side, inside hands joined, left side to center of room. The third dance, (Santa Claus), stands behind the two, dancing in the same direction. He reaches forward and takes in his hands the outside hands of the two reindeer, which they extend backward.

Music: The tune, "Jingle Bells" is the music for this rhythm.

Procedure: "Dashing through the snow" - on these words the two reindeer make a pawing movement with their right feet, three times.
"In a one-horse open sleigh, " - paw with the left foot on the words.
"O'er the fields we go, laughing all the way!" - all walk forward in rhythm with the music.
"Bells on Bobtail ring, making spirits bright,
What fun it is to ride and sing a sleighing song tonight!" -
All skip forward, stopping on the word night.

Chorus:
"Jingle bells, jingle bells, jingle all the way!
The two reindeer turn about to face Santa. All clap in in rhythm with the words.
"Oh what fun it is to ride"
Santa takes the right hand of the reindeer on his right with right hand and they skip around in place, once.
"Jingle bells, jingle bells, jingle all the way!"
Santa goes back to his own place, once.
"Jingle bells, jingle bells, jingle all the way"
Santa goes back to his own place and all clap the rhythm as before to those words.
"Oh what fun it is to ride, in a one-horse open sleigh!"
All join hands in a little circle of three and skip around to the left. Finish in the starting position, ready to do the rhythm over again from the beginning.

"Dear Old Santa" - To the tune of "All Around the Mulberry Bush"

1. Santa goes down the chimney flue, the chimney flue, the chimney flue,
Dear Old Santa (Arms raise to make flue, stoop slowly as going down the flue.) (Cross arms over chest and hug yourself on 'Dear Old Santa'.)
2. He opens up his bag of toys, bag of toys, bag of toys----
3. He takes out a horn that says toot-toot----
4. He takes out a doll that says mama----
5. He takes out a bell that says ding-dong----
6. He takes out a car that says honk-honk----
7. He takes out a train that says chug-chug----

8. He takes out a gun that says bang-bang----
9. He takes out a duck that says quack-quack----
10. He takes out a drum that says boom-boom----
11. Santa goes up the chimney flue, the chimney flue, the chimney flue, Santa goes up the chimney flue, Good-bye Dear Old Santa.

RHYTHMS

The Kindergarten Book   Ginn & Co.

Let's Dance Around the Christmas Tree, p. 84;
Christmas Tree March, p. 85 (Children may carry decorations as they march around the tree);
Bells of Christmas, p. 78 (Children play this rhythm with sleigh bells);
Jingle Bells, p. 82 (Have children ring sleigh bells when music suggests jingle bells);
Santa's Helpers, p. 83 (Have children use rhythm sticks when music says to tap);
Galloping Reindeer: Sicilienne. From "Armide", p. 16 (Victor Rhythm Album One);
Christmas Jumping Jacks: Jumping. Salto Mortale, p. 22 (Victor Rhythm Album Two);
Teddy Bear Walking: Let's Take A Walk, p. 23;
Christmas Orchestra: Happy And Light. From "Bohemian Girl", p. 14 (Rhythm sticks, bells, jingle sticks, drums, wood blocks) (Victor Rhythm Album Two);
Santa's Elves: Tiptoe. (Amaryllis), p. 21 (Tripping like elves);
Toy Soldiers: March, p. 25 (Victor Album Two); Military March, Tin Soldiers Marching, p. 28 (Victor Album Two);
Roll Christmas Ball: (Use a red ball) Harvest Home, p. 29;
Ice Skating: Waltz, p. 31, The Reaper's Song, p. 32 (Victor Rhythm Album Two);
Rocking Horse: p. 52 (Victor Rhythm Album One); Presto. Op. 31, No. 3, p. 53; Knight Of The Hobby Horse, p. 54 (Victor Rhythm Album Three);
Riding a Stick Horse, p. 57;
Rocking Christmas Dolls, p. 61 (Victor Rhythm Album Three);
Spinning Top, p. 127 (Victor Listening Album One);
Dancing Dolls, p. 129.

Romp In Rhythm   Seatter, Minnis, The Willis Music
         Wallace   Co.

The Jumping Jacks, p. 22; The Jack In The Boxes, p. 23; The Train, p. 24; Rag Doll Dance, p. 27; French Doll Dance, p. 28; The Rocking Horse, p. 29.

Games, Rhythms, Dances   Barnett   George Stanley Co.
                 1225 S. Biscayne Pt. Rd.
                 Miami Beach, Florida

A Visit To The Toy Shop, p. 44; Did You Ever See Dear Old Santa, p. 12; Here We Go Round The Christmas Tree, p. 14.

Music For Early Childhood   New Music Horizons

    Jack In The Box, p. 62; Round The Christmas Tree, p. 104;
    The Orchestra, p. 72.

Rhythmic Activities   Stuart-Ludlam   Burgess Publishing Co.

    Jingle Bells, p. 41; Dance Of The Snowflakes, p. 39; Shoe-
    maker's Dance, p. 89.

RECORDINGS

Children's Record Guild and Young People's Records. Greystone Corp.,
100 Sixth Avenue, New York 12, N.Y.
    "The Merry Toy Shop"   R.P.M. 45-78

Phoebe James Records, Box 124, Pacific Palisades, Calif.
    "Santa Claus and Reindeer"

Bowmar Records, Inc., 10515 Burbank Blvd., North Hollywood, Calif.
    "Holiday Rhythms"

POETRY

Time For Poetry   Arbuthnot   Scott, Foresman Co.

    An Old Christmas Greeting, p. 170; Christmas, p. 170; Christmas
    Pudding, p. 170; Carol, Brothers, Carol, p. 170; Bundles, p. 170;
    A Visit From St. Nicholas, p. 171; Here We Come A-Caroling,
    p. 172; In The Week When Christmas Comes, p. 172; For Christ-
    mas Day, p. 173; Song, p. 173; Cradle Hymn, p. 173; A Christ-
    mas Carol, p. 174.

Let's Say Poetry Together   Rasmussen   Burgess Publ. Co.

    Bundles, p. 57; Christmas Carol, p. 62; Christmas Carol, p. 57;
    Christmas Cookies, p. 60; Christmas Hearth Rhyme, p. 61;
    Christmas On The Heart, p. 60; Long, Long Ago, p. 57; My
    Christmas Wish, p. 60; Santa Claus, p. 58; Santa Claus, p. 61;
    Why Do Bells For Christmas Ring?, p. 59.

Choral Speaking   Hemphill   Educational Publ.
                                                                     Co.

    A Welcome To You, p. 17; The Bells, p. 26; My Christmas
    Gift, p. 29; A Shepherd Tells The Story, p. 36; The Christmas
    Story, p. 39.

The Sound Of Poetry   Austin   Allyn & Bacon

    Santa Claus, p. 374; Christmas, p. 375; Christmas Is Coming,
    p. 375; The Friendly Beast, p. 376; The Barn, p. 377; Cradle
    Hymn, p. 378; The Christmas Candle, p. 380; Why Do The Bells
    Of Christmas Ring, p. 381; The First Christmas, p. 381; A
    Christmas Carol, p. 382

Poems	Govoni-Smith	Golden Press

An Old Christmas Greeting, p. 38; Christmas, p. 38; Bundles, p. 39; Here We Come A-Caroling, p. 39; White Fields, p. 40.

One Thousand Poems For Children	Sechrist	Macrae-Smith Co.

The Christ Candle, p. 175; My Gift, p. 175; Santa Claus, p. 176.

Sing A Round	Harrington	Macmillan Co.

Xmas Song, p. 170; A Christmas Folk Song, p. 171; Long, Long, Ago, p. 174.

Travel

Children enjoy telling about the places they have visited. Because so many people take movies of their trips and snapshots of their travels, this project is one in which small children show a great deal of interest. Most children have daily experiences with things that go.

SUBJECT MATTER

Methods of Travel

Talk about the different ways animals use to get places:
Hop, walk, crawl, fly, jump, etc.
Talk about animals that help people travel:
Horses, camels, donkeys, ponies, dogs, etc.
Relate how people get places:
Walk, ride in cars, travel in busses, use bicycles, wagons, etc.
Talk about how people travel long distances:
By bus, car, plane, boat, etc.

Travel By Land

Trains

Ask children to tell about train trips they have taken. Discuss different kinds of trains:
Passenger, freight
Talk about the different kinds of cars on a passenger and freight train:
Baggage, pullman, diner, mail, coach, observation, box, refrigerator, tank, stock, etc.
Discuss the various types of engines used:
Steam, electric, diesel.
Tell about the workers on the train and at the station:
Conductor, brakeman, waiter, engineer, fireman, porter, chef, mailman, waiter, station agent, red caps, dispatcher.

Travel By Water

Boats

Have children tell about many different kinds of boats they have seen, traveled in, or heard about.

Freighters, row boats, canoes, speed boats, ocean liners, sail boats, submarines, river boats, ferry boats, tugs, yachts, fishing boats, navy ships, etc.

Travel By Air

Airplanes

Talk about the many different kinds of planes children have seen.

Transports, jets, army planes, privately owned.

Encourage children to tell about rides they have taken.

Discuss the fastest way of traveling.

Talk about the workers that help in air travel:

Pilot, co-pilot, stewardess, mechanic, weather man, baggage man, radio operator, dispatcher, telegraph operator.

ACTIVITY PERIOD

Collect pictures from the children for a class scrapbook on the various forms of travel.

Suggest children bring toys from home to show the different way to travel. Let children tell about them.

Engage in dramatic play with blocks and toys. Construct a train from large blocks or apple crates. Build a round house with trains going in and out. Construct a station.

Engage in playing train. Choose an engineer, conductor, passengers. Have children make tickets, money, food, etc. to be used on the trip.

Construct a boat from building blocks or from crates. Engage in dramatic play on the boat, choosing people to work on the boat.

Construct a large bus from packing boxes. Put it on wheels so children can ride from room to room.

Use crayons or paint to make a frieze about the different modes of travel. Paint in the background using land, air, and water. Let the children cut and color various modes of travel and attach to the frieze in the proper place; include air, land, and water.

Color pictures of the different animals used in travel.

Allow children to paint and color pictures of trips they have taken.

Model animals from clay. These can be animals that help us in moving from place to place. These can be painted when dry. Plasticine may also be used in this way.

Draw pictures of vehicles that help us travel.

Take an excursion to the station and watch the train come in. If an appointment is made ahead of time, and time reserved, an employee will show the children around the station and the train.

If possible, take a train ride. It may be best to go by car one way and return by train. This is an excellent time to have a tour of the train and actually see workmen at their jobs.

After children have had a ride on the train they will want to draw and paint pictures of this experience.

An excursion to the bus depot is also advised. They enjoy seeing a bus being loaded with baggage and passengers. Some bus companies take the children back to school in a large bus so they have the experience of riding on one.

Encourage a visit from the Safety Patrol Officer telling about bike safety.

RHYTHMS

Playing Train: Run, Run, Run by Giuseppe Concone, p. 11, Kdg. Bk.
(Victor Rhythm Album Two)
Dance of the Moorish Slaves by Giuseppe Verdi.
The Train: Romp In Rhythm by Seatter. The Willis Music Co.
Riding On A Bus: The Knight Of The Hobby Horse by Robert Schumann.
(Victor Rhythm Album Three)
The Bus Ride: Romp In Rhythm by Seater. The Willis Music Co.
Playing Airplanes: Running Game by Cornelius Gurlitt, p. 12, Kdg. Bk.
(Victor Rhythm Album Two)
Gigue by Arcangelo Corelli, p. 13 Kdg. Bk.
(Victor Rhythm Album One)
The Airplane Ride: Romp In Rhythm by Seatter. The Willis Music Co.
Walking: The Little Traveller by A. Gretchanioff, p. 24, Kdg. Bk.
Roller Skating: The Reaper's Song by Robert Schumann, p. 32, Kdg. Bk.
Horseback Riding: Hunting Song by Robert Schumann, p. 42, Kdg. Bk.
(Victor Rhythm Album One)
Pony: Galloping Horses by Clara Anderson, p. 52
(Victor Rhythm Album One)
Donkey: Presto by Ludwig van Beethoven, p. 53, Kdg. Bk.
The Nodding Donkeys: Romp In Rhythm by Seatter. The Willis Music Co.
Flying Airplanes: Flying Birds by Clara Anderson, p. 106, Kdg. Bk.
(Victor Rhythm Album One)
Roller Skating: Skater's Waltz by Waldteufel, p. 134, American Singer.
Galloping: The Wild Horseman by Schumann, p. 128, American Singer.
Airplane by Reinhold, p. 116, American Singer.

RECORDINGS

Children's Record Guild and Young People's Records. The Greystone Corporation, 100 Sixth Avenue, New York 13, N. Y.
Visit To My Little Friend   Trains And Planes

Phoebe James Records, Box 134, Pacific Palisades, Calif.
Trains, Boats and Harbor.

Childhood Rhythms, Series 1, Ruth Evans, 326 Forest Park Ave.,
Springfield, Mass. Airplanes, rowboats, horses, bicycles.

Rhythm Time Records, Vol. 4, P. O. Box 1106, Santa Barbara,
Calif. Train.

Estamae MacFarlane Records, 2829 7th Ave., Pueblo, Colorado
Album 1. Trucks, trains, rocking horse, donkeys, cowboy,
roller skates, tricycles, airplanes.

Bowmar Records, 4921 Santa Monica Blvd., Los Angeles 29, Calif.
Record 1551-A. Jet Planes.

MUSIC

American Singer Bk. 1.   American Book Co.

Be Careful, p. 25; Crossing the Street, p. 25; My Airplane,
p. 26; Conductor's Call, p. 26; Transportation, p. 27; Wait For
The Wagon, p. 28, The Freight Train, p. 29; Playing Train,
p. 30; The Auto, p. 31.

Kindergarten Book   Ginn & Co.

I Am A Big Train, p. 131; Train, p. 132; All Aboard, p. 133;
Airplane, p. 134; I'm An Airplane, 134; In A Bus We Come,
p. 134, I'd Like To Be, p. 135; Tugboat, p. 135; Watch The
Lights, p. 136; Who Will Ride The Bus?, p. 136.

More Singing Fun   Webster Publishing Co.

Little Airplane, p. 54; Little Old Train, p. 52; Lonely Little
Sailboat, p. 2; Ferryboat, p. 6; Over The Deep Blue Sea, p. 1;
Bell Buoy, p. 3; Billowing Sails, p. 4; Seashore, p. 7; Faithful
Lighthouse, p. 8; Ferryboat Is Coming, p. 9.

Singing Fun   Webster Publishing Co.

Little Engine, p. 43;   A Big Truck, p. 44; My Rocket Ship,
p. 45; The Windshield Wiper, p. 46.

Music For Young Americans   American Book Co.

When I Am Big, p. 28; Streamline Ttrain, p. 29; Choo Choo,
p. 31; I Like A Bike, p. 31; The Big Truck, p. 31; Sailing, p. 32;
Little Ships, p. 32; Pull The Oars, p. 33; Tugboats, p. 33; The
Horn On The Bus, p. 34; Galloping, p. 35; Wait For The Wagon,
p. 36.

Music For Early Childhood   Silver Burdett Co.

Our Windshield Wiper, p. 22; Here Comes The Train, p. 22; Let's
Take A Little Trip, p. 23; Busy Trucks, p. 24; The Allee Allee O!,
p. 25.

My <u>Picture</u> <u>Book</u> <u>Of</u> <u>Songs</u>   M. A. Donohue & Co.

    The Motor Boat, p. 19; Tony's Pony, p. 23; Choo! Choo! Choo!,
p. 23; I'm A Pilot, p. 49; The Air-O-Plane, p. 49.

<u>Singing</u> <u>Time</u>   The John Day Co.

    Pony Song, p. 42; The Canoe, p. 33; The Sail Boat, p. 32; The
Ferry Boat, p. 31; The Row Boat, p. 30; The Train, p. 29;
Down By The Station, p. 28.

<u>Songs</u> <u>To</u> <u>Grow</u> <u>On</u>   W. Sloane Associates

    The Mail Boat, p. 13; I Saw Three Ships, p. 58; Galloping
Horses, p. 74; I've Been Working On The Railroad, p. 6;
The Rock Island Line, p. 90.

STORIES

TITLE	AUTHOR	PUBLISHER
Pony Tales	Watson	Doubleday & Co.
Creeper's Jeep	Gramalky	E. M. Hale & Co.
Little Toot	Gramalky	E. M. Hale & Co.
How Do You Travel	Schlein	Abingdon Press
Whistle For The Train	MacDonald	Doubleday & Co.
The Two Cars	d'Aulaire	Doubleday & Co.
The Pie Wagon	Budd	Lothrop, Lee Shepard
Two Little Trains	Brown	Wm.
Little Sea Legs	Barker	E. M. Hale & Co.
This Is A Road	Curren	Follet Publ. Co.
What Can A Horse Do	Crowell	McGraw-Hill
Little Old Automobile	Ets	Viking Press
Mystery Of The Broken Bridge	Friskey	Childrens Press
Perky Little Engine	Friskey	Childrens Press
The Lost Tugboat	Hagner	E. M. Hale & Co.
Loopy	Gramalky	E. M. Hale & Co.
Chuggy & The Blue Caboose	Freeman	E. M. Hale & Co.
The Boats On The River	Flack	Viking Press
At The Airport	Colonious	Melmont Publ.
Big Book Of Real Boats & Ships	Zoffo	Grosset & Dunlap

TITLE	AUTHOR	PUBLISHER
Sails, Wheels, Wings	Liliethanl	Grosset & Dunlap
Airplane Andy	Tousey	Doubleday & Co.
Little Train	Lenski	Oxford Univ. Press
The Little Sail Boat	Lenski	Oxford Univ. Press
The Little Red Caboose	Potter	Charles Merril
I Like Trains	Wooley	Harper & Co.
I Want To Be A Train Engineer	Greene	Childrens Press
I Want To Be A Ship Captain	Greene	Childrens Press
I Want To Be A Pilot	Greene	Childrens Press
I Want To Be A Bus Driver	Greene	Childrens Press
The Man, The Boy & The Donkey	Evans	Whitman Co.
Jamie And The Dump Truck	Sinnikson	Maxton House
The Noon Balloon	Brown	Harper & Bros.
How Engines Talk	Burleigh	Follet Publ. Co.
ABC Of Cars & Trucks	Alexander	Doubleday & Co.
Cloud Hoppers	James	Childrens Press
Piggyback	Burleigh	Follet Publ. Co.
Shoofly	Burleigh	Follet Publ. Co.
The Little Engine That Laughed	Evers	Grosset & Dunlap
The Wonder Book of Trucks	Peters	Wonder Books, Inc.
Wheels and Noises	Elting	Wonder Books, Inc.
The Terrytoon Space Train	Waring	Wonder Books, Inc.
Benjie Engie	Devine	Rand McNally Co.
All Aboard	Conger	Simon & Schuster
Boats	Lachman	Golden Press
Roundabout Train	Wright	Whitman Publ. Co.
The Rattle-Rattle Train	Geis	Wonder Books, Inc.
Away We Go	Harris	Garden City Publ.
Saturday Flight-Saturday Ride	Wright	Cadmus
City Boy, Country Boy	Schlein	Childrens Press
Listen To My Seashell	Steiner	Knopf

TITLE	AUTHOR	PUBLISHER
How Do You Travel	Schlein	Abingdon Press
The Little Engine That Could	Piper	Platt & Munk
Surprise On Wheels	Friskey	Albert Whitman & Co.
Mike Mulligan And His Steam Shovel	Burton	Houghton-Mifflin
Davy Goes Places	Lenski	Henry Z. Walck, Inc.

FINGER PLAYS

Rhymes For Fingers And Flannelboards	Scott & Thompson	Webster Publ. Co.

Here Is The Engine, p. 20; Railroad Train, p. 20; The Airplane, p. 21; Five Little Sailors, p. 23.

POETRY

Now We Are Six	Milne	Dutton Publ.

The Engineer, p. 42; The Old Sailor, p. 36.

There I No Rhyme For Silver	Merriam	Atheneum Publ.

Flying, p. 17

Let's Say Poetry Together	Rasmussen	Burgess Publ. Co.

Airplane, p. 106; Bus, p. 108; Cars Go Fast, p. 107; Ferry Boats, p. 107; The Jet, p. 110; Motor Cars, p. 109; Trains, p. 105; Trucks, p. 108.

Time For Poetry	Arbuthnot	Scott, Foresman & Co.

From A Railway Carriage, p. 72; Trains At Night, p. 72; The Ways Of Trains, p. 72; Travel, p. 73; Up In The Air, p. 73; Taking Off, p. 73; Silver Ships, p. 73; Cockpit In The Clouds, p. 74, Boats, p. 74; Ferry Boats, p. 74; Whistles, p. 75; A Sea-Song From The Shore, p. 75; Sea-Fever, p. 76; Stop-Go, p. 77; Motor Cars, p. 78; Taxis, p. 78; Moving, p. 78; Roads, p. 80; Travel, p. 82.

Childcraft Vol. 1		Field Enterprises

Maps, p. 196; Western Wagons, p. 199; Good Green Bus, p. 202; Motor Cars, p. 203; City Streets And Country Roads, p. 204; Country Trucks, p. 205; The Ways Of Trains, p. 206; Trains At Night, p. 206; I'd Like To Be A Lighthouse, p. 209; Where Go The Boats?, p. 209; Up In The Air, p. 210; Otherwise, p. 218.

Choral Speaking   Hemphill   Educational Publ. Co.

Water, p. 15; The Subway Train's Story, p. 16; Clickety-Clack, p. 26; Forced Landing, p. 26; The Train, p. 27; The Freight Train, p. 40; Our Traffic Song, p. 42.

My Poetry Book   Huffard-Ferris   Winston Publ. Co.

Riding In A Motor Boat,   Taxis,   Travel,
The Locomotive,   The Railroad Cars Are Coming,

The Sound Of Poetry   Austin   Allyn & Bacon

Bridges, p. 160; A Modern Dragon, p. 160; There Are So Many Ways Of Going Places, p. 161; B's The Bus, p. 162; Motor Cars, p. 163; Taxis, p. 164; City Streets And Country Roads, p. 165; Roads, p. 166; Song Of The Train, p. 166; Wings And Wheels, p. 168; Passenger Train, p. 169; The Ways Of Trains, p. 170; Trains, p. 171; Engine, p. 172; The Dirigible, p. 173; Up In The Air, p. 173; Aeroplane, p. 174; Taking Off, p. 175; The Old And The New, p. 175; Space Travel, p. 177; Ferry Boats, p. 178; I'd Like To Be A Lighthouse, p. 179; Ships, p. 179.

Poems   Govoni & Smith   Golden Press

Skyscrapers, p. 18; Motor Cars, p. 18; Taxis, p. 19; Whistles, p. 22; Boats, p. 22; I'd Like To Be A Lighthouse, p. 23; Ferry Boats, p. 23; Fog, p. 23; From A Railway Carriage, p. 24; Trains, p. 25; Taking Off, p. 25.

GAMES

Music For Early Childhood New Music Horizons   Silver Burdett

Who's That Knocking At My Door, p. 14; The Old Brass Wagon, p. 64; Willowbee, p. 65.

Physical Education For The   South Dakota State
Elementary School, Bulletin 73   Course of Study

Stop And Go, p. 23; Parachute Landing, p. 24; Bicycling, p. 25; Johnny Over The Water, p. 59.

Play Activities For   C. V. Mosby Co.
Elementary Grades   Nagel

Traveling, p. 38; Automobile Relay, p. 78; Over The Waves, p. 95; Locomotive, p. 115.

Springtime

After a beautiful spring day or morning children are very much interested in springtime activities and the awakening of nature. If we wait and introduce this unit when children are able to see some of these signs for themselves, nature takes on a new meaning for them.

SUBJECT MATTER

Birds

What birds return to us first in the spring?
(Robins, swallows, sparrows, etc.)
Where have they been all winter?
(In the warmer climates.)
Why are there such few birds here in the winter?
(Because they can't find food and they need the warmth.)
How can we tell different birds?
(By their color, size, call, nests.)
Where do the different birds live?
(In nests, trees, ground, cliffs.)
What birds build mud nests?
Robins -- color, size, nest, food.
Wood thrush -- color, size, nest, food.
Barn swallow -- color, size, nest, food.
What birds build with twigs?
Catbird -- color, size, nest, food.
Cardinal -- color, size, nest, food.

Rain

Why do we need rain?
(It waters the earth's plants, washes buildings, washes plants, and trees free from dust, fills cisterns, and washes the air.)
What happens when we have too little rain?
(We have a drouth, things dry up, and the crops are poor.)
What happens when we have too much rain?
(We have floods, rust forms on the crops, etc.)

Wind

What is the wind's work?
What is wind?
(Air in Motion.)
What does wind do to things?
(Dries puddles, flies kites, turns windmills, blows things around, sails boats.)

Gardens

How is the soil prepared?
(Plowed, raked, etc.)

What kind of ground is needed?
  (Rich soil, black dirt.)
How is the soil prepared?
  (Raked, plowed, dragged.)
What tools are used?
  (Plow, rake, hoe, harrow, disc.)
When are crops planted and cared for?
  (After frost is out of the ground.)
How do plants grow?
  (From seeds, bulbs, slips.)
How do we help seeds grow?
  (Water them, keep them weeded.)

DEVELOPMENT

Telling Time
At the beginning of this unit, let the children name the birds they have seen and tell what they can about them. There are some excellent pictures to show about the birds that can be used to stimulate discussion of the birds.

Boys and girls like to tell of their experience in the rain. Most have had the experience of wading after a storm, carrying an umbrella and walking in the rain.

Children will enjoy telling about their experiences while planting a garden.

Activity Period
Crayons and Paint
Draw pictures of spring activity - the wind, pussywillows.
Paint and color kites.
Paint or draw a picture about walking in the rain.
Use colored chalk on real pussy willows.
Make a frieze of spring activities such as drying clothes, planting gardens.

Clay and Plasticene
Model birds and their nests and make all kinds of garden tools.

Paper Tearing and Cutting
Cut and tear likenesses of the birds that have returned.
Cut and tear bird nests and houses. Also cut garden tools.
Cut and tear spring flowers.

SONGS

The Kindergarten Book   Ginn & Co.

Like A Leaf, p. 97; Spit, Spat, Spatter, p. 97; The Wind Is Singing, p. 99; The Leaves, p. 99; Down, Down, p. 100; Busy, Buzzy Bee, p. 107; My Pretty Butterfly, p. 108; Little Bug, p. 109.

Music For Early Chilhood   New Music
                                                     Horizons

The Woodpecker, p. 6; Little Wind, p. 7; April, p. 7; Little Redbird in The Tree, p. 9.

Singing Time   Coleman-Thorn   The John Day Co.

> Spring Song, p. 10; Sing O Sing, p. 11; A Story Of Four Little
> Birds, p. 12; The Robin, p. 22; Swing Song, p. 37; Rain Song,
> p. 38; The Little Bunny, p. 39

My Picture Book of Songs   Dalton-Ashton   M. A. Donohue
                                                              & Co.

> Skating, p. 11; My Kite, p. 45; The March Wind, p. 45; Easter
> Morning, p. 51; Fluffy Bunny, p. 51; Pitter Pat, p. 53; Little
> Drippy Drops, p. 53; The Bumble Bee, p. 55; Pretty May
> Flowers, p. 55; Sunshine, p. 57; Clouds, p. 59.

More Singing Fun   Wood   Webster Publ. Co.

> Spring Is On Its Way, p. 40; Springtime Story, p. 41; Whirlwind,
> p. 42; Four Robins, p. 43; Fly, Kite, Fly, p. 44; Five Kites,
> p. 46; Little Bird, p. 48 Little White Cloud, p. 49; Easter Music,
> p. 50; An Easter Basket, p. 51.

The American Singer, Book 1   American Book Co.

> Roller Skating, p. 135; My May Basket, p. 66; It's Easter Today,
> p. 67; A Rainy Day, p. 39; March, p. 40; Spring Is Here, p. 41;
> April, p. 42; Pussy Willow, p. 43; It's Raining, p. 44; Working,
> p. 45; Planting My Garden, p. 46; The Robin's Call, p. 47; Our
> Garden, p. 47; Blackbirds, p. 48; The Bluebird, p. 48; The Little
> Bird, p. 50; Wading, p. 51; The Robin, p. 52; The Oriole, p. 54.

Singing Fun   Wood   Webster Publ. Co.

> Easter Bunny, p. 29; A Green Frog, p. 30; My Easter Bonnet,
> p. 31; Pussy Willow, p. 32; Little Seeds, p. 33; Springtime, p. 34.

Happy Songs For Happy Children   Siebold   G. Schirmer, Inc.

> Raining, p. 24; Rubber Boots, p. 23; Birdies And Apple Blossoms,
> p. 19; My Parasol, p. 5; April Showers, p. 16; The Bouquet, p.
> 14; Teeter-Totter, p. 14; The Swing, p. 13; Guess, p. 26, Pansies,
> p. 27; The Merry Wind, p. 26.

RHYTHMS

The Kindergarten Book   Ginn & Co.

> Running and hopping like a robin, p. 10 and 11.
> Making hands or feet patter like rain, p. 11.
> Skipping to the garden to pick flowers, p. 13, Gigue.
> Dancing raindrops. Happy and Light. From "Bohemian Girl",
>   p. 14.
> Hopping like rabbits. Skip, p. 15 (Victor Rhythm Album One).
> Pedaling bikes: Sicilienne. From "Armide", p. 16.
> Bouncing ball: Dance It Merrily, p. 17.
> Swinging: Waltz, p. 31. Roller Skating (The Reaper's Song),
>   p. 32.
> Hopping like bunnies: "The Rabbit", Gounod, p. 92.

Growing plants and flowers: Nature's Dream (Arabesque), p. 104.
Bird on the Wing: Flying birds, p. 106.
Birds in flight: Birdling (Voglein), p. 107.
Buzzing Bees: The Bee, Schubert (Victor Listening Album Three).
Flying like butterflies: Papillons No. 8 (Victor Rhythm Album Three).

Music For Early Childhood   New Music
                                             Horizons

Bouncing Balls, p. 38; Skipping Merrily, p. 38

Happy Songs For Happy Children   Siebold   G. Schirmer, Inc.

Out Walking, p. 30; The Swing, p. 13; Teeter-Totter, p. 14;
The Bouquet, p. 14; April Showers, p. 16; The Fairies, p. 11.

Romp In Rhythm   Seatter, Minnis,   The Willis
                                 Wallace   Music Co.

Walk To Church, p. 32; Easter Skip, p. 34; Waddling Ducks In
Spring, p. 36; Dance Of the Breezes, p. 38; Spring Winds, p. 40;
Rain, p. 41; Sunbeams, p. 42; The Posy Dance, p. 44; Fairy
Dance, p. 46.

Games - Rhythms - Dances   Barnett   George Stanley Co.

This Is The Way, p. 4; Planting A Garden, p. 40; The Wind,
p. 39.

RECORDINGS

Bowmar Records, Inc., 10515 Burbank Blvd., North Hollywood, Calif.
"Holiday Rhythms" - Easter.

POETRY

Childcraft Vol. 1   Field Enterprises

The Winter Is Past, p. 54; Spring Wind, p. 55; Spring Morning,
p. 56; The Year's At The Spring, p. 57; Barefoot Days, p. 58;
March, p. 66; April, p. 66; May Morning, p. 67; Rain, Rain, Go
Away, p. 89; Rain, p. 89; The Umbrella Brigade, p. 91; Rain In
The Night, p. 92; Singing, p. 93; Drums Of The Rain, p. 93; In
Time Of Silver Rain, p. 94; The Woodpecker, p. 120; Trees,
p. 122; Dandelions, p. 125.

Let's Say Poetry Together   Rasmussen   Burgess Publ. Co.

April First, p. 99; Return Of Birds, p. 99; Winds, p. 99; Spring
Signs Out, p. 100; May Day, p. 101; Merry Sunshine, p. 103.

The Sound Of Poetry   Austin   Allyn & Bacon

The Seasons, p. 306; Directions, p. 306; Daffodils, p. 306;
Daffadowndilly, p. 307; How The Flowers Grow, p. 307; Little
Grey Pussy, p. 308; City Rain, p. 309; In Time Of Silver Rain,
p. 310; It Is Raining, p. 311; Rain, p. 312; Who Is Tapping At My

Window, p. 313; Down The Rain Falls, p. 314; Rain Riders, p. 314; Very Lovely, p. 315; Rain, Rain, Go Away, p. 315; The Rainbow, p. 316; The Winter Is Past, p. 317; March Winds, p. 317; The Merry Month Of March, p. 317; The Coming Of Spring, p. 318; April, p. 319; A Summer Morning, p. 319.

Everything And Anything   Dorothy Aldis   Minton, Balch & Co.

Clouds, p. 11; The Storm, p. 23; Early, p. 35; The Rain, p. 67"; Brooms, p. 73; The Sprinkler, p. 93; The Puffer, p. 97; Skipping Rope, p. 99.

Poems   Govoni-Smith   Golden Press

My Kite, p. 20; Brooms, p. 30; Rain, p. 30; Spring Rain, p. 31; Mr. Rabbit, p. 35.

One Thousand Poems For Children   Sechrist   Macrae-Smith Co.

My Garden, p. 67; Happy Thought, p. 67; The Secrets Of Our Garden, p. 68; The Gardner, p. 69; The Swing, p. 73; The Robin, p. 107; Sir Robin, p. 107; Bob White, p. 108; The Brown Thrush, p. 109; Song Of The Chickadee, p. 109; The Bluebird, p. 111; The Humming Bird, p. 111; The Swallow, p. 112; Green Tings Growing, p. 121; Jack-In-The Pulpit, p. 131.

Sing-A-Round   Harrington   Macmillan Co.

Kites Flying, p. 19; Chickadee, p. 81.

STORIES

BOOK	AUTHOR	PUBLISHER
Jonathan And The Rainbow	Blanck	Houghton-Mifflin Co.
Hi, Mister Robin	Tresselt	Lothrop, Lee & Shepard
The Round Robin	Holland	T. S. Denison & Co.
Rain Drop Splash	Tresselt	Lothrop, Lee & Shepard
Green Is For Growing	Lubell	Charles Scribner's Sons
The Storm Book	Zolotow	Harper & Bros.
Please Pass The Grass	Adelson	David McKay & Co.
Pussy Willow	Brown	Simon & Schuster
The White Bunny And His Magic Nose	Duplaix	Simon & Schuster
My Bunny Book	Cross	Garden City Books
Joe The Bluejay And Carl The Cardinal	Dugo	E. M. Hale & Co.
Johnny And The Birds	Munn	Rand McNally Publ. Co.
Funny Bunny	Learnard	Simon & Schuster

A Tree Is Nice	Udry	Harper & Bros.
Easter	Wiese	E. M. Hale & Co.
Wonders Of Nature	Watson	Golden Press
Easter Kitten	Konkle	Childrens Press
My Hopping Bunny	Bright	Doubleday & Co.
The Golden Egg Book	Brown	Simon & Schuster
The Easter Bunny That		Lothrop, Lee &
Overslept	Friedrich	Shepard
I Like Butterflies	Conklin	Holiday House
Umbrella	Yashima	Viking Press
Story Telling With The		T. S. Denison
Flannel Board	Anderson	& Co.

The April Calendar, p. 144; The Child Who Found Easter, p. 193; The Lavender Bunny, p. 199; A Spring Story, p. 241.

FINGER PLAYS

Rhymes For Fingers and
    Flannelboards   Scott & Thompson   Webster Publ. Co.

Making Kites, p. 124; The Wind, p. 125; Raindrops, p. 125; The Rain, p. 125; Yellow Daffodil, p. 126; Relaxing Flowers, p. 126; Purple Violets, p. 126; Daisy Clocks, p. 127; Flowers, p. 127; Pretending, p. 128; Five Little May Baskets, p. 128.

GAMES

Bunny Bunny
    Children are seated in a circle. One child is chosen to be the bunny. He holds two fingers up to his ears for rabbit ears and hops around the circle and stops at one of his friends. He says to his friend: "Bunny, bunny how's your neighbor?" The child replies: "I don't know but I'll go see." He continues hopping around the circle until he comes to another child and asks the same question.

Kindergarten Book   Ginn & Co.

Five Little Chickadees, p. 37.

Suggested Program by Seasons

FALL

Family Life In The Home

        Type of homes
        Number in family
        Occupations
        Duties of members
        Food in the home

Seasonal Activities

    Preparing for winter
      Animals and people
    Collect fall flowers
    Gather leaves, pods, seeds, nuts, grains, weeds, berries,
      flowers
    Collect and observe caterpillars
    Observe birds and squirrels
    Celebrate Halloween
    Prepare for Thanksgiving
    Christmas
      The real meaning
      Santa Claus
      Toy shops
      Gift exchange
      Tree

WINTER

Observe changes in the weather - Take walks in snow
Outdoor play in winter - safety at play
Observe length of days
Transportation
By land, by water, and by air
Celebrate St. Valentine's Day
Community life
Schools, church, police, firemen, mailman

SPRING

Watch for signs of spring - birds, pussywillows
Necessary work in the home - house cleaning, gardening
Outdoor play with marbles, kites, ropes
Celebrating Easter and May Day
Study the wind
Plant gardens
Study the rain and the sun
Excursions to observe the changing seasons
April Fool's Day
Talk about Arbor Day
Visit a hatchery - greenhouse to observe new life

Chapter 9

A TYPICAL
ACTIVITY PERIOD

This period is made up of any art material the child would care to use.

PLANNING - 5-10 minutes

Usually the child will not have to be told what to do in the work period, and gradually the teacher will help him develop his own ability to plan an activity that will contribute to his growth. When he selects his material he will plan what he expects to do with it. At this time the teacher can make use of the records she has kept of the child's work, to check his group participation and his individual experiences. If the teacher feels that this particular child is too active, she may suggest he work at the tables, or if she feels the child is in need of other experiences, she may suggest building with blocks or playing in the doll house, but for the most part the child does the initiating. He decides on his undertaking.

CARRYING OUT THE PLANS - 30 minutes

Whatever work the child has decided upon, the teacher should see that he carries it out to the best of his ability. He should be encouraged to finish what he begins. The child's part in this period is being able to respond to the different art materials before him, and to suggestions made by the teacher. As far as he is able he should carry out his own plan and learn when to ask for help. The teacher's part is to move about among the children, discussing individual problems with them, and make suggestions on how to improve the work. A teacher should be able to raise the children's standards of work by giving help in technique, and by suggestions. She may have to present certain problems when the child has none of his own. A teacher will overlook many mistakes especially those that the five-year-old is not capable of understanding. It is better to call attention to only one or two weaknesses.

CRITICISM OF WORK - 15 minutes

As the children are working at different projects about the room, the teacher uses this time to acquaint herself with their problems. When the group comes together, she brings out the main problems noticed in the various groups. Children soon learn how to accept and use suggestions both from the teacher and school friends. At the beginning of the year, and until the time the child has had an opportunity to work with many art materials, a teacher must be careful not to include too much adverse criticism of the work. However, anything worth doing should be evaluated in some way. Children enjoy telling what they like about another child's work, and may be able to include a suggestion or two on how to improve it. During this discussion period, the teacher will be helping the children meet the goals

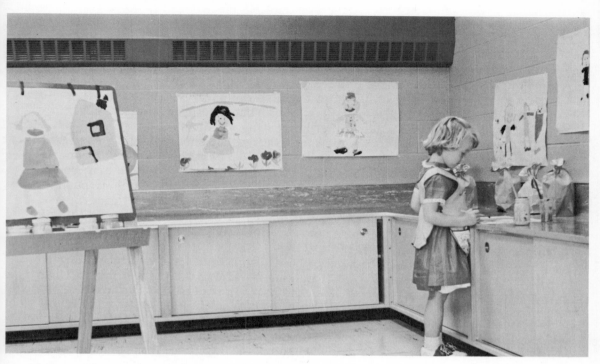

of the work period. Many times this is a difficult period as small children are
not too interested in another child's problems. At first it is perhaps better
to shorten this period a little, and give each child encouragement in what he
has been able to accomplish.

CLEAN-UP - 5 minutes

After the first week or two of school, most children know where the
materials are kept and enjoy putting them away as much as getting them out
for work. This is a very valuable part of the training of the work period.
Children trained in this way soon learn what is expected of them during this
period and if available space is supplied for their materials they will become
accustomed to taking care of them. At clean-up time some teachers let the
children make up a tune as they pick-up and clean-up. Other pieces of equipment can be substituted or other toys, as clay, paint, blocks, etc. in this
rhyme.

> We're working together
> We're working today;
> Let's pick up our blocks
> And put them away.
>
> Let's pick up and pick up,
> And pick up some more;
> Let's pick up and clean up
> The table and floor.

Painting and Drawing

Kindergarten children vary the most in their ability to draw and paint, but they love to do it. Most children love to paint. It is one of the best means still within the power of children to express themselves. When the five-year-old first starts to paint, he often just dabs, but with practice in using this material, he is able to make many interesting pictures.

There are certain techniques in painting that should be discussed with beginners. We need to show the five-year-old how to hold a brush properly in order that the motion comes from the arm. To assure ample arm room, many teachers train the children to stand at the table with his chair pushed against it. If you want children to paint large have them stand, give them large paint brushes and large pieces of paper to work with. We help the kindergartener improve his muscle coordination when we give him materials which will help develop big muscles.

At first boys and girls need to be shown how to handle paint so that it will not run down the brush. This is done by wiping the paint brush against the side of the paint jar. Also when the paint is poured into the jar it should not go above the metal band on the paint brush. This also helps to prevent dripping.

Since many children scrub when they paint, they will need to be shown how to use just the tip of the paint brush and how to take more paint when it is needed.

It is very important also that the children put the right brush into the right color of paint. If the paint brush handles are of the same color as the jar of paint to be used, the color problem is simplified.

In initiating kindergarteners to painting and drawing we must help them find subjects. We can do this by giving them the opportunity to see things and to engage in activities. To create a picture is difficult if a person has had no experience with the object. An excursion offers many opportunities for children to observe things around them. Another way to encourage beginners is to have them draw and paint pictures that tell a story. Although we are prepared to help them with technique when they are ready for it and ask for it, we are in the beginning much more interested in their own efforts in self-expression.

Children's drawing usually lacks perspective. Youngsters seem to draw what they know about the object they see before them, and as a rule they draw many outlines and many details. Not much mass drawing is found in the kindergarten.

After a few tries at painting, children soon learn that paper with wet paint should be allowed to dry before it is moved; otherwise the paint runs and the paper tears. To protect the children's clothing, many schools suggest that the parent send with the child one of the brother's or father's old shirts that have had the sleeves shortened, or a smock with the child's name on it.

Water colors are sometimes introduced for variety in painting before the year is over. It is more difficult for kindergarteners to get bright clear colors with water colors and this may be one of the reasons for using powdered or mixed paint. When mixing the powdered paint for children to use, try two tablespoons to a small jar. Mix the powder and water to make a paste, and then dilute it. After the paint has been mixed, cover the jars with lids that have been painted the color of the paint in the jars. Add only enough water to the paint to come to the top of the metal ring on the paint brush. Another method of mixing dry paint is to add this proportion to a jar and add the water and shake putting your hand over the mouth of the jar. If large quantities are to be mixed at one time such as orange and black at Halloween, or red and green at Christmas, this is a time saving method.

Some teachers prefer not to mix the paint at all but furnish each child with a jar of clear water and let them dip directly into dry powder paint that is on the table. Milk bottle tops can be used to hold the various kinds of colors of paint.

<u>Finger painting</u> is usually introduced later on in the year. It excells as a means of creative expression because it makes use of the large arm muscles and makes it possible for the child to achieve a finished piece of work. To the child the results are very satisfactory. It is possible to use home-made fingerpaints and shelf paper but the results are not as interesting. For the kindergartner the teacher uses a sponge and wets the paper with water. A tablespoon of paint is then placed in the center of the wet paper. You may want to suggest that the child smooths out the lumps and spreads it over the paper. Soon the kindergartener sees his own print in the paint and tries other movements. One of the advantages of finger paint is it can be wiped out or rubbed out and something new begun again. When you are ready to leave a design on the paper, you will thumb tack it to the bulletin board immediately and prevent curling. If curling does take place, use a flat iron that is only slightly warm to iron out the curls.

Have you ever used <u>paint crayon</u>? Children love to draw their pictures with the paint crayons and then go over their drawing with a brush dipped in water. After working with these crayons a few times children soon learn how much water is needed to make the most attractive picture.

<u>Paper tearing</u> is one of our greatest helps in developing finger dexterity. Children enjoy illustrating a story they have read or part of a unit they are discussing at this time. Material is no object for they can use old newspapers or unprinted newsprint as well as the more gaily decorated papers. Boys and girls can rearrange their torn pieces on colored paper and they become very interesting. If some of the children have difficulty tearing the paper tell them to hold the sheet between the forefinger and the thumb of the left hand, and tear the paper with the same fingers of the right hand keeping the fingers close together. All children can tear paper and learn to do it well if given a chance to tell a story in this way.

<u>Crayons</u> are usually not new to the kindergartner. Before boys and girls start to school they usually have used crayons either in a coloring book or on separate sheets of paper. Some children do better with crayons than with any other art material because they have had so much experience using them. One of our aims in the kindergarten is

to acquaint boys and girls with many art mediums and to allow them to experiment freely. An accumulative effort throughout the year assures beginners of experience and the "know how" to use many different art materials.

Spray painting is another medium boys and girls enjoy trying out. It is fun to do this with leaves in the fall, and at Christmas time as a different approach to art.

Combinations of materials used are both interesting and rewarding for five-year-olds. Combining painted faces on children with wall paper clothes or adding a color wash to a favorite crayoned Halloween picture all add up to enjoyment.

Sponge painting is enjoyed by all boys and girls in the kindergarten. Try using an ordinary sponge that has been cut in quarters. The sponge is dipped into the paint and then pressed on the paper. Trees with various colored leaves are very effective when made in this way.

Potato and carrot printing can be done in the kindergarten. A section of a potato or carrot can be used to print designs. At Christmas time they can be used for wrapping paper. Each child must first make a design and then they must draw it on the end of the potato or carrot. The part not needed is then cut away. The designed end is then dipped in the paint and stamped on the paper.

Clay and Plasticine

Working with clay or plasticine is sure to hold a child's attention. This material stimulates a child to do creative work, and fascinates him more and more as he uses it. Because it is pliable, it gives him a chance to feel and a chance to do. The first time some kindergarteners use clay they like to just feel it in their hands and may not make anything recognizable with it, but with continued use they mold it and pat it and "mark it with T".

Clay like finger painting, is reminiscent of mud pie days and appeals to the five-year-old for that reason. This manipulative stage comes first, just as it does in all other art mediums. A child's natural response to any new material introduced to him is just to experiment with it and find out its possibilities. He begins to use it as a means of self-expression.

Kindergarten teachers use both the coil and the mass technique in modeling. It may be easier for the very young child to model from the mass, as there are not so many pieces involved and they are less likely to break off. If the children use small pieces, they naturally produce small objects. Another advantage is that an object in clay is more easily painted if it is all in one piece.

For a lesson of this sort, be sure to mix the clay powder several days in advance. Most of the older formulas suggest a mixture or four parts of clay flour to one part of water. Knead this and cover tightly. Twenty pounds should be sufficient for an average size group. Be sure to keep it covered and moist in an earthen jar until ready for use. The newer type of clay can be purchased already moist. Another kind can be selected that comes in a kneading bag and can be made by the teacher herself.

Do not confuse clay with plasticine, for plasticine is no substitute for clay. Some children choose clay rather than plasticene as they like to paint it and find more enjoyment in working with it.

When plasticine is used, many teachers ask each child to bring a plastic bag with a clip to hold his own ball of plasticine. Still others have children keep the clay in match boxes with their name on it. The use of plasticine over and over again involves the question of sanitation. Some teachers want each child to have his own piece of clay, and some prefer to keep all of it in a stored metal container which can be covered or left open as desired. All colors are stored together in large rolls. This problem, largely an individual one, depends a great deal upon the amount of space available for storing materials.

When either of these materials is used, kindergarten tables must be protected. This can be done by providing cardboards, tagboards, oil cloth squares, or paper towels as covering. The advantage in using oil cloth squares seems to be that they can be used over and over again. The advantage in using brown paper towels seems to be that when the children are through working, the towels will clean their hands easier than using soap and water, so they serve a two fold purpose. Many teachers use old peg boards very effectively as a mat for clay and plasticine.

Chapter 10

HEALTH ACTIVITIES

The use of the toilet room is a health activity that should be explained carefully to the children. When they first enter kindergarten, they should be told what is expected of them. They should be trained to use the toilets properly before they go outside for recess or during the period that is provided for this purpose. The habit of washing hands after using the toilet should be discussed with them and for a time it may seem advisable to so station yourself to make sure that this part of the period is carried out. Furthermore, they should understand that one towel is sufficient if time is taken to use it correctly, and that it should be deposited in the waste basket provided and not thrown on the floor. They should also understand that the recess time is to be used for toilets and washing hands and whatever time that is left can be used for play.

If the groups are not too large, all the girls may go to their toilet room together, taking turns. If the rooms are not connected to the kindergarten, both groups may go at the same time, providing it is possible for you to see what the two groups are doing. If the rooms are not connected or close to one another, the boys may be chosen to go next, and a short game can be played by the girls while waiting, or one child may be chosen to show and tell about a favorite library book or one that has been brought from home. Many kindergarten teachers prefer to have this toilet period over before other primary grades have their recess. This is essential if toilet rooms are shared. It is easier in this way to establish good habits and it is also less confusing because of the number of children involved.

An ideal situation exists when the toilets are a part of the school room, for the children can use them as the occasion arises. Since no teacher wants a constant procession at any one time, it is easier to check on this when they can be seen and supervised. If, however, there are no room facilities provided, the foregoing suggestions may somewhat systematize the procedure.

After the children have been to the toilets and have washed their hands, they should be encouraged to take a drink at the fountain before returning to the room or to their place. If there is a fountain in your room, the kindergartener may drink whenever he is thirsty.

Rest Period

If time is to be taken during the day for rest, it should result in relaxation for the children. These children need room to stretch and relax and for this reason they should be encouraged to bring rugs from home when they come the first day of school. It is easier for them to rest on rugs or cots than at a table. The rugs should be sent home several times during the school

year to be washed unless a kinder-mat is used. A good time to send them is just before a vacation period such as Christmas, Easter, or whenever there is a need. If you plan to have children bring rugs ask each parent to send a washable rug to rest on at rest time. 24" x 48" is a good size. Be sure that the child's name is on a strip of cloth sewn to a corner of the rug. The larger the better as it is very difficult to find a small marking on any rug. The kinder-mat* is a sanitary rest pad made especially for small

*Peerless Maid Plastic, Inc., Farmington, Minnesota.

children.   Each mat has a name tab attached.   The pad size is 20" x 48" and it folds to 12" x 20" for easy storage.   The covering is made of hard finished embossed vinyl.   It is easily cleaned with warm water and soap.   They are sold mostly in dime stores and variety stores.

Some teachers enjoy using a cleaning bag for resting.   Use the long cleaning bag, staple the hanger to the top.   Then fill the bag with newspaper and staple the bottom.   Have the child make his own outline on paper or print his name on it.   These can be used instead of rugs.   They are very easy to hang and children recognize their own.   They are also nice to use in a school room where cupboards have not been provided for storage.

Teachers find that it is very stimulating for the five-year-old to be in a large group of children, especially when he has been used to playing alone or in smaller groups, and the child needs a short rest period in which he can relax.   Many emotional difficulties may be avoided if the child is helped to re-lax in a quiet atmosphere.   However, do not make resting time so short that it is practically useless.   The longer children rest the quieter they become. Although the rest periods vary in length from five to fifteen minutes, it is felt that the longer the rest time, the more valuable it becomes.

Try to carefully balance your program to have the active periods alter-nate with the less active ones and schedule the resting period near the middle of the session.

At the beginning of the school year some of the timid kindergarteners will just sit or rest their heads on a table while the braver ones will attempt the rugs.   When the children are experiencing a rest period for the first time the newness of it all is like to motivate them to cooperate nicely.   For this reason it is important to establish good rest habits in the beginning because in a little while some children begin to get a little bored with the resting time and use their time in disturbing others.

If the teacher herself uses this time to relax or to be with a child that is restless instead of resorting to cleaning out her desk or cupboard, she will find that the children will have more interest in doing the same.

Usually there is not enough time during the day to do everything you want to do, so try using the rest period as a time to use some of the poems or finger plays children love to hear, or to listen to a quiet story such as "The Sleepy Forest".   This kind of rest is very easy and comes naturally for the children.

FOR NAP TIME

I know it's best
To take a rest
So I've a little key;
I'll lock the door.
    (Children lock lips)
Pull down the shades.
    (Children close eyes)
I cannot talk or see!

Encourage the children to relax and listen comfortably in one place in-stead of moving about on the floor so it will be quiet enough for all the children to rest. You may want to talk about the rag doll and call attention to its limp and relaxed arms and legs. You may want to lift some of the children's arms and legs to see whether they too are relaxed. To help make this idea more meaningful, a real rag doll could be taken from the doll house and the teacher might use any poem about a rag doll such as the following:

LET'S PLAY RAG DOLL

"Let's play rag doll, don't make a sound!
Fling your arms and your body loosely around.
Fling your hands, fling your feet, let your head go free.
Be the raggedest rag doll you ever did see."

Then there is the rest which gives time for listening to music. Music, either played on the piano or victrola, may be introduced, preferably after all are quietly resting. You may even want to suggest to the children that they listen for some particular sound or instrument. One very good record is "Time to Relax" - Album C104, Jeri Productions, 3212 Glendale Blvd., Los Angeles 39, California. Other records for resting and quiet time might include:

"Heather Rose"	Schubert
"Meditation"	Hayden
"Cradle Song"	Oesten
"Moonlight Sonata"	Beethoven
"Minuet in G"	Mozart
"Humoresque"	Dvorak

Setting the stage for the rest period is sometimes done with singing. Most children love a resting song to sing before they are expected to rest quietly, and they enjoy singing it. "This Is My Sleepy Time", and "Now It's Time To Rest" from The Kindergarten Book by Ginn & Co. is a very good example.

Once in a while it is fun just to listen to a favorite music box play especially if it is playing "Silent Night", or "Happy Birthday."

Milk Lunch

Now the children are ready to drink their milk and to enjoy a conversation time about topics that relate to the group. They have fun arranging the tables, counting the napkins, and serving the milk. The group enjoys saying a short prayer that they have learned for this particular time. Many of these prayers will fit in very nicely with a unit you are working on. A prayer that is sometimes used in the Spring of the year when children are thinking about birds and their nests is:

Thank you for the sun so bright.
Thank you for the stars at night.
Thank you for the lovely spring.
Thank you for the birds that sing.

There are other favorite prayers that may be said at other times through out the entire year such as:

> I have two little eyes to look to God.
> I have two little ears to hear His word.
> I have two little lips to speak His praise.
> I have two little feet to walk His ways.
> I have two little hands to do His will.
> And one little heart to serve Him still.

Even though a child drinks milk at home many teachers feel that he will benefit from the mid-morning small half-pint bottle of milk. Sometimes a child who refuses to drink milk at home will do so at school with the other children. The milk period has many social advantages, along with the health benefits it affords.

Many excellent health habits are established at this time such as: washing hands before eating, not starting to eat until all are served, talking together about foods that help us grow and that are good for us.

Since milk is ordered a week in advance, and each child brings his money on one designated day such as Friday or Monday, it is usually customary not to accept milk money on the remaining days of this week. This makes the bookkeeping much easier. When the child brings money to school he must share the responsibility for getting it there. It also makes him aware of the different money denominations and what they are made up of. If a child brings a dollar to school, he may suggest that the ten dimes are the same as a dollar and will buy milk for a month. In this way children are learning the value of money, the various denominations and combinations of money, and the responsibility involved in being allowed to bring money to school.

This period helps the child develop good motor control. He must give his undivided attention to what he is doing in order to carry his milk to his place without spilling it. If trays are used for this purpose he must be able to balance the tray and carry the milk to the tables.

It provides an excellent opportunity for group planning and conversation relative to things that relate to the group. Planning parties, helping prepare and serve food, taking the responsibility for being on some committee such as the food or clean-up committee, all find chances for advancement at this time.

It helps develop social poise and grace as children show courtesy in using their napkins, etc. It is an excellent time to learn to say "thank you", "please", and "you are welcome". It also gives an opportunity for a child to be a host or hostess to the group when he brings a treat to school.

Chapter 11

SONG PERIOD

Most five-year-olds have a great interest in music and find much pleasure and relaxation in singing. Music becomes an outlet for their emotions, and music becomes for them a means of expression.

All kindergarten teachers know that the ability to sing varies in any group. Very few children have much native singing ability or acquire accurate pitch. The important thing is that most of the other children will sing with just a little encouragement and with a great deal of pleasure. As teachers, we must help the child acquire self-confidence if we are going to help him learn to sing. We should avoid criticizing him and reminding him that he is off tune. Mothers who sing with their children and to them, help them become interested in music as a natural means of expression.

Music is to the kindergarten day what frosting is to the cake. It's fun to enjoy and fun to participate in. Singing comes into the daily program in the kindergarten in many different ways. Sometimes it follows the milk lunch period or is utilized to a very good advantage at resting time, along with the regular time set aside for it.

These varied experiences are of real help to the beginning child:

Group singing is an excellent means of giving the children confidence. As it does not require as much initiative on their part, most children love to fit into this group pattern of acceptance. Many teachers use this particular period to vary the seating arrangement of the boys and girls. Some use several rows of chairs for singing time at which time the poorer singers are seated closer to the piano and the better singers are in the back row, giving the poorer singers practice in listening and ear training. Different rows of children can be called upon at different times to sing together giving other children a chance to listen to each other.

Tone drills and phrases can be used as a game to help those needing practice with their sense of pitch. This helps the teacher hear individuals sing alone without the child becoming self conscious and frightened. These drills often include activities in which the class is participating or they may be related to games played in the room, or they may be an imitation of an animal, train, or instruments. Many kindergarten songs lend themselves to tone matching some of which are: "Big Brass Drum", "My Dog", "Valentines" and "Jack O'Lantern", which are listed in Tone Matching Tunes by Coit and Bompton, Flammer, Inc., N. Y. Most music periods in the kindergarten include a variety of drills and songs. A tone drill is of great help to the monotone. While intended primarily for the monotone, these songs will help all children with pitch.

A good music period also includes songs children have learned before coming to school. An old song, either suggested by the teacher or chosen by the children, is greatly enjoyed. Several times a week an appreciation song could be included. Many teachers like to present it as the new song for the coming week. This gives the children an opportunity to hear it several times before they are asked to learn it. Many times these songs are played on the piano, sung with the piano, or played on the victrola.

Before the year is over children will enjoy making up original songs from their own experiences. Sometimes children are motivated to do this by substituting their own names in the songs they already know.

Several new songs should be introduced every week. If the song is short, consisting of only one or two phrases, it is sung completely through when first introduced. If it is a longer song, it may be necessary to work on the more difficult phrases when it is first introduced. When the song is first taught to the children be sure not to slow the tempo and sing it as you expect the children to sing it later when they know it.

If the song is very short most teachers teach the whole song method and use the phrase method for the longer more difficult ones.

Songs and Seasons

Through music and song the kindergarten makes an attempt to enrich children's backgrounds and experiences. These are some of the songs that could be used at certain seasons of the year.

FALL

Days of Make Believe
  The Whirling Leaf
  The Busy Squirrels
  The Wind And Sun
  The Caterpillar

My Picture Book Of Songs
  Crunchy Leaves
  Whirley Twirley

Sing A Song
  The Milkman
  Housework

The Kindergarten Book
  The Leaves
  Down! Down!
  Wind Is Singing

Singing Time
  Falling Leaves
  Baking Apples
  Rain Song
  October
  Apple Tree

More Songs For Happy Children
  Johnny Took A Tumble

HALLOWEEN

Happy Songs For Happy Children
  Halloween

My Picture Book Of Songs
  Boo!
  Mr. Jack O'Lantern

Days Of Make Believe
  Jack-O-Lantern
  Harvest

The Kindergarten Book
  I'm A Jack O'Lantern
  Halloween Has Come
  Halloween Is Coming
  See My Big Eyes

American Singer
  Funny Witches
  Brownies And Witches

Rhythm Fun For Little Folks
Halloween Brownies
Halloween Cat

THANKSGIVING

The Kindergarten Book
Thanksgiving Is Coming
Company Is Coming
A Big Fat Turkey
Prayer
Gobble, Gobble

American Singer
Gobble
Thanking God

Rhythm Fun For Little Folks
Indian Dance

Sing A Song
What The Turkey Said
Thanksgiving

CHRISTMAS

Sing A Song
On Christmas Day
Talking Doll
Busy Santa

The Kindergarten Book
Santa's Helpers
Away In The Manger
Let's Dance Around The
Christmas Tree
Silent Night

Days Of Make Believe
Santa Claus
Bein' Good
My Christmas Stocking
Decorating The Tree
Dolly's Lullaby
Christmas Toys

American Singer
The Christmas Tree
Jingle, Jingle

Sing A Song
Mr. Jack O'Lantern

Sing And Sing
Jack O'Lantern

Singing Time
The Big Tall Indian

Our First Music
The Turkey
Over The River
Thank Thee, Lord

Small Songs For Small Singers
Mr. Duck And Mrs. Turkey

Merry Songs
The Turkey Gobbler

Sing And Sing
Snowman

Sing A Song
On Christmas Day
The Snowman

Merry Songs
A Pop Corn Song
The Snowman

Songs For Early Childhood
Round The Christmas Tree

Singing Time
Christmas Bells
Happy New Year

WINTER

Happy Songs For Happy Children
Snow
Snowman
Jackie Frost

American Singer
Winter
Coasting
The North Wind
Skating

The Kindergarten Book
I'm Glad It's Snowing
Skating

Rhythm Fun For Little Folks
Shoveling Snow
Snowflakes

Music For Early Childhood
The Snowman

VALENTINE'S DAY

My Picture Book Of Songs
My Valentine
The Postman

Happy Songs For Happy Children
A Valentine

The Kindergarten Book
A Valentine For You
When You Send A Valentine

Singing Time
The Postman

Another Singing Time
A Valentine Song

American Singer
Valentine
Making Valentines

Our First Music
Valentine Questions

SPRING

American Singer
The Seasons
Pussy Willows
Spring Is Here
Leaves
March

Kindergarten Book
Seeds and Flowers

Singing Time
Spring Song
Sing O Sing
Rain

Walk The World Together
March Winds

Sing A Song
In My Garden
Fat Robin Red Breast
I Can Tell
When Springtime Comes

Music For Early Childhood
Little Wind

My Picture Book Of Songs
My Kite
The March Wind

Merry Songs
Pussywillow
Little Robin Redbreast

Small Songs For Small Singers
Bluebird

Happy Songs For Happy Children
Spring
Raining

The Kindergarten Book
A Bird In A Pear Tree
A Blue Bird
A Getting Up Song
Five Little Chickadees

EASTER

My Picture Book Of Songs
    Easter Morning
    Fluffy Bunny

The Kindergarten Book
    Easter Eggs
    Mrs. Hen And Mrs. Chick

Another Singing Time
    A Song About A Rabbit
    Easter Eggs

Our First Music
    Easter Eggs

Merry Songs
    Meeting The Easter Bunny

Sing A Song Again
    My Yellow Duck

Kindergarten Book
    Bunnies

Singing Time
    The Little Bunny

Happy Songs For Happy Children
    Easter Bunny

Song Books

This list of song books is suitable for use in a kindergarten. Many of these songs suggested in this book are to be found in this list of books.

BOOK	AUTHOR	PUBLISHER
Songs And Stories About Animals	Crowinshield, Ethel	The Boston Music Co., Boston, Mass.
Stories That Sing	Crowinshield, Ethel	
Songs To Grow On	Landeck, Beatrice	Wm. Sloane Associated, Inc., New York
Music For Early Childhood	Nelson & Tipton	Silver Burdett Co.
Music Time	Hunt, Evelyn	The Viking Press, New York, N. Y. (1947)
Children Come And Sing	Lyden, Clara	E. M. Hale & Co. Milwaukee, Wisconsin
Songs For The Nursery	MacCarteney	Willis Music Co. Cincinnati, Ohio
Small Songs For Small Singers	Neidlinger, Albertina	G. Schirmer, Inc. New York, N. Y. (1925)
The Kindergarten Book	Pitts, Glenn, Watters	Ginn and Co., Chicago, Ill.
Happy Songs For Happy Children	Siebold, Meta	G. Schirmer, Inc. New York, N. Y. (1928)
Sing A Song	Glenn, Leavitt	Ginn and Company Chicago, Ill.

BOOK	AUTHOR	PUBLISHER
Walk The World Together	Crowinshield, Ethel	The Boston Music Co. Boston, Mass.
Days Of Make Believe		
Our First Music	Armitage	Birchard & Co.
Sing Mother Goose	Wheeler, Opal	E. P. Dutton & Co., Inc. New York, N. Y. (1945)
Fifty Songs For Boys & Girls	Gomez, Winnifred	Follet Publishing Co. Chicago, Ill. (1949)
Songs Of The Child World	Gaynor	John Church & Co. Philadelphia, Pa.
My Picture Book of Songs	Dalton, Arlene	W. A. Donohue Co. New York, N. Y.
Another Singing Time	Coleman, Satis Thorn, Alice	The John Day Co. New York, N. Y.
The New Singing Time	Coleman, Satis	The John Day Co. New York, (1950)
Singing Time	Coleman, Satis Thorn, Alice	The John Day Co. New York, N. Y. (1935)
Sing A Song Of Safety	Caesar, Irving	Irving Caesar New York, N. Y. (1937)
Twenty Little Songs	Carter, Jessie	The Willis Music Co. Cincinnati, Ohio
The American Singer	Beattie, Wolverton, Wilson, Hinga	American Book Co. Chicago, Ill. (1944)
Sing And Sing Again	Boesel, Ann	Oxford Press New York, N. Y.
My Picture Book Of Songs	Dalton, Ashton, Young	M. A. Donohue & Co.
Timothy's Tunes	McCall, Adeline	The Boston Music Co. Boston, Mass.
The Land Of Pretend	Johnson	Birchard, Boston, Mass.

Chapter 12

STORY TIME

    This is the time when children listen to a new story or to a familiar one. The children settle down to enjoy hearing a story read to them as they see the pictures unfold before their eyes. Sometimes they listen to the teacher tell a story because some stories are best told. When children know the story better and have heard it several times they may want to play or act it out. At first it is kept very simple, and as the year goes on it may become more detailed. Many teachers begin by having the children tell parts of the story, or just the part that is familiar to them. Many chances for dramatization should be given in the kindergarten through-out the entire year. Pictures sometimes serve as reminders when children are attempting to play a role. Questions from the teacher may provoke a response also. Children like the familiar things rather than the strange. For this reason Mother Goose serves as a good introduction for dramatization. These rhymes are very simple and yet have so much rhythm to them that children enjoy them.

    Do not forget that the best known and the best loved stories like "Peter Rabbit" or "The Three Bears" are told and retold again and again and the children are encouraged to retell them and play them. As children mature they learn to tell their experiences well, but they do need practice in story telling without help. Have you tried using the flannel board for just such a purpose? It is one of the easiest ways to motivate boys and girls to take an active part in story telling. This flannel board, known by various names can either be purchased or made. Many teachers prefer to make theirs because they can make them larger than most commercially made boards. There are not too many stories that can be purchased for use on this board, but any ingenious teacher can buy two linen story books at the dime store, paste heavy sand paper strips or felt on the back of the cut-out pieces of the story and use on the flannel board. The reason for buying two books alike is that you will want to use some of the pictures on the backs of the story pages.

    Try using the opaque projector to help the five-year-old develop ease and freedom of expression. You will find that it also helps in developing a speaking vocabulary. Soon the children begin to realize there is a sequence in stories and that pictures tell a story that is easy for them to understand. In this way their interest is vitalized.

    During the year when the children have had a chance to tell parts of stories make a tape recording of it. Children will become more conscious of their mistakes when the tape is played back to them, and you will have the opportunity to notice speech defects and clarity of expression.

    Poems and finger plays are added to the story time because they enrich its value and add so much to the enjoyment of it. However, poems and finger plays should not be substituted for it. When this is done the children are apt to feel that something has been omitted.

Some children can repeat lines or the whole of very short poems almost immediately, and the ones they enjoy the most are very easy for them to master.

Stories, poems, fingerplays, and choral reading are all an important part of the kindergarten program. They help to bring about a realization that the print below the picture tells the story; they help teach left-to-right sequence, top to bottom, front to back, as well as the association of ideas, and most of all they further a child's desire to read. From the time children learn to talk they want to know what it says under the picture. They are beginning at this early age to acquire a reading vocabulary. The training we give the children in our kindergarten determines in a large measure the ease with which they will learn to read.

The suggestions has been made several times that one thing at a time be added to the kindergarten routine. The same thing should be said of books. If books are added one at a time, like art materials and manipulative toys, children will be ready for them and will look forward to hearing the story.

You will want to have some books that the children themselves may handle and look at with little or no supervision. This will require a shelf or two in your own room along with a reading table. The children will enjoy having something all their own, and they can be taught to care for books and return them when they are through. Respect for books which includes many habits can best be taught at this time.

The teacher of the five-year-old will also want to have a book shelf for herself where special books are kept which may be read or told aloud to the children.

The content of children's books is very important. Since books and children must be considered together, it is impossible to place a book at a certain age level. These groupings are only approximate listings. As selections should be made with care, a few rules may be helpful in choosing in this age of lavish advertising.

1. Look for the kind of print, preferably black ink on ecru.
2. Learn the better children's publishers and illustrators and include many of these books.
3. Books should always be chosen with a permanent purpose. Cheap books are not a good investment.
4. Picture books should be bound sturdily enough to stand the wear and tear of the child's handling.
5. Beginning story books should have an element of realism about them and should be within the child's own experience of homes, animals, and transportation.
6. Stories for the young child should be short and vivid, so that it is possible to hold his attention. As the year progresses and listening power increases, longer stories may be told; also many more of them.
7. A child's book should have an interesting theme.

The five year old enjoys listening to stories read and told to him. He loves to hear simple poetry and is very much at home when he has the opportunity to look at picture books. Ideas are necessary to understand books and ideas are gained by handling things, by observation and by asking questions about them. The teacher of five-year-olds needs to provide many opportunities for children to name and talk about pictures, to make up stories, to play them, and most of all to enjoy them. Gradually the kindergartner gains a rich background for reading and grows toward a readiness for reading in the first grade. Much experience with rhymes, choral reading, and stories is valuable in kindergarten mainly for the literary experience involved. If children can live richly during the kindergarten year they can not help but be better ready to read.

Every kindergarten teacher will want to be able to tell several stories, especially the classics. Sometimes children are deprived of hearing some of these stories unless the teacher can tell them. One advantage in telling a story to your group is that it brings you closer to them. The book sometimes becomes a barrier between you and the children. Children are able to watch your gestures and facial expressions better when you tell them the story. It does take preparation on the part of the teacher of five-year-olds, but once the story has been learned it is not difficult to retell it. In the past story telling was a much loved art in the kindergarten. Of course there were not as many lovely picture books from which to choose, however, there is still a great deal to be said for telling stories at this day and age. Perhaps it is sufficient to say do not use one technique to the exclusion of another.

It is a very enjoyable experience when boys and girls can enjoy hearing a story told to them and also see the pictures that tell about it. This type of story telling also calls for preparation on the part of the teacher. You must be familiar with the content of the story so that the boys and girls are atune to the story itself. This is very difficult to achieve unless some time is given to reading the story through and becoming familiar with its content.

Early in the year you will want to set the stage for the technique to be used at story time. It lends little to have children adding things to the story as you go along. Tell them that their turn will come at the end of the story after you have had your turn to tell it to them. When you have finished telling the story listen to their comments and suggestions and ask pertinent questions relating to it.

Stories to Read to Children

BOOK	AUTHOR	PUBLISHER	PRICE
A Kiss Is Round	Budney	Lothrop	$2.50

"This book helps sharpen a child's perception of form, but first of all it is great fun."

| Angus And The Ducks | Flack | Doubleday | $1.50 |

"Angus, a Scotch Terrier puppy, becomes curious and he slips under the hedge to see the outside world."

| Autumn Harvest | Tresselt | Lothrop | $2.00 |

"A recreation of all the sights, sounds, and smells of a beautiful fall season."

| Big Snow | Hader | Macmillan | $2.75 |

"Story of the little old man and woman who lived in the only house on the hillside and how, during the long winter they put out pans of food for the animals."

| ABC | Gag | Coward-McCann | $3.00 |

"An alphabet book which tells in verse the story of a little rabbit's adventures."

| When The Root Children Wake Up | Fish | Stokes | $2.00 |

"It tells the story of how the root children wake up in their underground home"

| Red Light, Green Light | MacDonald | Doubleday | $2.00 |

"A picture book in which the truck, the car, the jeep, the horse, the boy, the dog, and the cat each comes out in the morning and sets forth upon his way."

BOOK	AUTHOR	PUBLISHER	PRICE

Golden Egg Book — Brown — Simon-Schuster — $1.50
"The brief text concerns a lonely bunny who found an egg which eventually hatched out a lonely little duck."

Johnny Crow's Garden — Brooke — Warne — $2.00
"The animal friends who come to Johnny Crow's Garden are unusual personalities."

Me And The Bears — Bright — Doubleday — $1.50
"About the little girl who loved the little bears of the zoo so much that she wished they'd come home with her."

Green Eyes — Birnbaum — Capitol — $2.50
"This story gives the high spots in the first year of a cat."

Pelle's New Suit — Harper — Beskow — $1.75
"The story of how Pelle earned his new suit."

Animals Everywhere — Aulaire — Doubleday — $2.00
"Introduces the child to the animals of the tropics and the arctic regions."

Growing Up — Fritz — Rand-McNally — $
"Tells how various animals grow up such as the kitten, giraffe, chicken, also children."

Brownies — Adshead — Oxford — $1.25
"A story of the brownies who helped the little old lady and man with their work."

Whistle For The Train — Brown — Doubleday — $2.50
"The rhythmic text describes a little train and the little animals who are warned by the whistle not to cross the track."

Big World And The Little House — Krauss — Harper — $2.50
"A story of a little tumble-down house that became a home."

Wake Up, City! — Tresselt — Lothrop — $2.50
"How a city wakes up - the traffic, the markets, and the people."

When It Rained Cats And Dogs — Turner — Lippincott — $2.00
"A picture book which will provide fun for children who like cats and dogs and one which may help them to identify different breeds."

A Tree Is Nice — Udry — Harper — $2.50
"The author sets forth reasons why trees are nice to have around."

Cunning Turtle — Wiese — Viking — $2.00
"Hidden In Mr. Buzzard's guitar, shy Mr. Turtle hitchhikes to a meeting of insect musicians. On the way home he falls out and cracks his shell, and that is why all turtles have cracks on their backs."

All By Himself — Clark — Plakie — $1.98
"A cloth bound book that helps the child in handling the more difficult aspects of dressing himself and gives him a chance to try a real zipper, button, buckle, and shoe lace."

132

BOOK	AUTHOR	PUBLISHER	PRICE
Tale Of Benjamin Bunny	Potter	Warne	$ .95

"Little Benjamin is a first cousin of Peter Rabbit, and this is the sequel to Peter's adventure in Mr. McGregor's garden. "

Tale of Peter Rabbit	Potter	Warne	$ .95

"All about the famous rabbit family consisting of Flopsy, Mopsy, Cotton tail and Peter Rabbit. "

Circus Baby	Petersham	Macmillan	$2.00

"Mother elephant was a bit over zealous in training her baby, and this is what happened when she tried to make him eat the way the clowns did in the circus. "

Blueberries For Sal	McCloskey	Viking	$2.50

"One day, Little Sal went with her mother to Blueberry Hill, to pick blueberries. On the other side of Blueberry Hill Little Bear came with his mother to eat blueberries and they all got mixed up together. "

Rooster Crows	Petersham	Macmillan	$2.75

"A collection of American rhymes and jingles, finger plays, rope skipping rhymes. "

Curious George	Rey	Houghton	$2.50

"Colored picture book describing the adventure of a curious small monkey and the difficulties he had in getting a job. "

The Biggest Bear	Ward	Houghton	$2.75

"All the other barns in the valley had a bearskin and Johnny hated for his to be different. He decided to shoot a bear. He met one, but he couldn't shoot it. He brought it home instead. "

Johnny Maple Leaf	Tresselt	Lothrop	$2.00

"The story of a little maple leaf and its life through the cycle of the seasons. "

White Snow, Bright Snow	Tresselt	Lothrop	$2.00

"From the first smell of snow in the air to the frost ferns on the window pane, the magical beauty of snowfall is described. "

Follow The Wind	Tresselt	Lothrop	$2.00

"With a great whoosh and bluster the wind runs away from everything even an airplane that follows it three times around the world. But, at last, tired and gentle, it rocks itself to sleep. "

Walter, The Lazy Mouse	Flack	Doubleday & Co.	$2.95

"A delightful story of young Walter Mouse who was very lazy. Children will relish Walter's story, from the ingenious mouse house to the games of real live leap frog. "

You And The World Around You	Selsam	Doubleday & Co.	$2.95

"In simple language, accompanied by beautiful illustrations, this book answers such questions as: where does the rain go and what does it do after it falls?"

BOOK	AUTHOR	PUBLISHER	PRICE

ABC Of Cars And Trucks — Alexander — Doubleday & Co. — $2.50
"An alphabet book with a car or truck to go with every letter, from auto trailer to zone truck, told in rhymes and gay pictures."

The Ugly Duckling — Andersen — Doubleday & Co. — $1.50
"The famous story about the Ugly Duckling has been boldly and colorfully illustrated by Tony Palazzo."

I Like Red — Bright — Doubleday & Co. — $1.75
"This story tells why it is fun to be a redhead (pint-size), with the author's gay drawings pointing out all the things in the world that make it fun."

Whistle For The Train — Brown — Doubleday & Co. — $2.75
"A little black train whistles and gives safety warnings to animals, children, grown-ups in this story."

Red Light, Green Light — Brown — Doubleday & Co. — $2.75
"This is about the cars, animals and people who stop at the traffic light during a day."

The Big Red Bus — Kessler — Doubleday & Co. — $2.00
"A shopping trip and a ride on the big red bus, complete with sounds, sights and feelings."

Crunch, Crunch — Kessler — Doubleday & Co. — $1.50
"A trip to the supermarket is full of fun when gaily described and illustrated."

The Day Daddy Stayed Home — Kessler — Doubleday & Co. — $2.00
"Special delights of a child's everyday world, when snow covered everything and daddy stayed home with his family."

Peter's Long Walk — Kingman — Doubleday & Co. — $2.75
"The poignant story of small Peter whose birthday wish for some playmates came true in a surprising way."

The Little Family — Lenski — Doubleday & Co. — $1.00
"Everyday family fun - simply told."

The Giant Nursery Book — Palazzo — Doubleday & Co. — $3.95
"A selection of nursery rhymes, stories, and poems which Tony Palazzo has colorfully illustrated."

Let's Go To The Circus — Palazzo — Doubleday & Co. — $2.95
"A book to familiarize and charm the youngest child with what he has already seen or can see in that world of wonders, the circus."

Story Telling With The — Paul S. Anderson — T. S. Denison
Flannel Board
"A collection of stories that are not found easily and adapt themselves to use with the flannelboard."

BOOK	AUTHOR	PUBLISHER	PRICE
A Fly Went By	McClintock	Random House	$2.19

"A little fly sits by the lake and a fly goes by. Other things go by too, such as a frog, cat, dog, pig, cat, and a fox; even a man with a gun went by, and they all waved good-bye."

White Snow - Bright Snow   Tresselt   Lothrop, Lee, Shepard Co. $2.50

"Everybody said that it looked like snow - the postman, the policeman, even the rabbit knew it would snow. Then, when everybody was asleep it stopped. Everything was covered with many inches of snow. After the big snow was over, everyone looked for the first signs of spring."

Let's Be Indians   Parish   Harper Row & Co. $2.75

"All projects in this book center around Indians. The reader can make and wear a complete costume from moccasins to headband."

Quack-Quack   Hader   Macmillan $3.50

"Quack-quack and a little wild duck take off on a lifetime adventure. From native marshland, to farmyard, to migration flying, to a free ride on an ocean liner, to Becky's back yard; the little wild duck goes and grows. And, when he becomes a handsome, green-headed mallard, he stretches his wings and wisely flies home; for wild ducks begin and belong in the marshland."

Rabbits' Wedding   Williams   Harper Row & Co. $3.25

"A really furry-looking rabbit and a tender story for the very young. Lovely pictures that lend themselves well for illustration.

Proud Pumpkin   Unwin   A Guild Book $2.00

"During the course of the story many things happen to the proud pumpkin and some of them are not so pleasant. As the weather grows colder and the Halloween season passes, the pumpkin becomes unattractive and seems to lose its usefulness; but the proud pumpkin is finally saved and restored to usefulness by a gopher who uses the pumpkin as his home."

I Would Like To Be A Pony   Baruch   Harper-Row & Co. $2.75

"This is a book of unusual poetry for the very young written by a noted psychologist."

One Morning In Maine   McClosky   Viking Press $2.98

"The story of a little girl and her small sister, who have gone clamming with their father, so they can have clam chowder for dinner. The little girl has a loose tooth and she wonders if other animals have loose teeth also. She is so busy talking her tooth falls in where her father is digging.

Award Winning Books

AWARDED	ARTIST	BOOK
1938	Dorothy P. Lathrop	Animals Of The Bible
1939	Thomas Handforth	Mei Li
1940	Ingri And Edgar Parin d'Aulaire	Abraham Lincoln
1941	Robert Lawson	They Were Strong And Good
1942	Robert McCloskey	Make Way For Ducklings
1943	Virginia Lee Burton	The Little House
1944	Louis Slobodkin	Many Moons
1945	Elizabeth Orton Jones	Prayer For A Child
1946	Maud And Miska Petersham	Rooster Crows
1947	Leonard Weisgard	The Little Island
1948	Roger Duvoisin	White Snow, Bright Snow
1949	Berta And Elmer Hader	The Big Snow
1950	Leo Politi	Song Of The Swallows
1951	Katherine Milhous	The Egg Tree
1952	Nicolas Mordvinoff	Finders Keepers
1953	Lynn Ward	The Biggest Bear
1954	Ludwig Bemelmans	Madeline's Rescue
1955	Marcia Joan Brown	Cinderella
1956	Feodor Rojankovsky	Frog Went A-Courtin'
1957	Marc Simont	A Tree Is Nice
1958	Robert McCloskey	Time Of Wonder
1959	Barbara Cooney	Chanticleer And The Fox
1960	Marie Hall Eta	Nine Days To Christmas
1961	Nicolas Sidjakov	Baboushka And The Three Kings
1962	Marcia Joan Brown	Once A Mouse
1963	Ezra Jack Keats	The Snowy Day
1964	Maurice Sendak	Where The Wild Things Are
1965	Beatrice de Regniers	May I Bring A Friend

Poetry

BOOK	AUTHOR	PUBLISHER	PRICE
Silver Pennies	Thompson	Macmillan	$1.50

"A nice understanding of children's appreciation of poetry is shown in the selection of these eighty modern poems."

Taxis And Toadstools	Field	Doubleday	$2.25

"Verses that have childlike quality and suggest new ways of seeing city and country to children who like to make rhymes of their own."

The Night Before Christmas	Moore	Lippincott	$1.75

"The pictures in this delightful book emphasize all the magic aboard in the air on Christmas Eve."

Fairies And Chimneys	Fyleman	Doubleday	$1.50

"Fanciful poems about fairies and their ways."

Now We Are Six	Milne	Dutton	$2.00

"A delightful book of verse for the very young child."

Very Young Verse	Geismer	Houghton	$2.50

"Two nursery school teachers have compiled this anthology out of their experiences with small children."

Sung Under The Silver Umbrella	Lit. Committee	Macmillan	$2.75

"A charming collection of about two hundred poems for young children. All the poems have been tried out with children. The grouping is by subject matter."

Sing Song	Rosetti	Macmillan	$1.35

"A nursery rhyme book first published in 1872 whose verses are brief and simple."

Child's Garden Of Verses	Stevenson	Scribners	$3.50

"Verses known and loved by generation after another. Poems full of music and rhythm by a poet who always kept his ability to live in a child's world."

Time For Poetry	Arbuthnot	Scott	$3.00

"An American poetry collection for children to be used in the classroom."

Time For Poetry Album	Arbuthnot		

Book Awards

The children's library association presents two awards each year. The John Newberry medal, awarded annually since 1922, gives recognition to the most distinguished book for children. It is awarded for the most distinguished contribution to American literature for children. (Text)

The Randolph Caldecott Award was given for the first time in 1938. This medal was named in honor of a great English illustrator of children's books. It is awarded to the illustrator of the most distinguished picture book for children published in the U.S.A. that year.

Helps for Parents

Parents often ask for help in making a study of children's literature and some of these books might prove helpful:

BOOK	AUTHOR	PUBLISHER	PRICE
Reading With Children	Eaton	Viking	$3.00
First Adventures in Reading	Becker	Stokes	$2.25
Proof Of the Pudding	Fenner	Day	$3.95
The Unreluctant Years	Smith	ALA	$4.50

Booklists

Basic Book Collection for Elementary Grades (Revised 1956), American Library Association, 50 East Huron St., Chicago 11, Illinois. $2.00

Bibliography of Books For Children (Revised Sept. 1958), Association for Childhood Education International, 1200 15th St. N.W., Washington 5, D.C. $1.50

Books Of The Year For Children. An annual list. Child Study Association Of America, Inc., 132 East 74th St., New York 21. $.25 a copy

Children's Books Suggested As Holiday Gifts. An annual list. New York Public Library, Fifth Avenue at 42nd St., New York 18. $.10

Children's Books Too Good To Miss (Revised 1953), The Press Of Western Reserve University, 2035 Adelbert Road, Cleveland 6. $1.00

Growing Up With Books. An annual list. R. R. Bowker & Co., 62 West 45th St., New York 36. $.10 a copy

Stories Anyone Can Tell (1957), A List for the beginner. New York Public Library, Fifth Avenue at 42nd St., New York 18. Free

Once Upon A Time. A storytelling booklet prepared by Augusta Baker, 1955 for the New York State Library Association. (Write Mrs. Augusta Baker, Donnell Library Center, 20 West 53rd St., New York 19, N. Y.

Notable Children's Books (of the year). An annual list compiled by the Children's Service Division of the American Library Association, 50 East Huron Street, Chicago 11. Free

Finger Plays

Have you tried any of these finger plays or poems in connection with school festivals or units?

THE FAMILY

This is the mother so happy and gay. (Point to thumb)
This is the father who works all the day. (Point to second finger)
This is the brother so strong and tall. (Point to middle finger)
This is the sister who plays with her doll. (Point to fourth finger)
This is the baby the sweetest of all. (Point to little finger)
That is the whole family great and small. (Point to all fingers)

THESE ARE MOTHER'S KNIVES AND FORKS

These are mother's knives and forks. (Fingers intertwined)
This is mother's table. (Back of hand)
This is grandma's looking glass. (Diamond with pointers and thumb)
And this is baby's cradle. (Cup hands and rock)

TWO LITTLE HOUSES

Two little houses closed up so tight. (Fists)
Open the windows and let in some light.
Ten little finger people so tall and straight.
Come straight to school so they won't be late.

THINGS FOR BABY

Here's a ball for baby, big and soft and round. (Make it with hands)
Here's the baby's hammer, oh, how he can pound. (Pound with hands)
Here's a big umbrella, keeps the baby dry. (Made with hands)
Here's the baby's cradle, rock-a-bye-bye. (Make cradle with hands)
Here's the baby's trumpet, toot-too-toot-too-too. (Play trumpet with hand)
Here's the way that baby plays, "Peek-a-boo", with you. (Play)

THE APPLE TREE

Way up high in the apple tree. (Hands way up in air)
Two little apples smiled down at me. (Hands around eyes like glasses)
I shook the tree as hard as I could. (Shake tree)
Down came the apples. (Motion to ground)
Umm, they were good. (Rub stomach)

HERE'S THE CHURCH

Here's the church. (Fingers interlocked, palms down)
And here's the steeple. (Index fingers rise to a point)
Open the door. (Keep fingers interlocked, but turn palms up)
And see all the people (Wiggle fingers)

AN OLD OWL

An old owl sat on the limb of a tree.   (Left arm extended for limb of tree)
(Left hand turned palm up to represent owl)
And he was as still as still could be.
It was night and his eyes looked just like this.
(Open eyes wide. Make rings around eyes with thumbs and forefingers)
He looked all around, and not a thing did he miss.
(Look all around with the big eyes)

Five little brownies crept upon the tree.
(The fingers of the right hand represent the five brownies)
And they were as still, as still could be.
(Use hushed voice and keep right fingers on the left arm)
(Hide hands quickly)
The old owl looked around and said, "who, who!"
And away went the brownies, away they flew.

TEN LITTLE FINGERS

I have ten little fingers
And they all belong to me.
I can make them do things
Would you like to see?

I can shut them up tight
Or open them wide
I can put them together
Or make them all hide.

I can make them jump high
I can make them jump low
I can fold them up quietly
And hold them just so.

FIVE LITTLE CHICKENS

Five little chickens lived in a pen.   (Hold up right hand)
The name of their mother was Mrs. White Hen.   (Hold up thumb of other hand)
The chickens went out for a walk one day.   (Hold up right hand)
Each of them went a different way.   (Spread fingers of right hand)
This little chicken saw a brown dog.   (Point to thumb of right hand)
This one saw a little green frog.   (Point to first finger of right hand)
This little chicken saw a big black cat.   (Point to middle finger or right hand)

This one saw a piggy quite fat.   (Point to fourth finger of right hand)
This one saw a little grey mouse.   (Point to little finger)
Running around the side of the house.
"Cluck, cluck, cluck," said Mrs. Hen.   (Hold up thumb of left hand)
Then all of the chickens ran home again.   (Rapidly move fingers of right
                                        hand toward left thumb).

THREE BALLS

Here's a ball. (Small circle made with thumb and index finger of one hand).
And here's a ball. (Larger circle made by using both thumbs and index finger)
And a great big ball I see. (Huge ball using both arms)
Shall we count them? Are you ready?
One! Two! Three! (Each of the circles is made as counted)

RESTING HANDS

These are my sun glasses. (Circle made around the eyes with thumb and
                            index fingers of each hand)
This is my great sun hat. (Hands over head forming pointed hat)
This is the way I fold my hands. (Hands clasped in the air)
And rest them, just like that! (Hands relaxed and resting in lap).

HANDS

Hands on hips, hands on your knees
Put them behind you, if you please
Touch your shoulders, touch your toes
Touch your knees and then your nose
Raise your hands way up so high,
And let your fingers swiftly fly
Then hold them out in front of you
While you clasp them one and two.

CROSSING STREETS

Stop, look and listen before you cross the street
Use your eyes (point to eyes) use your ears (point to ears)
And then use your feet (point to feet).

TEN TINY REINDEER

(Dance fingers and thumbs on table)
Ten tiny reindeer ready to go;
Ten tiny reindeer pawing in the snow.

(Wave right thumb in air)
Rudolph has a shiny nose;
He decides which way the sleigh goes.

(Tap finger on table)
Dasher and dancer paw with their hoofs
They're in a hurry to get to the roofs.

(Hold middle fingers in the air)
Prancer and Vixen hold their antlers high;
At Santa's signal, they're ready to fly.

(Rest finger on table)
Comet and Cupid patiently stand;
They're the quickest of Santa's band.

(Wave little fingers in the air)
Donder and Blitzen, jingle bells to say,
"Children, listen, Santa's on his way."

(Hold up left thumb)
And who should be bringing up the rear;
But number ten, a tiny new reindeer.

THANKSGIVING TURKEY

"Gobble, gobble," said Mr. Turkey
"Soon 'twill be Thanksgiving Day.
How you treat me, would you eat me?
I think I'd better run away."

(Make a turkey with the hands. Place the fist of one hand against the open palm of the other. Thumb of the fisted hand forms the turkey head. Fingers of the open hand form the turkey tail. On the words "Gobble, gobble" wiggle the thumb or head. On the line, "I think I'd better run away," move the hands up over right shoulder as if the turkey were running away).

FIVE LITTLE FARMERS

Five little farmers (Fingers closed tightly over thumb)
Woke up with the sun,
For it was early morning
And chores must be done.

The first little farmer (Use thumb upright - make motion of milking cow)
Went to milk the cow.

The second little farmer (Use finger next to thumb)
Thought he'd better plow.

The third little farmer (Use next finger)
Fed the hungry hens.

The fourth little farmer (Use next finger)
Mended broken pens.

The fifth little farmer (Use little finger)
Took his vegetables to town -
Baskets filled with cabbages
And sweet potatoes brown.

When the work was finished (Hands are again closed tight)
And the western sky was red,
Five little farmers
Tumbled into bed.

FIVE LITTLE KITTENS

Five little kittens
Sleeping on a chair,
One rolled off,
Leaving four there.

Four little kittens,
One climbed a tree
To look into a bird's nest,
Then there were three.

Three little kittens
Wondered what to do,
One saw a mouse,
Then there were two.

Two little kittens
Playing near a wall,
One little kitten
Chased a red ball.

One little kitten
With fur as soft as silk,
Left all alone,
To drink a dish of milk.

Make 5 for each child.
Cut out the head, fold
hat part back and paste
tabs back so that it fits
on the finger.

FIVE LITTLE PUMPKINS SITTING ON A GATE

1st one said, "My, it's getting late." (Point to fingers)
2nd one said, "There are witches in the air."
3rd one said, "Ha! We don't care."
4th one said, "Let's run, let's run."
5th one said, "Isn't Halloween fun?"
OOOOOO! went the wind
Away went all light
Those five pumpkins ran quickly out of sight.

FIVE LITTLE PILGRIMS

Five little Pilgrims on Thanksgiving Day:
The first one said, "I'll have cake if I may."
The second one said, "I'll have turkey roasted,"
The third one said, "I'll have chestnuts, toasted."
The fourth one said, "I'll have pumpkin pie."
The fifth one said, "Oh cranberries I spy,"
But before they ate any turkey or dressing,
All of the Pilgrims said a Thanksgiving blessing.

(The hands should come together as in prayer on the last two lines.)

FIVE VALENTINES

One little valentine said, "I love you."
Tommy made another; then there were two.
Two little valentines; one for me;
Mary made another; then there were three.

Three little valentines said, "We need one more."
Johnny made another; then there were four,
Four little valentines, one more to arrive;
Susan made another; then there were five;
Five little valentines all ready to say,
"Be my valentine on this happy day."

Let the class make valentines. Five children are chosen to hold up their valentines one by one as the poem is said. Substitute the names of the children chosen. All five may say the last line. Each other child in the class holds up a closed fist and extends a finger when another valentine is added.

THE ENGINEER

I ride in the engine. (Point to self proudly)
The whistle I blow (Pull imaginary whistle
I do all the things that will make the train go. (Pull out throttle)
Whoo! Whoo! says the whistle! (Put hands to mouth and draw out whoo,
                        whoo)
Chug! Chug! say the wheels! (Use arms as wheel motions)
I'm chief engineer 'til I'm called for my meals. (Pat chest proudly)

MISS MUFFET'S SPIDER

A spider one fine summer day
(Hold left hand up with fingers as spider's legs)
Made Miss Muffet run away.
(Bring left hand toward right hand which runs away on two fingers)
But I sit down to watch him spin
(Put right fist in front of you and left left hand to make spider spin a web)
A lacy web with thread so thin.
I wonder if Miss Muffet knew
(Place hands and arms in a thinking pose and hold for last line)
That God made little spiders too?

FIVE LITTLE SNOWMEN

Five little snowmen, happy and gay. (Point to fingers)
First one said, "What a beautiful day."
Second one said, "We'll never have tears."
Third one said, "We'll stay here for years."
Fourth one said, "But what will happen in May?"
Fifth one said, "Look! We're melting away."

TEN LITTLE FRIENDS

Two little houses across the street. (Hold up hands, fists closed)
Open the doors and ten friends meet. (Open fingers)
How do you do, and how do you do. (Fingers bow to each other)
Such nice sunny weather.
Off they hurried to kindergarten.
Ten little friends together. (Hurry into your lap)

Poems

Have you tried using any of these selected poems especially for kindergarten children? You may enjoy them at various times of the year, and in connection with different units of work.

SAFETY

CROSSING STREETS

Remember when you cross the street,
That cars are swifter than your feet.
So if you see one coming fast
Wait a bit 'til it has passed.

TRAFFIC LIGHTS

The traffic lights we see ahead
Are sometimes green and sometimes red.
Red on top and green below.
The red means STOP, the green means GO.
Green below -- Go, Go, Go
Red on top -- Stop, Stop, Stop.

STOP AND GO

The green light tells the cars to stop
And I can go ahead.
For soon I know the light will change again to red.
The cars will stop, and I can go ahead.

FALL

LEAVES

Leaves are floating softly down
They make a carpet on the ground,
Then swish, the wind comes whirling by,
And send them dancing to the sky.

SQUIRRELS

A little squirrel runs up a tree - scamper, scamper, skip.
He jumps about from branch to branch, hippity, hippity, hip.
A little squirrel runs down a tree.
He has no time to stop
He's getting nuts you can see, hippity, hippity, hop.

RAKING LEAVES

What jolly fun to rake the leaves,
And see the pile grow higher.
But we must wait 'til daddy comes,
Before we light the fire.

HALLOWEEN

THE WITCH

The witch is on her broomstick
Riding very fast.
OOOOoooo--Oooooo
Halloween at last!

THE PUMPKIN SEED

We planted common pumpkins,
But wonderful indeed,
Two great big eyes, a nose, and mouth,
Grew from that pumpkin seed.

TONIGHT IS HALLOWEEN

We're happy as can be.
The witches and the goblins come,
Oh just you wait and see.
With eyes of red and pumpkin heads,
With sheets and gowns of white
If you should meet one in the dark,
I think you'll shake with fright.

HALLOWEEN MASK

Who am I behind this mask,
With nose so big and whiskers too?
Who am I behind this mask
Who is it that is asking you?

A JACK O'LANTERN

A face so round and eyes so bright.
A nose that glows
My, what a sight!
A fiery mouth
With a jolly grin.
No arms, no legs
Just hat to chin.

JACK O'LANTERN

I used to be a pumpkin all orange and big and round.
I used to live some place else, growing on the ground.
Now, I have a mouth, nose, and eyes; I'm different, but I'm the same size.
I have a candle in me and it's very plainly seen,
You see, I am a jack-o-lantern for your Halloween.

CHRISTMAS

FIVE LITTLE BELLS

Five little bells hanging in a row.
The first one said, "Ring me slow."
The second one said, "Ring me fast."
The third one said, "Ring me last."
The fourth one said, "I'm like a chime."
The fifth one said, "Ring me at Christmas Time."

SANTA

When he comes down my chimney,
I should like to peep.
But he'll never come, no never,
Until I'm fast asleep.

CHRISTMAS

Twinkle, twinkle, twinkle, twinkle,
All the stars shine bright.

Twinkle, twinkle, twinkle, twinkle,
Santa comes tonight.

CHRISTMAS TREE

I'm a little Christmas tree.
Glittering, glittering, merrily.
A star at my head, gifts at my feet,
And on all my branches, candy canes sweet.

SECRETS

Secrets are fun at Christmas time.
I have some wrapped with ribbon and twine.
I will keep them all hidden far back out of sight.
Until time to open on Christmas night.

SPRING

ON A WALK

Taking a walk was so much fun.
We didn't hurry, we didn't run.
We watched for birds, we watched for bees.
We looked for all the budding trees.

THE SUN

The sunshine does so many things,
Like changing winter into spring.
He makes days long and all things grow,
So that is why I do love him so.

UMBRELLA

Put up the umbrella,
To keep baby dry.
Put up the umbrella,
There's rain in the sky.

DANDELIONS

Dandelions yellow, hiding in the grass.
Dandelions pretty, nodding as I pass.
Dandelions silver, dandelions gray.
Dandelions pretty, I'll blow your hair away.

A KITE

I often sit and wish that I,
Could be a kite up in the sky,
And ride upon the breeze and go,
Whichever way I chanced to blow.

BLUE-JAY

I put a little feeding tray upon my window sill.
My first guest was a blue-jay
Oh my, what a thrill!

BIRDS

Once I saw a little bird,
Come hop, hop, hop.
So I cried: "Little bird
Will you stop, stop, stop, stop?"

And I was going to the window
To say: "How do you do."
But he shook his little head
And far away he flew.

RAIN

On storm days
When the wind is high
Tall trees are brooms
Sweeping the sky.

They swish their branches
In buckets of rain.
And swash and sweep it
Blue again.

ROBIN

A pair of busy robins
Build a soft warm nest.
Where the mother and her baby birds
Can softly rest.

SPRING

The melting snow says, "Drop, drop."
The little frog goes, "Hop, hop."
The little bird says, "Peep, peep."
The little vine goes, "Creep, creep."
The little bee says, "Hum, hum."
The little flower says, "Spring has come."

PUSSY WILLOW

Pussy willow, pussy willow
In your coat of gray.
Happy now are we to see you.
Spring is on the way.

WOODPECKER

I put a little feeding tray
Upon my window sill,
My first guest was a woodpecker,
Oh my what a thrill.

EASTER

EASTER EGGS

Easter eggs are prettier,
Than any I have seen.
One is red, and one is blue,
And one is white and green.

EASTER

Easter is the time of year,
That hearts are glad and full of cheer.
We go to church on Easter Day,
For friends and neighbors always pray.

BUNNY

Creeping, creeping, creeping,
Comes the kitty cat.
But the bunny with his great long ears,
Jumps like that.

EASTER

Easter nests and bunnies, too.
Tinted chicks and bonnets, blue.
Candy eggs, chocolate bunny.
Day of joy, bright and sunny.
Singing birds, playground breezes,
Make our Easter one that pleases.

Bibliography

Finger Plays And How To Use Them, Tessa Colina, Standard Publishing
    Co., Cincinnati, Ohio.
Fascinating Finger Fun, Eleanor Doan, Zondervan Publishing House, Grand
    Rapids, Michigan.
Let's Play With Fingers, Florence Summer, Albert Whitman & Co.
Finger Plays, Songs and Rhythms For The Very Young Child, Helen V.
    Salisbury, Cowman Publications, Los Angeles, California.
Finger Plays For Nursery And Kindergarten, Emilie Poulsson, Lothrop,
    Lee, and Shepard Co.

Chapter 13

READING READINESS

Readiness is a composite of many things and so it has to be measured in many different ways. It is not a thing to be taught, neither can it be purchased in a box or developed with a crayon on a piece of paper. It is an individual state. Children are constantly involved in different degrees of readiness. They are called to meals and they linger; they are put on their feet to walk and they fall down. There are signs for being ready and for not being ready.

In the spring of the year many people think of readiness as something that must happen to children during the season preceding first grade, but we know that readiness is a long slow process built on many experiences over a long period of time.

Picture Books

The kindergarten room should be well supplied with colorful, well selected picture books for children to examine. They should be placed on low shelves where they can be reached easily. It is in this atmosphere that boys and girls learn that books are sources of wonderful information and pleasure. Interest in reading and the desire to undertake it are aroused by this exposure to picture books. Using books by both the teacher and the child, gives an acquaintance with the appearance of symbols. There are many informal and incidental contacts with symbols that children need and can have. By exposing boys and girls to reading situations they become acquainted with the fact that reading symbols really stands for meaning. There are many ways to accomplish this without interfering in the least with the informal kindergarten program.

Through the library and story hours, children come to have an interest in books and a regard for their care and handling. They learn how to keep books clean and neat along with the proper way to open and close the pages in a book.

Dramatization: Dramatic play should be included as often as possible in the kindergarten day. It is very helpful in stimulating imagination and inspires children to observe more carefully. It is very valuable in developing language, as it is here that language becomes alive. Dramatization helps children understand what is happening in the story by pointing out details. Dramatic play for five-year-olds is very simple. Few costumes or props are needed, but praise should be given, no matter how little they actually achieve.

Dramatization does much to develop and enrich children's personalities. It provides satisfactory experiences in cooperation and motivates the organization and expression of thoughts and feelings.

The flannel board has many uses and is very versatile as far as the kindergartener is concerned. When it is used in relating the parts of a story, children identify themselves as the characters in the story. Manipulation is a part of their reading readiness program. Along with this, they are also made to feel the sequence of events in the story as they participate in this activity. They recognize the beginning of the story, what comes next, and how it ends. They learn to place the characters in their proper order and relationships.

Much experience is necessary with poetry, jingles and rhymes. By saying rhymes and jingles, we help in the rudiments of phonetic analysis. Rhymes bring out enjoyment of similar sounds and it is hard to beat them for limbering tongues and lips. Rhymes are excellent for making children aware of and able to hear the vowel and consonant sounds.

Young children learn more about their language from one to five years of age than they will at any other time in their lives. The children are mastering spoken language as they recall sensory impressions verbally as they use language creatively to tell what they know, see, do, hear, feel, or think. Without a doubt the most rapid growth in the ability to speak well, comes from practice in free oral expression during the "Show and Tell" time. The development of a fairly wide speaking vocabulary is important in training pupils to read.

Kindergarten children are not yet ready to write down words for themselves, but they love to dictate letters and stories to be written down by their teacher.

A wealth of experience is extremely important as it is a vital prerequisite for reading. The child must know as much about ducks as the author of the book expects him to know if he is to read about ducks with understanding.

The Skill of Observation

If boys and girls are to learn from their surroundings, beginnings in the skill of observation must be made in the kindergarten. When they become close observers and find out things for themselves, they develop a wider understanding of things around them.

Children are curious about the changes taking place in the out-of-doors.

Children can develop visual readiness by noticing objects around them and how these objects change from day to day.

VISUAL DISCRIMINATION

An awareness and understanding of likenesses and differences may be developed by using puzzles.

The Zoo unit was an added experience in visual discrimination. We included such words as big, bigger, tall, taller, thin, thinner, also things that look alike and things that look different.

We often talk about how things are different and how they are alike. We have used flannel and placed it on the flannel graph. Each line has one thing on it that is different either larger, smaller inverted, or designed.

By watching the teacher as she reads and by having the fact specifically called to their attention, children learn that the eye movement for reading is from left to right. This eye movement children practice in their own play reading - or develop it as they watch the teacher write in manuscript on a chart the recipe they will follow when they stir up a batch of sugar cookies.

Understanding Your Environment

Children experience pleasure in anticipating the weather. We give them an opportunity to look at the thermometer and observe how it moves up and down as the temperature becomes warmer or colder.

Small children are interested in changes in the weather as they affect their play and the clothes they wear.

As children dramatize family living in the doll house, their play expands to include the people who come into the home or who are met in the community. They become aware of our dependence upon many people in the community who contribute to the daily needs of folks in the home. Probably of greatest interest to most kindergarteners are the fireman, grocer, and policeman. Information found about the fireman can serve to introduce new ideas or clarify false concepts.

Kindergarteners are interested in travel. They live in a world where it takes just a short time to go great distances. A study of travel should acquaint them with the ways people and goods are moved from place to place, and should make them want to know more about it. From their pictures on travel they can generalize about the action and can draw a conclusion.

Children grow in citizenship and love for their country as we say our Pledge of Allegiance and sing America.

The months of the year, days of the week, and the time of the day are all very important to the kindergarten child. Many opportunities must be offered to him if he is to be able to recognize these learnings.

A new calendar is made each month in keeping with some special day that is being celebrated and each child receives a chance to mark it in some way and at some time. Doing this over and over again throughout the year the child becomes acquainted with our calendar.

Along with the months of the year, birthdays are also very important. The color train on the top of the bulletin board signifies the name of each month. It is also used as a birthday train and carries the name and birthdate of the children in the room. Very early the child is able to identify his own name and birthdate. The names of the days of the week are learned very easily in the kindergarten year. It is possible to link the situation they are about to view to their own experience. Monday - wash day, Tuesday - we iron our clothes, etc.

Emotional Responses

Recognizing emotional reactions is important. The well-rounded child has to experience both emotionally and intellectually.

All children in kindergarten enjoy looking at pictures and models of animals. We can help them see relationships. They can see a relationship between animals and between animals and people.

Color

Words indicating color are met early in reading. Many rich experiences are to be desired in the kindergarten if the child is to know his colors. Various colors of finger paint were introduced to the children and they were encouraged to make their movements on paper to music. The skip and the walk were stressed especially. The records used were from the album Childhood Rhythms arranged and recorded by Ruth Evans.

Holidays

Discussions of new bonnets or Easter eggs are evidence of the children's delight in the Easter holiday. Walks around the neighborhood to observe signs of spring help children to understand the true meaning of Easter and the reawakening of life.

Motivation

A bulletin board of zoo animals could offer an opportunity for learning. It would arouse curiosity and children could identify the word with the name of the animal.

Fun With Speech

Accuracy in enunciation and pronunciation helps children form good habits in the first reading experiences and helps to eliminate the need of corrective exercises later on.

Listening

Listening is the reciprocal part of speaking. Without skill in listening, communication is impossible. Too many times we focus all our attention on speaking and neglect to develop its more passive part, listening.

Culminary Statement

There are many skills and habits to be formed before the child is able to interpret symbols. However, as we look back over the year on the things that seemed important to reading readiness perhaps the greatest thing we have given the child is the desire to learn to read.

Chapter 14

LESSON PLANS FOR A YEAR IN KINDERGARTEN

First Week

CONVERSATION TIME

Use much of this time to get acquainted. Do not venture out of the room until children are better adjusted.

Wear name tags to help get acquainted. Use these for the first few weeks of school.

Look at stuffed animal on the desk. (This may be a stuffed dog, cat, rabbit.) Let children feel of it. Pass it around.

Let children tell about the pets they have at home. Discuss color of pets, size, and names.

Talk about food a pet likes to eat. Show pictures of pets eating food. Let children tell what they feed their pets, and how their pets eat and drink.

Look at pictures of pets. Place them on the bulletin board.

Mount a picture of a pet. Feel of it, and put it on the easel.

Mount a picture of another pet. Look at it, feel of it, put it on the easel. Give it a name.

Show picture "Starting to School" from chart #1 - The Basic Health and Safety Program.

WORK PERIOD

Go to the work tables and eat a graham cracker. Mention the toilet. Return to the circle again.

Get acquainted with the room. Find out where the rugs are kept, aprons, crayons, scissors, paste, paint, etc. Do this for several days. Have materials placed low enough so children can get them out and put them away.

SONGS AND RHYTHMS

Sing many nursery songs children may have learned before they came to school such as: Mary Had A Little Lamb; Twinkle, Twinkle, Little Star; Jack And Jill, etc.

Listen to records of these nursery rhymes.

Clap to the music.

Introduce a march. Walk around the room.

Walk around the circle and clap to the music.

Tap to the music using two fingers in palm of hand.

STORIES

Use very short stories at first about things children have had some experience with such as:

This Is The Way The Animals Walk	Gale Parks	E. M. Hale & Co.
Harry The Dirty Dog	Gene Lion	Harper & Bros.
Hello Peter	Morrell Gipson	Doubleday & Co.
All About Dogs, Dogs, Dogs	Grace Skaar	Cadmus
Is It Hard Is It Easy	Maru Green	William R. Scott
Joan Wanted A Kitty	Jane Gemmill	E. M. Hale & Co.
The Very Little Dog	Grace Skaar	Cadmus
A Dog Came To School	Lois Lenski	Oxford Press

Do not substitute poems and finger plays for a story but include as many as possible. If children are asked what they learned in school they often reply with a poem or finger play. Include such as:

Rhymes For Fingers And Flannelboards, Louise Scott & J. J. Thompson, Webster Publ. Co.

Ten Little Ducklings, p. 27; Five Little Chickens, p. 29; Little Kittens, p. 31; Five Little Pussy Cats, p. 31; Kitty And Bunny, p. 32; Creepy Crawly, p. 33; Five Kittens, p. 33; Piggies, p. 34; Once I Saw A Beehive, p. 35; Puppy Jumps Over A Stick, p. 35; Five Little Puppies, p. 36; Frisky's Doghouse, p. 36.

GAMES

Dog And Bone
Bounce the ball and catch it.
Bounce the ball to a child. Have him say his name.
Roll the ball to children seated in the circle.

Second Week

CONVERSATION TIME

Talk about school helpers: Discuss the ones in the building; Principal, janitors, nurse, secretary, librarian, etc.

Go on a tour of the building. Show children where all the helpers can be located. This helps to make children feel acquainted so if they are asked to take a note or the attendance slip they feel more confident.

Take another tour of our own room and talk about where materials are kept. Suggest getting out materials and putting them away. Show them how to do this.

WORK PERIOD

Introduce each material separately, one at a time, so boys and girls will know how you expect them to use the material and what they are to do with it when finished.

Introduce plasticine. Show children how to use it. Discuss its properties. Decide if you will work with paper towels on the tables or on clay boards. Tell them exactly the procedure you expect them to follow when they use the material and when they put it away. (Decide where it is to be kept, in a jar, can, individual plastic bags, etc.) Let them manipulate the clay and find out what they can do with it.

SONGS & RHYTHMS

Learn an opening song: Good Morning, p. 44, The Kindergarten Book, Ginn & Co.

Include in the opening such songs as: Our Flag, or Glory To The Flag, p. 121, Music For Young Americans, American Book Co.

Learn to sing: America, p. 87. The Kindergarten Book, Ginn & Co.

Teach children to say the Pledge of Allegiance.

Walk around the room to music - Basic Rhythms.

March around the room - use a record.

Continue with clapping; clapping in time to the music, clapping with fingers on palms of hand, clapping loudly and softly.

STORIES

Tommy On Time	Virginia Novinger	Albert Whitman & Co.
Let's Play	Lois Lenski	Oxford Univ. Press
Where Are You Going?	Charlotte Steiner	Doubleday & Co.
Once There Was A Kitten	Janet Konkle	Childrens Press
The New Pet	Marjorie Flack	Doubleday & Co.
Come Summer Come Winter	Terry Shannon	Whitman & Co.
A Dog Came To School	Lois Lenski	Oxford Univ. Press
Tabby's Kittens	Janet Konkle	Childrens Press
Cinder, The Cat	Meriam Huber	American Book Co.
Percy, Polly, and Pete	Clare Newberry	Harper & Bros.
Run, Run, Run	Clement Hurd	E. M. Hale & Co.

FINGERPLAYS & POEMS

Rhymes For Fingers And Flannelboards, Louise Scott & J. J. Thompson, Webster Publishing Co.

The Puppets, p. 39; The Mouse, p. 39; Little Rabbit, p. 41; The Butterfly, p. 46; One Two, p. 47; Learning To Count, p. 49; One And Two, p. 50; Three Little Nickels, p. 50; I See Three, p. 51; Honey Bears, p. 52; The Woodchopper, p. 52; Fred And His Fishes, p. 53; Follow Me, p. 56; How Many, p. 56.

GAMES

Review - Dog And Bone.

Bounce the ball and catch it.

Bounce the ball to a child. Have him say his name.

Roll the ball to children seated in a circle.

Introduce - The Farmer In The Dell.

Third Week

CONVERSATION TIME

Talk about Safety coming to and from school.

Invite the school patrol to talk to the children and tell them what is expected
of them. Have them explain their duties, and how they help at the corners.
Invite the school safety officer to speak to the group. He may also have
some movies to show on school safety.
Take children to the street corner and show them how to watch for turning
cars, how to cross at the corner, how to walk in the cross-walk, etc.
Discuss safety in the school room. Have children illustrate how to carry
a chair correctly, how to carry scissors, etc.
Talk about keeping feet folded and out of the way of performing children,
particularly at rhythm time. Mention that we walk in the halls and pick
up our feet in the classroom. Bring out the suggestion that we keep
crayons, paste, plasticine, paint out of our mouths. Mention that we
all go the same direction when we play games or execute rhythms.
Make a game out of our fire drill. Show children where they are to go and
why we do it this particular way.

WORK PERIOD

Introduce crayons. Decide ahead of time where they are to be kept and tell
children how to care for them in the manner you select. (Individual
boxes, separate colors, put into coffee cans, etc.)
Let each child draw a picture of himself crossing the street at the corner.
Keep these first pictures to show to the children at the close of the year.
Using crayons, draw a picture of a stop sign.
Make a fireman's hat from red construction paper. Let children wear them
when they play the fire drill game.

SONGS & RHYTHMS

Learn the song: Let The Ball Roll, and An Automobile Has Two Big Eyes,
p. 19 and 10 from Sing A Song Of Safety by Gerald Marks, published by
Irving Caesar.
Learn the song: I'm A Traffic Cop, p. 64 from The Kindergarten Book,
published by Ginn & Co.
Introduce the song: The Traffic Policeman, p. 23 from Music For Young
Americans, published by the American Book Co.
Review the opening song learned last week, also Our Flag, and America.
Introduce rhythm sticks. Give each child two rhythm sticks; have them
keep time to a march. Use a record.
Review basic rhythms: walk, march.

FINGERPLAY AND POEMS

ABC Music Series. American Book Co. Where Is Thumbkin, p. 12.

Rhymes For Fingers And Flannelboards, Louise Scott & J. J. Thompson,
Webster Publ. Co.

Marching Soldiers, p. 22; Ten Little Soldiers, p. 22; Five Little Firemen,
p. 25; Five Strong Policemen, p. 25.

Choral Speaking, Irene Hemphill, Irene Hemphill, Educational Publ. Co.
Our Traffic Song, p. 42; The Firemen, p. 62.

STORIES

Safe All Day With The Happies	Josephine Pease	Rand McNally & Co.
Safety Is Fun	A Bonnie Book	James & Jonathan Inc.
Safety Can Be Fun	Monroe Leaf	Stokes & Co.
Safety Town Stories	Mildred Roberts	Lyon & Carnahan
Five Little Firemen	Margaret Wise Brown	Simon & Schuster
Firemen And Fire Engines	Lisa Peters	Wonder Books
Rosa-Too-Little	Sue Felt	Doubleday & Co.

GAMES

Review: Dog And Bone
Review: The Farmer In The Dell
Introduce: <u>Play</u> <u>activities</u> <u>for</u> <u>elementary</u> <u>grades</u>, published by C. V.
   Mosby Co., Animal Story, p. 3, also Lost Child, p. 5.
Bounce the ball and catch it.
Bounce the ball to a child. Have him say his name.
Roll the ball to children seated in the circle.
Introduce: Traffic Safety Puzzle, Guess Who And Guess What, and Sing
   A Song Of Safety, p. 44, 45, 46.
      <u>Activities</u> <u>That</u> <u>Teach</u> <u>Health</u>, Cleo Carter, F. A. Owen Publ. Co.

Fourth Week

CONVERSATION TIME

This is the time of the year when we can begin to look for signs of Fall.
Take a walk to look for signs of Fall.
Discuss the different kinds of leaves and what is happening to them.
   (Falling from the trees, turning color, drying up, etc.)
Talk about how nature prepares for winter. (Fall flowers, bees, cocoons,
   seeds, bulbs, birds, squirrels, etc.)

WORK PERIOD

Prepare a science table. Have children bring leaves, pods, cocoons,
   bulbs, etc.
Children can draw fall fruits and cut them out. These may be used later
   in a horn of plenty as a bulletin board motif.
Have children gather different kinds of leaves and press them between
   waxed paper.
Make three large paper trees, all of a different variety. Have children
   cut appropriate leaves. Fasten onto the trees and use as a bulletin
   board. When leaves begin to fall, take down a few each day and place
   at the bottom of the board.
Make leaf people and animals by using the real leaf as the body of the
   person or animal to be represented.

Pin leaves onto colored paper, spray with spray gun using colored ink or paint.

Introduce paint. Explain to children where paint materials are to be found and demonstrate how to use them. Let children experiment. Do this in small numbers at first.

Make scrap books with pictures cut from magazines of fall flowers, vegetables, fruit, trees, etc.

SONGS & RHYTHMS

Review safety songs learned last week.

Review the songs learned for our introduction.

Introduce: ABC Music Series, published by the American Book Co. Leaves, p. 42 also The Shivers, p. 44.

Introduce: More Singing Fun, published by Webster Publ. Co. Autumn Is Here, p. 10, also Autumn Leaves, p. 11.

Introduce: Stories That Sing, published by Boston Music Co. The Apple Tree, p. 1.

Make up story plays and have children pretend they are:
Jumping in a pile of leaves, dancing, twirling, and falling like a leaf. Pretend to rake up a large pile of leaves. Light a bonfire. Jump up and down to keep warm.

STORIES

A Tree Is Nice	Janice Udry	Harper & Bros.
(Also use record and film strip)		
All Ready For Winter	Leone Adelson	David McKay & Co.
Three Smart Squirrels	Margaret Friskey	David McKay & Co.
Follow The Fall	Maxine Kumen	C. P. Putman's Sons
Squeaky, The Squirrel	Gene Darby	Benefic Press

FINGERPLAYS & POEMS

ABC Music Series, published by The American Book Co., "Knock At The Door", p. 11.

Rhymes For Fingers and Flannelboards, Louise Scott & J. J. Thompson, Published by Webster Publ. Co.

Little Leaves, p. 119; The Apple Tree, p. 119; Three Little Oak Leaves, p. 119; Five Red Apples, p. 120; What Jack Frost Taught Me, p. 120.

GAMES

Review: Dog And Bone; Farmer In The Dell; Animal Story; Lost Child.

Introduce: Play activities for elementary grades, published by C. V. Mosby Co., This Is My Nose, p. 10.

Fifth Week

CONVERSATION TIME

Continue talking about signs of Fall.

Discuss with the children how our weather is getting colder, leaves are falling down and changing color, frost is nipping our gardens and flowers, the birds are leaving.

Have the children tell about rides they have taken and changes they have noted.

Talk about home activities and how mother is getting the home ready for winter by canning, cleaning, etc.

Discuss how father is getting ready for winter by putting on storm windows, raking the yard, getting the car ready, etc.

Relate how animals get ready for winter. Discuss how their fur gets thicker, some hide food to be eaten later, and some animals hibernate.

WORK PERIOD

Do some canning in the home economics room or kitchen. Put it away for a future party. Children enjoy canning peaches, applesauce, pears.

Make jelly. Store it away for future use.

Go for a walk and try to find pods and dried weeds. Bring them back and let children paint them for a room decoration or for gifts to parents.

Make a frieze showing what the family does to get ready for winter.

Model squirrels from clay, paint them when dry.

Introduce finger painting. Let children use their fingers. Tell children exactly how to use the material and how it is to be cared for. Decide this ahead of time.

Use regular school paint and paint fall trees. Instead of a brush, use sponges. Use many colors for the leaves.

SONGS & RHYTHMS

Review fall songs learned the previous week.

Introduce: The Kindergarten Book, Ginn & Co. The Leaves, p. 99 also Down, Down, p. 100.

Use rhythm sticks again to tap out music to a march.

Make up a story play. Have children pretend to pick up autumn leaves and put them in a basket; also rake them into a pile. Use record - Victor Rhythm Album One.

STORIES

All Falling Down	Gene Zion	E. M. Hale & Co.
Now It's Fall	Lois Lenski	Oxford Univ. Press
Autumn Harvest	Alvin Tresselt	Lothrop, Lee & Shepard
All Ready For Winter	Leone Adelson	E. M. Hale & Co.
Hurry, Skurry & Flurry	Mary Buff	Viking Press

FINGERPLAYS & POEMS

Let's Say Poetry Together, Carrie Rasmussen, Burgess Publishing Co.

Apple Song, p. 81; Autumn Fancies, p. 81; Baby Seeds, p. 78; Jack Frost, p. 80; Autumn Fires, p. 95; Fall, p. 96; Fresh October, p. 93; North Wind Doth Blow, p. 95; What The Leaves Said, p. 94; Jack Frost, p. 98.

Rhymes For Fingers and Flannelboards, Louise Scott & J. J. Thompson, Webster Publishing Co.

What the Animals Do, p. 88; Five Little Squirrels, p. 88; Squirrel In A Tree, p. 89; Where Are The Baby Mice?, p. 89; Sleepy Caterpillars, p. 91; Eeency Weency Spider, p. 91.

GAMES

Review: Dog And Bone; Farmer In The Dell; Animal Story; Lost Child; This Is My Nose;
Introduce: Play activities for elementary grades, published by C. V. Mosby Co. Hot Potato, p. 42.

Sixth Week

CONVERSATION TIME

Talk about the frost in the air, the bittersweet, and fall flowers and leaves.
Talk about Halloween. Look at the calendar and find out when it comes; mark it on the calendar.
Let children tell whom they expect to meet on Halloween.
Mention witches, cats, bats, spooks, goblins, ghosts, etc.
Relate something about the origin of Halloween.
Let children tell how they expect to dress on Halloween.

WORK PERIOD

Make a spook tree. Make a large one. Cut a branch from a bush, paint it. Set it in a can of sand or into a pot filled with hardening clay. Let children make Halloween designs to hang onto the branches. (Make witches, hats, ghosts, pumpkins, jack-o-lanterns, etc.)
Color large pumpkins, cut them out.
Paint large pumpkins and make them into a jack-o-lantern.
Let children illustrate some of the Halloween songs.
Carve a jack-o-lantern from a real pumpkin. Scoop it out. Let children help. Plant some of the seeds and grow a vine.
Make orange Halloween lanterns with black handles from paper.

SONGS & RHYTHMS

Learn this song - Tune: Mulberry Bush
"I'm going to ride the witch's broom,
The witch's broom, the witch's broom.
I'm going to ride the witch's broom,
High up to the moon."

Introduce: <u>Singing</u> <u>Fun</u>, Lucille Wood, published by Webster Publ. Co.
In A Pumpkin Patch, p. 9; Three Little Pumpkins, p. 6; Halloween's
Coming, p. 7; I'm A Jack-O-Lantern, p. 8.
Work on basic rhythms, skip, hop, walk, and run.
Use rhythm sticks while marching around the room.
Gnomes (Victor Album 1) Pretend to steal from house to house and scare
people with false faces and spooky costumes.
<u>Romp</u> <u>In</u> <u>Rhythm</u>, Elizabeth Seatter & Enola Minnis, The Willis Music Co.
Ringing The Bell, p. 10; Scampering, p. 12; Jack-O-Lantern March,
p. 13.

STORIES

Mary's Scary House	Edith Hurd	E. M. Hale & Co.
Georgie And The Robbers	Robert Bright	Doubleday & Co.
Georgie's Halloween	Robert Bright	Doubleday & Co.
Wobble, The Witch's Cat	Mary Calhoun	Wm. Morrow & Co.
Danny's Luck	Lavinia Davis	Doubleday & Co.

FINGERPLAYS AND POEMS

<u>Let's</u> <u>Say</u> <u>Poetry</u> <u>Together</u>, Carrie Rasmussen, Burgess Publishing Co.

Halloween, p. 51; Halloween Song, p. 53; The Magic Vine, p. 53; This
Is Halloween, p. 52;

<u>Rhymes</u> <u>For</u> <u>Fingers</u> <u>And</u> <u>Flannelboards</u>, Louise Scott & J. J. Thompson,
Webster Publishing Co.

Halloween, p. 59; Ten Little Pumpkins, p. 60; Three Little Witches,
p. 61; Five Little Goblins, p. 61.

GAMES

<u>Games</u>, <u>Rhythms</u>, <u>Dances</u>, Jean Barnett, George Stanley Publ. Co.

Pumpkin Man And Brownie, p. 32, also This Is The Way, p. 4.

Review: Dog And Bone; Farmer In The Dell; This Is My Nose; Hot Potato.
Introduce: <u>Games</u>, <u>Rhythms</u>, <u>Dances</u>, Jean Barnett, George Stanley Co.
The Leaves, p. 17 and Pussy Cat, p. 9.

Seventh Week

CONVERSATION TIME

Continue talking about Halloween.
Talk about going "Tricks or Treating". Discuss why we do this, and some
of the safety measures involved.
Tell about pumpkins. Discuss where they grow, shape, color, etc.
Discuss the difference between a pumpkin and a jack-o-lantern.
Talk about having a Halloween party; make plans for the party.
Appoint various committees such as: food, games, story, etc.

WORK PERIOD

Make a place mat for the party. Use brightly colored paper, fringe the sides and paint on a jack-o-lantern.

Make a basket to hold the food, such as popcorn, candy, etc.

Make paper masks to wear at the party. These masks can be made from paper sacks and decorated or from colored construction paper.

Color pumpkins and cut them out to use around the room.

Make a frieze using a Halloween fingerplay as the main idea.

Make a Halloween favor using suckers covered with white paper napkins, tied at the neck with yard. Children can color on the face. Make them stand up by putting the stick into a large gum drop.

Cut and paste orange and black paper chains. Decorate the room with them, also the windows.

Make a color wash about Halloween. Have children first color a Halloween story. Tell them to press hard so colors will be bright. Make a color wash of diluted black paint. Use a sponge to apply to entire colored picture.

SONGS & RHYTHMS

Review Halloween songs learned last week.

Introduce the following songs: The Kindergarten Book, Ginn & Co.
I'm A Jack-O-Lantern, p. 75; Halloween Is Coming, p. 73; See My Big Eyes, p. 73.

Use recording: Songs From The Kindergarten Book, Album K, Side 6
Use this record after children have first learned to sing the above songs.

Use recording: Childhood Rhythms Series One by Ruth Evans, Witches, Giants. Record No. 106.

STORIES

Punkin's First Halloween	Esther Reinecke	T. S. Denison
Which Witch?	Robert Lasson	David McKay & Co.
Tell Me Mr. Owl	Doris Foster	Lothrop, Lee & Shepard

A Holiday Book - Halloween   Lillie Patterson   Garrard Publ. Co.
Included are the following stories: It's Halloween; How It All Began; The Apples of Ponona; Ghosts, Ghosts, Ghosts; Witches and Black Cats; Wee Folk Halloween Customs; Magic Tests; Halloween Comes To America.

The Teeny Tiny Woman, Old English Take from Story Telling With The Flannel Board, Paul Anderson, p. 28, T. S. Denison & Co.

Queer Company, Frances Wickes, Story Telling With The Flannel Board, Paul Anderson, p. 21, T. S. Denison & Co.

Peter Pumpkin   John Ott   Doubleday & Co.

FINGERPLAY AND POEMS

Choral Speaking   Irene Hemphill   Educational Publ. Co.

The Owl And The Pussy Cat, p. 42.

Rhymes For Fingers And Flannelboards, Louise Scott & J. J. Thompson, Webster Publ. Co.

Tall And Small, p. 98; The Elf's Coat, p. 99; Said This Little Fairy, p. 100; The Fairies Wash Day, p. 100; Follow The Leader, p. 108; Fun With Hands, p. 110.

GAMES

Games, Rhythms, Dances   Jean Barnett   George Stanley Pub. Co.

Review: Pumpkin Man And Brownie, p, 32; This Is The Way, p. 4; The Leaves, p. 17; Pussy Cat, p. 9.
Introduce: Looby Loo, p. 5.

Eighth Week

CONVERSATION TIME

Talk about our homes and why we have them.
Let children tell about the kinds of homes they live in.
    Apartment, trailer, basement, duplex, rambler, etc.
Discuss the different kinds of materials used in building a home.
    Stone, brick, wood, steel, etc.
Take a walk to a home that is being built in the neighborhood.
Talk about the different rooms in a house.
    Living room, dining room, recreation room, kitchen, etc.
Talk about the helpers needed to build a house.
    Contractor, carpenters, brick layers, electricians, etc.

WORK PERIOD

Dramatic play in the doll house. Allow children to dress up in old clothes.
    Let them bring dolls and old clothes to school. Let one be the mother, father, and children.
Cut pictures from magazines showing different kinds of homes, also different rooms in the homes.
Make a scrap book of these pictures.
    Let each child draw a picture of his home.
    Stress knowing our street address.

SONGS & RHYTHMS

Introduce: I Have A Little Sister, p. 46, The Kindergarten Book; What Are Babies Made Of?, p. 47; Bed Time, p. 55; Pinky Winky Baby, p. 47.
Review: Nursery Rhymes learned the first week of school - Jack and Jill; Mary Had A Little Lamb; Twinkle, twinkle, Little Star.
Review: walking and marching, p. 46, The Kindergarten Book, Ginn & Co. Also use (Victor Rhythm Album Two)

STORIES

The Buttons Go Walking	Edward Mammen	Harper & Row
The Little House	Virginia Burton	Houghton Mifflin Co.
Everybody Has A House	Mary Green	William R. Scott
My Own Little House	Merriman Kaune	Follett Publ. Co.
I Live In So Many Places	Jane Hengesbaugh	Childrens Press
Homes	Virginia Parsons	Doubleday & Co.

FINGERPLAY AND POEMS

Let's Say Poetry Together   Carrie Rasmussen   Burgess Publ. Co.

Bedtime, p. 74; Clock, p. 69; Mitten Song, p. 71; My Hands, p. 76; The Nursery, p. 76; Politeness, p. 70; Only One Mother, p. 74; One Thing At A Time, p. 75; Song for A Little House, p. 73; Stars, p. 71; What Shall I Buy?, p. 75.

Rhymes For Fingers And Flannelboards, Louise Scott, J. J. Thompson, Webster Publishing Co.

My Family, p. 78; See My Family, p. 78; This Is The Father, p. 78; Here Is Baby's Tousled Head, p. 78; Five Little Babies, p. 79; Here Are Mother's Knives and Forks, p. 80; This Little Boy, p. 80; These Are Grandmother's Glasses, p. 81; Thee Thee That, p. 81; Houses, p. 86.

GAMES

Review: Dog And Bone; Farmer In The Dell; This Is My Nose; Hot Potato; The Leaves.

Introduce: Play activities for elementary grades, Charles Nagel, C. V. Mosby Co. Red Light, p. 69

Ninth Week

CONVERSATION TIME

Talk about the members of the family. Let children tell about the number in their family and their names.

Discuss the duties of the various members of the family:
father, mother, brothers, sisters.

Mention how boys and girls can help at home.

WORK PERIOD

Draw pictures of the various members of the family.

Paint pictures showing where father works.

Let children draw a picture of what they would like to do when they grow up.

Make a scrap book about babies - cut out magazine pictures.

Do some cooking. Have each child bring one vegetable and make vegetable soup.

SONGS & RHYTHMS

Review: I Have A Little Sister, p. 46, The Kindergarten Book; What are Babies Made Of?, p. 47; Bed Time, p. 55; Pinky Winky Baby, p. 47.

Introduce: My Picture Book Of Songs, Dalton, Ashton, Young, M. A. Donohue & Co. Publ.; My Grandmother, p. 25; Helping Mother, p. 25

Introduce: Singing Fun, Lucille Wood, Webster Publ. Co., How Many People Live At Your House?, p. 49.

Review a tip-toe march.

Jumping (Victor Rhythm Album Two)

STORIES

About Family Helpers	Elaine Hoffman	Melmont Publ.
Mommies	Lonnie Carton	Random House
Grandfather And I	Helen Buckley	Lothrop, Lee & Shepard
Mommies At Work	Eve Merriam	Alfred A. Knopf
Your Family Tree	Jean Komarco	Parents' Magazine Press
Let's Play House	Lois Lenski	Henry Z. Walck, Inc.
Papa Small	Lois Lenski	Henry Z. Walck, Inc.
What's A Cousin?	Helen Olds	Random House
When You Were A Baby	Rita Eng	Golden Press

FINGERPLAYS AND POEMS

For A Child   Wilma McFarland   Westminster Press

Do You Know, p. 8; Our House, p. 7; Shoes, p. 8; A Wonderful Man, p. 14; Kitchen Tunes, p. 16.

Rhymes For Fingers And Flannelboards, Louise Scott & J. J. Thompson, Webster Publ. Co.

See My Clothes, p. 56; Fred And His Fishes, p. 53; Tall and Small, p. 98; Stretch, Stretch, p. 111.

GAMES

Review: Red Light; The Leaves; Hot Potato; Squirrel In The Trees.

Introduce: Play activities for elementary grades, Charles Nagel, C. V. Mosby Co. Coffee Grinder, p. 108.

Tenth Week

CONVERSATION TIME

This is the month when the fruits and vegetables have been gathered in. Talk about gathering in the harvest. Discuss what this means.

Tell the children why we have Armistice Day.

Talk about the Indians: Discuss what they eat, where they live, how they dress, what they look like, etc.

WORK PERIOD

Make patriotic hats for Armistice Day and decorate them.
Make Indian head bands.
Make an Indian face and head band.
Make an Indian suit from a large paper sack. Decorate it.
Make moccasins from a small paper sack.
Make wigwams from manilla paper, color wash the picture.

SONGS & RHYTHMS

Introduce: Let's Play Indians, p. 10; Indians In A Teepee, p. 11; How Many Feathers, p. 12 from Singing Fun, Lucille Wood, Webster Publishing Co.
Introduce: Rhythm Band.
    Use record: Let's Have A Rhythm Band, Columbia MJV 4-167 -2, 45 45 RPM.
Review Basic Rhythms: Run, walk, skip, and hop.

STORIES

Indian Two Feet	Margaret Friskey	Childrens Press
The Little Indian Pottery Maker	Ann Clark	E. M. Hale
The Mighty Hunter	Berta Hader	Macmillan Co.
Around The Year	Tasha Tudor	Oxford Univ. Press
The Nicest Time Of Year	Zhenya Gay	Viking Press
Now It's Fall	Lois Lenski	Henry Z. Walck, Inc.
One Mitten Lewis	Henel Kay	Lothrop, Lee & Shepard
The Brave Little Indian	Bill Martin	John Winston Co.
Let's Play Indian	Madye Chastain	Wonder Book
Good Hunting Little Indian	Peggy Parish	Young Scott Books

FINGERPLAYS AND POEMS

For A Child   Wilma McFarland   The Westminster Press

The Woodpecker, p. 12; Whisky Frisky, p. 34; Trees, p. 54.

Let's Say Poetry Together   Carrie Rasmussen   Burgess Publ. Co.

Fall, p. 96; Autumn Fires, p. 95; What The Leaves Said, p. 94; The North Wind Doth Blow, p. 95; Indian Children, p. 92; Autumn Fancies, p. 81; Jack Frost, p. 80; The Song On The Way, p. 79.

GAMES

Review: This Is My Nose; Hot Potato; The Leaves; The Farmer In The Dell; Looby Loo.

Introduce: <u>Play</u> <u>activities</u> <u>for</u> <u>elementary</u> <u>grades</u>, Charles Nagel, C. V. Mosby Co. Colors, p. 1

Eleventh Week

CONVERSATION TIME

Talk about another holiday that comes this month. (Thanksgiving)
Tell about the first Thanksgiving.
Let children tell one thing they are thankful for.
Compare our homes with those of the pioneers.
Talk about who attended the first Thanksgiving feast.

WORK PERIOD

Make a place mat for our Thanksgiving party.
Make a favor for the party. Use pine cones for turkeys. Go for a walk to gather pine cones. Use pipe stem cleaners and pheasant feathers to make them into a turkey.
Draw the head of a lady Pilgrim, also a man.
Use your hand and draw around it to make a turkey. Color it brown, making the fingers various colors like the turkey tail. The thumb is the gobbler and head. Color it accordingly.
Paint turkeys and cut them out. Make a barnyard scene for the bulletin board.
Make turkeys by painting paper plates a brown color. Add a tail by cutting feathers of different colored construction paper.

SONGS & RHYTHMS

Little Pilgrims, p. 14, <u>Singing</u> <u>Fun,</u> Lucille Wood, Webster Publishing Co.
Foolish Questions, p. 16, Webster Publishing Co.
Thanksgiving Dinner, p. 27, " " "
My Thank You Prayer, p. 27, <u>My</u> <u>Picture</u> <u>Book</u> <u>of</u> <u>Songs</u>, Dalton, Ashton, Young, M. A. Donohue Publ.
Use The Wood Sticks, p. 137, <u>Kindergarten</u> <u>Book</u>, Ginn & Co.

STORIES

The Story Of Thanksgiving, <u>Story</u> <u>Telling</u>, Paul S. Anderson, p. 37, T. S. Denison & Co.
The Big, Big, Turnip, <u>Story</u> <u>Telling</u>, Paul S. Anderson, p. 46, T. S. Denison & Co.
Tommy Turkey, <u>Story</u> <u>Telling</u>, Paul S. Anderson, p. 62, T. S. Denison & Co.
The Scarecrow, <u>Story</u> <u>Telling</u>, Paul S. Anderson, p. 77, T. S. Denison & Co.
The Runaway Cookies, <u>Story</u> <u>Telling</u>, Paul S. Anderson, p. 68, T. S. Denison & Co.
Gobble, Gobble, Gobble, Mary Ellis, T. S. Denison & Co.

The Magnificent Pumpkin, Valdine Plasmate, E. M. Hale
A Very, Very Special Day, Frances DeArmand, Parents' Magazine Press

FINGERPLAYS AND POEMS

For A Child, Wilma McFarland, Westminster Press

A Popcorn Song, p. 74; First Thanksgiving Of All, p. 85; Autumn Tourists, p. 84; Come, Little Leaves, p. 83.

Let's Say Poetry Together, Carrie Rasmussen, Burgess Publ. Co.

For God's Gifts, p. 56; Happy Thank-You Day, p. 56; Pilgrims Came, p. 54; Thanksgiving Magic, p. 55; There's A Big Fat Turkey, p. 56.

GAMES

Review: Looby Loo; Red Light; Coffee Grinder; Colors; Farmer In The Dell.
Introduce: Cat And Mice, p. 60, Play activities for elementary grades, Charles Nagel, C. V. Mosby Co.

Twelfth Week

CONVERSATION TIME

Talk about the new month of December. Use the calendar. Mark the days on the calendar.
Talk about the special day coming up this month. (Christmas)
Talk about how our city has been preparing for Christmas. Encourage children to tell about the decorated streets, the Christmas windows, house decorations.
Have children tell how mother prepares for the special day.

WORK PERIOD

Make red and green chains for the room.
Paint a Santa. Cut him out. Use him for a room decoration.
Make some Christmas cookies. Put them away for the party.
Cut a Christmas stocking, fill it with toys.
Let children color a picture of what they want Santa to bring.
Have children dictate a letter to Santa.

SONGS & RHYTHMS

Introduce: Santa Claus Is Coming, p. 116; Christmas Is Coming, p. 116; O Christmas Tree, p. 117; We Wish You A Merry Christmas, p. 118; Christmas Day, p. 119, Music For Young Americans, American Book Co.
Learn: Santa Claus, p. 29; Bein' Good, p. 29; My Christmas Stocking, p. 31, My Picture Book of Songs, Dalton, Ashton, Young, M. A. Donohue.
Introduce Galloping Reindeer - Use any gallop music.

STORIES

The Smith's Christmas, p. 252; The Jingle Bells, p. 247; The Thirty-nine Letters, p. 212; Pedro's Christmas Flower, p. 185; The Boy Who Grew A Halo, p. 171; Wee Ann, p. 137.

Story Telling With The Flannel Board, Paul S. Anderson, T. S. Denison & Co.

Star Of Wonder	Robert R. Coles	McGraw-Hill Book Co.
The Christmas Story	Annie Cameron	Lyons & Carnahan

FINGERPLAYS & POEMS

For A Child	Wilma McFarland	The Westminster Press

Christmas Coming!, p. 89; Old Christmas Carol, p. 89; Long, Long Ago, p. 90; Christmas Morning, p. 91.

Time For Poetry	May Arbuthnot	Scott, Forseman & Co.

An Old Christmas Greeting, p. 170; Christmas, p. 170; The Christmas Pussing, p. 170; Carol, Brothers, Carol, p. 170; Bundles, p. 170; Here We Come A-Caroling, p. 172; Ceremonies For Christmas, p. 172; In The Week When Xmas Comes, p. 172, For Christmas Day, p. 173; Song, p. 173; A Christmas Folk-Song, p. 174; A Christmas Carol, p. 174.

GAMES

Review: Cat And Mice; Colors; Coffee Grinder; Red Light; Looby Loo. Introduce: Bibbety, Bobbety, Boo, p. 9, Play activities for elementary grades, Charles Nagel, The C. V. Mosby Co.

Thirteenth Week

CONVERSATION TIME

Talk about what Christmas means to me. Tell the children why we celebrate His birthday.
Let children tell how their families are getting ready for Christmas.
Talk about reindeer: their habits, where they live, etc.

WORK PERIOD

Go for a walk around the building to see bulletin boards other children have prepared.
Draw a reindeer. Make Rudolph the Red-Nosed reindeer. Use this on the bulletin board.
Make a Christmas card to be given to mother and father. Let each child draw around his hands. Cut them out and place them on colored con-

struction paper. Use a spray gun and spray around the hands. Put a calendar of the new year at the bottom of the card.

Decide to make a gift to be taken home. Give each child a ball of hardening clay. Model it into a round ball and place colored marbles in it before the clay hardens. The clay may be painted when dry. It can be taken home to be used as a paper weight.

Have children finger paint using red and green paint. When dry, let them draw semi-circles and shape them into bells.

SONGS & RHYTHMS

Introduce: Bells of Christmas, p. 78; Christmas Song, p. 78; The Angels, p. 79; O Little Town of Bethlehem, p. 79; Away In A Manger, p. 80; Silent Night, p. 81, The Kindergarten Book, Ginn & Co.

Review: Santa Claus Is Coming; Christmas Is Coming; O Christmas Tree; We Wish You A Merry Christmas; Merry Christmas, Music For Young Americans.

Have two children gallop together, holding hands, the third person is Santa and takes a hold of the reindeer's hands.

Dance around the circle - make believe the tree is in the center of the circle, p. 84, The Kindergarten Book.

STORIES

The Runaway Angel	Rosalind Welcher	Doubleday & Co.
It Happened On A Holiday Twelve short stories	Lavinia Davis	Doubleday & Co.
Baby Elephant And The Secret Wishes	Sesyle Joslin	Harcourt, Brace & World, Inc.
Christmas Miniature	Pearl S. Buck	The John Day Co.
On Christmas Eve	Margaret Wise Brown	Young Scott Books
Petunia's Christmas	Roger Duovisin	Alfred A. Knopf
Deck The Stable	Ivy Eastwick	David McKay Co.
Rudolph The Red-Nosed Reindeer	Robert May	Maxton Publishers
The Christmas Bunny	Will & Nicolas	Harcourt, Brace & Co.
Christmas In The Barn	Margaret Wise Brown	Thomas Y. Crowell Co.

FINGERPLAYS AND POEMS

Let's Say Poetry Together   Carrie Rasmussen   Burgess Publ. Co.

A Christmas Carol, p. 62; Santa Claus, p. 61; Christmas Hearth Rhyme, p. 61; My Christmas Wish, p. 60; Christmas In The Heart, p. 60; Christmas Cookies, p. 60; Why Do The Bells of Christmas Ring?, p. 59.

GAMES

Review: Farmer In The Dell; Cat And Mice; This Is My Nose; Colors.

Introduce: Frog In The Middle, p. 57; Slap Jack, p. 59; Physical Education for Elementary Grades, S. D. State Course of Study Bulletin No. 73.

Fourteenth Week

CONVERSATION TIME

Talk about Santa Claus and why he is so busy.

Mention Santa's helpers.

Discuss again the true meaning of Christmas: why we have it, and what happened on the first Christmas.

Talk about having a Christmas party. Plan the committees: games, story, food, clean up, etc.

Talk about Christmas trees: where they grow, different kinds.

WORK PERIOD

Walk to a lot and buy a Christmas tree.

Decorate your own tree.

Make Christmas cookies and decorate them for the party.

Make a party place mat.

Decorate a napkin.

Make Christmas trees. Decorate them. Cut from a magazine, the picture of a toy you want Sant to bring. Paste it on the "Wishing Tree".

Make jello using green lime flavor. Pour it into cone shaped paper cup liners. Unmold for party. These will be shaped like a tree.

SONGS & RHYTHMS

Review: Bells of Christmas; Christmas Song; The Angels; O Little Town Of Bethlehem; Away In A Manger; Silent Night, The Kindergarten Book, p. 78-81.

Introduce: Dolly's Lullaby, p. 33; Christmas Toys, p. 33, My Picture Book Of Songs, Dalton, Ashton, Young, Donohue Co.

Review: Santa Claus Is Coming; Christmas Is Coming; O Christmas Tree; We Wish You A Merry Christmas; Merry Christmas, Music For Young Americans, American Book Co.

Galloping reindeer: use bells on wrists, Kindergarten Book, p. 18, (Allegro Sonata No. 13)

Dance Around The Christmas Tree, p. 84; Christmas Tree March, p. 85, The Kindergarten Book, Ginn & Co.

STORIES

The Elves And The Shoemaker	Hilda Milache	Whitman Publ. Co.
The Happiest Christmas	Jessie Fairweather	Whitman Publ. Co.
The Santa Claus Book	Irene Smith	Franklin Watts
Paddy's Christmas	Helen Monself	Alfred A. Knopf
A Christmas Stocking Story	Hilary Knight	Harper & Row Publ.
The Christmas Manger	Hugh McCandless	Charles Scribners Sons
A Tree For Teddy	Marion Holland	E. M. Hale
The Christmas Donkey	Wilma Swedburg	Augsburg Publ. House

| The Littlest Angel | Charles Tuzewell | Wonder Books |
| Benjamin Brownie | Geraldine Ross | Whitman Publ. Co. |

FINGERPLAYS AND POEMS

Rhymes For Fingers And Flannelboards, Louise Scott & J. J. Thompson
Webster Publishing Co.

The Angel On My Christmas Tree, p. 65; Five Bright Stars, p. 65; The
Toy Shop, p. 66; This Baby Piggie, p. 66; In Santa's Workshop, p. 67;
Eight Tiny Reindeer, p. 68; Santa's Reindeer, p. 69; Christmas Presents,
p. 69.

For A Child, Wilma McFarland, The Westminster Press

The New Year, p. 92; Tomorrow, p. 92

GAMES

Review: Bibbety, Bobbety, Boo; Coffee Grinder; Red Light; Looby Loo;
Colors.

Introduce: How Sure, p. 17, Play activities for elementary grades,
Charles Nagel, The C. V. Mosby Co.

Fifteenth Week

CONVERSATION TIME

Allow children to tell about the presents they received for Christmas.
Have children bring one toy they received for Christmas.
Talk about the New Year: the number of months in a year, name them,
count the days in January. Talk about the calendar.
Talk about the four seasons: fall, winter, spring, summer.
Discuss the characteristics of the different seasons. Relate it to the
food we eat, the clothes we wear, the places we go.

WORK PERIOD

Draw a picture of a Christmas toy received this year.
Paint a seasonal picture.
Have children tear a picture of a toy they received.
Cut snowflakes. Make them six pointed.
Divide children into groups. Have each group cut a portion of a large
snowman from brown wrapping paper. Paste the snowflakes onto the
large snowman. Cut eyes, nose, mouth and buttons.

SONGS & RHYTHMS

Introduce: Old Mother Goose, p. 43; The Shivers, p. 44; The North
Wind's Song, p. 42, Music for Young Americans, American Book Co.
Review Nursery Rhyme Songs learned the first of the year.
Introduce: Dance Of The Snowflakes, p. 15, Romp In Rhythm, Seatter,
The Willis Music Co.

STORIES

Big Snow	Berta Hader	Macmillan Co.
I Like Winter	Lois Lenski	Oxford Univ. Press
The Summer Snowman	Gene Zion	E. M. Hale & Co.
Around The Year	Tasha Tudor	Oxford Univ. Press

The Three Tops From Story Telling With The Flannel Board, Paul S. Anderson, T. S. Denison & Co., p. 244.

| Kiki Skates | Charlotte Steiner | Doubleday & Co. |
| The Day Daddy Stayed Home | Ethel Kessler | Doubleday & Co. |

FINGERPLAYS AND POEMS

The Sound Of Poetry, Austin & Mills, Published by Allyn & Bacon

New Year's Day, p. 360; Winter, p. 333; First Snow, p. 333; No Sky At All, p. 333; First Winter's Day, p. 334; Falling Snow, p. 336.

Rhymes For Fingers And Flannelboards, Louise Scott & J. J. Thompson, Webster Publishing Co.

In Winter Time, p. 120; What Jack Frost Taught Me, p. 121; Ten Little Snowmen, p. 122; The Snowmen, p. 123; Snowflakes, p. 122; I Am A Snowman, p. 123.

GAMES

Review: Cat And Mice; Colors; Coffee Grinder; Red Light; Looby Loo.
Introduce: Button, Button, p. 6, Play activities for elementary grades, Charles Nagel, C. V. Mosby Co.

Sixteenth Week

CONVERSATION TIME

Talk about snow. Discuss what it is. Go outside and catch some on a black cloth. Observe the shapes of the flakes.
Talk about cold weather: how we dress, how we eat, etc.
Talk about the thermometer. Move it up and down as the weather varies.
Talk about marking our clothing such as mittens, scarfs, etc.
Stress putting on and taking off our own clothing.

WORK PERIOD

Cut colored snow flakes. Put them up around the room.
Learn to fold a six pointed flake. Cut them out.
Make snowmen using chalk: put on scarfs, buttons, pipes, etc.
Model snowmen from plasticine and clay.
Use white paint and a sponge. Make trees in the winter time.

SONGS & RHYTHMS

> Introduce: The Snowman, p. 6, Music For Early Childhood, New Music Horizons Series. Mr. Snowman, p. 37, The Sleigh Ride, p. 37, My Picture Book Of Songs, Dalton, Ashton, Young, M. A. Donohue.
> Review: Old Mother Goose, The Shivers, The North Wind's Song, Music For Young Americans, pp. 42-44.
> Work on the rhythm band: Use The Orchestra, p. 72, Music For Early Childhood, New Music Horizons Series.

STORIES

Come Summer Come Winter	Terry Shannon	Albert Whitman & Co.
When Winter Comes	Charles Fox	Reilly & Lee Co.
All Ready For Winter	Leone Adelson	David McKay Co.
The True Book Of Little Eskimos	Donalda Copeland	Childrens Press
A Dog Team For Ongluk	Terry Shannon	Melmont Publishers

FINGERPLAYS AND POEMS

> Time For Poetry, May Arbuthnot, Scott, Forseman & Co.

> Winter Night, p. 176; Stopping By Woods On A Snowy Evening, p. 176; Velvet Shoes, p. 177; Winter Night, p. 177; Waiting, p. 177

> The Sound Of Poetry, Austin & Mills, Allyn & Bacon, Inc.

> Falling Snow, p. 336; The Snowman's Resolution, p. 337, Crumbs, p. 66; The Snow Bird, p. 63; Poor Robin, p. 62; A Story In The Snow, p. 63.

GAMES

> Review: Button, Button; How Sure; Dog And Bone; The Farmer In The Dell; This Is My Nose.
> Introduce: Two In The Middle, p. 30; Rose, Rose And Up She Rises, p. 32, Music For Early Childhood, New Music Horizons Series.

Seventeenth Week

CONSERVATION TIME

> Talk about things that go. Discuss things that are on wheels. Skates, wagons, bicycles, scooters, etc.
> Relate how animals travel such as the rabbit, mole, fish, etc.
> Have children tell how they travel: by car, bus, airplane, walk, skate, etc.
> Allow children to tell of trips they have taken and how they have traveled.
> Make plans to take a train trip to a nearby town and return.

WORK PERIOD

Draw a car. Use construction paper in various colors. Cut them double. Use saran wrap for windows.

Paint pictures of children skating, coasting in a wagon, horse back riding, etc.

Model a horse from plasticine or clay. If clay is used, paint it when dry.

SONGS & RHYTHMS

Our Windshield Wiper, p. 22; Let's Take A Little Trip, p. 23, Music For Early Childhood, New Music Horizons Series.

Introduce: American Singer, American Book Company. Walking, p. 111, Sonata, Op. 14 No. 2.

Roller Skating, p. 143 (Waltz); The Blue Danube Waltz, p. 145; The Auto, p. 31; Rocking Horse, p. 142; Wait For The Wagon, p. 28.

STORIES

This Is The Way The Animals Walk	Gale Parks	E. M. Hale & Co.
Pony Tales	Nancy Watson	Doubleday & Co.
Peter's Long Walk	Lee Kingman	Doubleday & Co.
Indian Two Feet And His Horse	Margaret Friskey	Childrens Press
What Can A Horse Do That You Can't Do?	Pers Crowell	McGraw-Hill Book Co.
The Two Cars	Ingri d'Aulaire	Doubleday & Co.

FINGERPLAYS AND POEMS

The Sound Of Poetry, Austin & Milles, Allyn and Bacon, Inc.

There Are So Many Ways Of Going Places, p. 161; Motor Cars, p. 163; Taxis, p. 164; Roads, p. 166.

GAMES

Review: Bibbety, Bobbety, Boo; Coffee Grinder; Hot Potato; Did You Ever See A Lassie; Red Light; Colors.

Introduce: Brownies and Fairies, p. 58; Follow The Leader, p. 58, Physical Education For Elementary Grades, S. D. State Course of Study Bulletin No. 73.

Eighteenth Week

CONVERSATION TIME

Talk about trains. Let children tell of their experiences going on a train.

Talk about the different kinds of trains: passenger, freight.

Tell about the kinds of cars on a passenger and a freight train.

Have children tell what they can about the workers on the train and at the station.

WORK PERIOD

Make charts showing the workers needed to keep trains running.
Take a train trip. Take a tour of the various cars.
Dramatic play with blocks and toys.
Build a train from packing boxes. Include an engine and a passenger
   coach.
Make products used in the dramatic play: toy money, tickets, baggage,
   etc.
Paint and crayon pictures illustrating trains.

SONGS & RHYTHMS

Introduce: Little Old Train, p. 52. Use rhythm instruments to make
   sound effects. More Singing Fun, Lucille Wood, Webster Publ. Co.
   Little Engine, p. 43. Use poem on same page and also sand blocks
   and a triangle. Singing Fun, Lucille Wood, Webster Publ. Co.
Review: Roller Skating, p. 143, The American Singer, American Book
   Co.

STORIES

Two Little Trains, Margaret Wise Brown, W. R. Scott.
Dobbin, p. 228, Story Telling With The Flannel Board, Paul S. Anderson,
   T. S. Denison.

Benjie Engie	Louise Devine	Rand McNally Book
The Little Engine That Laughed	Alf Evers	Wonder Books
Train Coming!	Betty Wright	Whitman Publ. Co.
Roundabout Train	Betty Wright	Whitman Publ. Co.
The Choo-Choo Train	Oscar Fabres	John Martin's House, Inc.
The Little Train That Saved The Day	Charlotte Steiner	Wonder Books
Animal Train	Elizabeth Roberts	Whitman Publ. Co.
The Rattle-Rattle Train	Carl Bobertz	Wonder Books
The Terrytoon Space Train	Barbara Waring	Wonder Books

FINGERPLAYS AND POEMS

The Way Of Trains, p. 72; Trains At Night, p. 72; From A Railway Carriage, p. 72; Trains, p. 72; The Subway Train's Story, p. 16; The Train,
p. 27; The Freight Train, p. 40, Time For Poetry, May Arbuthnot,
Scott, Foresman & Co.

GAMES

Review: The Farmer In The Dell; Two In The Middle; Rose, Rose And Up
   She Rises; This Is My Nose; Button, Button.
Introduce: Airplanes, p. 138, Physical Education For Elementary Grades,
   S. D. State Course Of Study Bulletin No. 73.

Nineteenth Week

CONVERSATION TIME

Discuss travel by air: helicopter, airplane, dirigible, balloon, etc.

Talk about airplanes: have children tell of different kinds of planes they have seen, read about, or traveled in: jets, passenger airplanes with propellers and jet engines, little airplanes, cargo planes.

Discuss uses we have for planes: carrying people, carrying things, using an airplane to spray crops, weathermen use airplanes, many kinds of planes are used to keep our country safe.

Have children tell about the view from an airplane.

Talk about the airport; who uses it and what is located there: terminal building, control tower, runways.

Have children tell about the workers at the airport: ticket agent, baggage man, mechanics, etc.

WORK PERIOD

Paint airplanes, cut them out, use on a bulletin board.

Model airplanes from plasticine or clay.

Cut an airplane, use a pin wheel for the propeller.

Build an airport with blocks. Use toy planes.

Take a trip to an airport.

Draw a picture of the trip to the airport.

SONGS & RHYTHMS

Introduce: The Train, p. 8; My Pony, p. 12, Happy Songs For Happy Children, Meta Siebold, G. Schirmer, Inc.

Review: Little Old Train, p. 52, More Singing Fun, Lucille Wood, Webster Publ. Co.

Little Engine, p. 43, Singing Fun, Lucille Wood, Webster Publishing Co.

Rhythm Band stressing the tambourine: Music For Early Childhood, New Music Horizons Series, Boutique Fantasque, p. 70.

Stress skipping: Help children who are having difficulty.

STORIES

Cloud Hoppers	Frederick James	Childrens Press
Saturday Flight	Ethel Wright	E. M. Hale & Co.
How Airplanes Help Us	Edith McCall	Benefic Press
Flyaway At The Air Circus,	Leone Adelson, p. 55,	Let's Read A Story
I Want To Be A Pilot	Carla Greene	Childrens Press
I Want To Be A Space Pilot	Carla Greene	Childrens Press

FINGER PLAYS AND POEMS

Taking Off, p. 73; Aeroplane, p. 73; Up In The Air, p. 73; Silver Ships, p. 73; Cockpit In The Clouds, p. 74, Time For Poetry, May Arbuthnot, Scott, Foresman & Co.

The Airplane, p. 21, <u>Rhymes</u> <u>For</u> <u>Fingers</u> <u>And</u> <u>Flannelboards</u>, Louise Scott & J. J. Thompson, Webster Publ. Co.

GAMES

Review: The Farmer In The Dell; Looby Loo; Hot Potato; Bounce The Ball And Say Your Name; Red Light.

Introduce: Run Rabbit Run, p. 59, <u>Physical</u> <u>Education</u> <u>For</u> <u>Elementary</u> <u>Grades</u>, S. D. State Course Of Study Bulletin No. 73.

Twentieth Week

CONVERSATION TIME

Discuss travel by water: boats, tugboats, sailboats, ocean liners, motor boats, cruisers, etc.

Let children tell about any experience they have had on a boat.

Tell about the people who work in a boat: captain, navigator, radio operator, engineer, seaman, etc.

Discuss how boats carry passengers and goods.

WORK PERIOD

Make a sail boat using white paper and tooth picks for the sails.

Make a frieze. Include three kinds of travel, land, water, and air. Have children color and paint the ways of traveling and cut them out, place on the frieze. Have them paint one section of the frieze as land, one part as water, and the other part, air.

Make folded boats, such as a row boat, sail boat, etc.

Draw and cut out pictures of ocean liners, make a scrap book of pictures children bring.

SONGS & RHYTHMS

Review: The Train, p. 8; My Pony, p. 12, <u>Happy</u> <u>Songs</u> <u>For</u> <u>Happy</u> <u>Children</u>, Meta Seebold, G. Schermer, Inc.

Little Old Train, p. 52, <u>More</u> <u>Singing</u> <u>Fun</u>, Lucille Wood, Webster Publishing Co.

Little Engine, p. 43, Singing Fun, Lucille Wood, Webster Publishing Co.

Introduce: I'd Like To Be, p. 135; Tugboat, p. 135, <u>The</u> <u>Kindergarten</u> <u>Book</u>, Ginn & Co.

Play Train: Dance Of The Moorish Slaves, Verdi, p. 132, The Kindergarten Book, Ginn & Co.

Play Airplane: Run, Run, Run, by Concone, p. 11, <u>The</u> <u>Kindergarten</u> <u>Book</u>, Ginn & Co.

STORIES

I Want To Be A Ship Captain	Carla Greene	Childrens Press
Little Toot	Hardie Gramalky	E. M. Hale & Co.

The Boats On The River	Marjorie Flack	Viking Press
The Little Island	Golden MacDonald	Doubleday & Co.
Little Sea Legs	Melvin Barker	E. M. Hale & Co.

FINGERPLAYS AND POEMS

I Saw A Ship Sailing, p. 64; I Love The Sea, p. 73, Choral Speaking, Irene Hemphill, Educational Publ. Corp.

Ferryboats, p. 46; Where Go The Boats?, p. 48; The Sea Shell, p. 48; Freight Boats, p. 49; At The Seaside, p. 49; I Saw A Ship Asailing, p. 49, For A Child, Wilma McFarland, The Westminster Press.

GAMES

Review: Lost Child; Animal Story; This Is My Nose; The Leaves; Squirrel In The Trees.

Introduce: High Windows, p. 61, Physical Education For Elementary Grades, S. D. State Course Of Study Bulletin No. 73.

Twenty-first Week

CONVERSATION TIME

Talk about our new month: when it comes during the year, its name, number of days in it.

Discuss the special days in the month: Lincoln's birthday, Washington's birthday, Valentine day.

Let children tell what they know of the life of George Washington.

Let children tell what they know about the life of Abraham Lincoln.

WORK PERIOD

Make a patriotic hat, red, white, and blue.

Make heart animals such as a cat, turtle, dog, bird, rabbit, etc.

Let children draw a flag.

Make a flag using chains of red, white, and blue. Put the chains on a rod so it can be hung up.

Make heart containers to hold the valentines children bring to school. Use two large hearts cut from red and white paper; lace these together.

Practice cutting hearts, also tearing hearts from newspaper.

Cut hearts and decorate them by pasting on colored paper to make a face.

Make red and white chains to decorate the room.

SONGS & RHYTHMS

Introduce: A Valentine, p. 120; Abraham Lincoln, p. 120; Our Flag, p. 121; Glory To The Flag, p. 121; George Washington, p. 122, Music For Young Americans, ABC Series.

Review: I'd Like To Be, p. 135; Tugboat, p. 135, The Kindergarten Book, Ginn & Co.

March around the room. Wear paper hats:
Marching, p. 102, ABC Music Series, Music For Young Americans.
Use rhythm sticks: Rhythmic These in F, p. 96, Music For Young Ameri-
cans, ABC Music Series

STORIES

The Story Of Tom Thumb, p. 37; The Princess Who Slept On A Pea, p. 43;
The Pancake, p. 49; Rumpelstiltskin, p. 74; The Fairy Tale Picture Book,
Nancy Dingman, Garden City Books; Lincoln's Birthday, p. 6; Washing-
ton's Birthday, p. 10; St. Valentine's Day, p. 8, Some Days To Remember,
Alma Reck, Melmont Publ.

FINGERPLAYS AND POEMS

Rhymes For Fingers And Flannelboards, Louise Scott, J. J. Thompson,
Webster Publishing Co.

My Soldiers, p. 21; Ten Little Soldiers, p. 22; Marching Soldier, p. 22;
Captain and Men, p. 53.

Let's Say Poetry Together, Carrie Rasmussen, Burgess Publ. Co.

Abraham Lincoln, p. 68; Like Washington, p. 67; Washington, p. 65;
Yankee Doodle, p. 66; Marching Song, p. 41; Lincoln, p. 63.

GAMES

Review: High Windows; Squirrel In The Trees; Animal Story; Run, Rabbit
Run; Red Light.
Introduce: Bird Catcher, p. 60, Physical Education For Elementary
Grades, S. D. State Course of Study Bulletin No. 73.

Twenty-second Week

CONVERSATION TIME

Make plans for a Valentine party: choose committees such as game,
clean-up, food, story, etc.
Talk about why we send and give valentines to each other.
Decide to send a valentine to someone absent or sick at home. Plan to
go to the store and; buy one, address it, and walk to the mail box to
mail it.
Talk about the mailman. Let children tell what they know about him.
Observe where he picks up mail and the route he takes.
Make plans to go to the post office; observe sorting of mail, etc.

WORK PERIOD

Take a large paper sack, add strips of brown wrapping paper as a strap
for the shoulder and use as a mailman's pouch.
Take an excursion to the post office to see men at work.

Make cookies for our party. Make an experience chart telling how we
  made the cookies.
Frost cookies made the day before, put a candy heart on them.
Make red fruit jello in paper cups to be used at the party; store in the
  refrigerator until the party.
Make a valentine place mat. Decorate with candy hearts.
Make a valentine head-band, decorate with cut-out red hearts.

SONGS & RHYTHMS

Introduce: A Valentine For You, p. 86; When You Send A Valentine, p. 86,
  The Kindergarten Book, Ginn & Co.
  Valentine's Day, p. 108, Music For Early Childhood, New Music Hori-
  zons Series.
Review: A Valentine, p. 120, Music For Young Americans, ABC Music
  Series.
Have children play they are ice skating: Skaters' Dance, p. 102, The
  Kindergarten Book, Ginn & Co.

STORIES

Contrary Woodrow	Sue Felt	Doubleday & Co.
Bubble Baths & Hair Bows	Mallen DeSantes	Doubleday & Co.
The Giant Story	Beatrice deRegniers	E. M. Hale & Co.
Tom's Magic T. V.	Andre Dugo	E. M. Hale & Co.
The Five Chinese Brothers	Claire Bishop	E. M. Hale & Co.
She Loves Me, She Loves Me Not	Robert Keeshan	Harper & Row

FINGERPLAYS AND PEOMS

Let's Say Poetry Together, Our Valentine, p. 64	Carrie Rasmussen	Burgess Publ. Co.
Time For Poetry	May Arbuthnot	Scott, Foresman & Co.

A Valentine, p. 178; My Valentine, p. 178; A Sure Sign, p. 177.

Rhymes For Fingers And Flannelboards, Louise Scott, J. J. Thompson

For My Friends, p. 71; How Many Valentines, p. 71; Valentines, p. 72;
Five Little Valentines, p. 72.

GAMES

Review: Bird Catcher; Red Light; High Windows; Did You Ever See A
  Lassie; Animal Story.
Introduce: Music For Early Childhood, New Music Horizons Series,
  Willowbee, p. 65.

Twenty-third Week

CONVERSATION TIME

Introduce the circus.   Begin to talk about the various animals.

Have children tell what they know about the polar bear. Discuss its habits, color, size, shape, characteristics, etc.

Discuss the seal; bring out something about its shape, characteristics, habits, etc.

Talk about the monkey: Let children tell about what they know about the monkey: bring out things about its habits, characteristics, etc.

Talk about other kinds of bears: the grizzly bear, black bear, etc.

WORK PERIOD

Take an excursion to see a collection of stuffed animals.   These animals include a polar bear, grizzly bear, seal, monkey.

Draw pictures of the different kinds of bears.   Cut them out.   Use them on a bulletin board.

Cut out seals from black paper.   Cut out colored balls.   Paste pictures on colored construction paper and use about the room.

SONGS & RHYTHMS

Introduce: Squeaker At The Zoo, pp. 129-135, Work on the elephants and the lions. Music For Young Americans, ABC Music Series.

Introduce: The Ringmaster, p. 46; Old Gray Horse, p. 47; The Hippopotamus, p. 48; The Tiger, p. 48, Music For Early Childhood, New Music Horizons Series.

The Bear Walk, p. 50; Galloping Movements, p. 51; Galloping Ponies, p. 54, Music For Early Childhood, New Music Horizons Series.

STORIES

If I Ran The Circus	Sr. Seuss	Random House
What Animal Is It ?	Anna Pistorius	Follett Publ. Co.
I Was Kissed By A Seal At The Zoo	Helen Palmer	Random House
Ten Little Monkeys	Jessica Broderick	Rand McNally & Co.
The Little Bear's Mother	Carl Memling	Ariel Books
Lost Bear	Ann Durell	Doubleday & Co.
Little Brown Monkey	Elizabeth Upham	Platt & Munk Co.
I Like Animals	Dahlov Ipcar	Alfred A Knopf
Me And The Bears	Robert Bright	Doubleday & Co.
Five Little Monkeys	Juliet Kepes	E. M. Hale & Co.
Buzzy Bear In The Garden	Dorothy Marino	Franklin Watts
The Littlest Circus Seal	Mary Gehr	Childrens Press
The Biggest Bear	Lynd Ward	Houghton Mifflin Co.
Third Monkey	Ann Clark	The Viking Press

FINGERPLAYS AND POEMS

Choral Speaking   Irene Hemphill   Educational Publ. Co.

Clowns, p. 18; At The Circus, p. 21; Come! Bring Your Nickel, p. 32; About Animals, p. 38; At The Parade, p. 76.

For A Child   Wilma McFarland   The Westminster
                                                          Press

Circus, p. 50; The Balloon Man, p. 53; Merry-Go-Round, p. 53.

GAMES

Review: Willowbee; Animal Story; The Farmer In The Dell; Bird Catcher; Red Light.

Introduce: Hickory, Dickory, Dock, p. 30, Rhythmic Activities, Frances R. Stuart, Burgess Publ. Co.

Twenty-fourth Week

CONVERSATION TIME

Talk about circus wagons: why we have them, what they look like, etc.

Discuss how a circus travels from place to place. Let children tell about experiences they have had watching the circus unload.

Mention the circus lion. Talk about his habits, color, size, characteristics, etc.

Introduce the elephant. Let children tell of their experiences at a circus. Talk about the elephant and its size, color, habits, etc.

WORK PERIOD

Make some circus wagons. Use shoe boxes. Line with colored paper grass. Use colored construction paper cut in strips to paste across the open part of the box. Place animals inside the box. Cardboard wheels can be made and attached to the wagons.

Use yellow construction paper to make the head of a lion. Draw one large circle and one smaller circle. Have children fringe between the two circles. Then cut colored construction paper for eyes, nose, and mouth.

Fold a grey piece of construction paper in half to make an elephant. Round the two corners on the fold of the paper. Cut two arches at the bottom of the paper to form the feet. Color in the eyes, mouth, etc.

SONGS & RHYTHMS

Review: Squeaker At The Zoo, p. 129-135. Finish the song Music For Young Americans, ABC Music Series.

The Ringmaster, p. 46; Old Gray Horse, p. 47; The Hippopotamus, p. 48; The Tiger, p. 48, Music For Early Childhood, New Music Horizons Series.

Introduce: Bear, p. 122; Elephant, p. 121; Lion, p. 120; Monkey, p. 120, The Kindergarten Book, Ginn & Co.

Elephants March, p. 121; Bear-Dance, p. 122, The Kindergarten Book, Ginn & Co.

STORIES

The Saggy, Baggy Elephant	K. B. Jackson	Golden Press
The Happy Lion	Louise Fatio	Whittlesey House
The True Book Of Animal Babies	Illa Podendorf	Childrens Press
The Tales Of Don Quixote	Tony Palazzo	Garden City Books
Elephant Herd	Miriam Schlein	William R. Scott
The Circus Baby	Maud Perersham	The Macmillan Co.
Daffy	Adda Sharp	The Steck Company
The True Book Of The Circus	Mabel Harmer	Childrens Press
The Sleepy Little Lion	Margaret Wise Brown	Harper & Bros.
George, The Discontented Giraffe	Phillip Steinberg	T. S. Denison & Co.

FINGERPLAYS AND POEMS

Time For Poetry	May Arbuthnot	Scott, Forseman & Co.

The Elephant's Trunk, p. 67; The Elephant, p. 68; Trot Along, Pony, p. 66; Holding Hands, p. 67; The Hippopotamus, p. 68; The Seals, p. 69; The Kangaroo, p. 69.

GAMES

Review: Willowbee; Bird Catcher; High Windows; Red Light; Bounce Balls.
Introduce: Pop Goes The Weasel, p. 74, Rhythmic Activities, Frances R. Stuart, Burgess Publ. Co.

Twenty-fifth Week

CONVERSATION TIME

Talk about the tallest animal in the circus: the giraffe.
Discuss the hippopotamus: tell about his habits, size, color, etc.
Have children tell what they know about the tiger.
Talk about ponies and horses. Let children tell what they know about them.
Relate what you know about the zebra.

WORK PERIOD

Use construction paper and cut a giraffe. Color in the spots brown, use clothes pins (pinch) for the legs.
Use a large piece of brown construction paper to make a hippopotamus. Cut paper double. Cut it the shape of a figure eight. Make a liner of

red construction paper for the mouth. Use a white crayon and color in teeth. Draw in the face of the hippo with black crayon.

Draw a picture of a pony; also a horse. Put a saddle on the horse. Cut the pictures out and use on the bulletin board.

Model a zebra from clay. Paint it when dry.

SONGS & RHYTHMS

Review: Squeaker At The Zoo, pp. 129-135. Music For Young Americans, ABC Music Series. Also introduce the record with this song included. Let children sing with the record.

The Ringmaster, p. 46; Old Gray Horse, p. 47; The Hippopotamus, p. 48; The Tiger, p. 48. Music For Early Childhood, New Music Horizons Series.

Bear, p. 122; Elephant, p. 121; Lion, p. 120; Monkey, p. 120, The Kindergarten Book, Ginn & Co.

STORIES

The Frightened Tiger	Golden MacDonald	Doubleday & Co.
World Full Of Horses	Dahlov Ipcar	Doubleday & Co.
Shoe For My Pony	Margaret Friskey	Childrens Press
The Horse Who Lived Upstairs	Phyllis McGinley	J. B. Lippincott
Fuzzy The Tiger	Mary Villanejo	Alfred A. Knopf
The Unhappy Hippopotamus	Nancy Moore	Vanguard Press
The Little Carousel	Marcia Brown	Charles Scribner's Sons
The Cloud Eater	Katherine Reeves	Rand McNally & Co.
Penny And The White Horse	Margery Bianco	Julian Messner, Inc.

FINGERPLAYS AND POEMS

Rhymes For Fingers And Flannelboards, Louise Scott & J. J. Thompson, Webster Publishing Co.

Ten Circus Wagons, p. 14; This Little Clown, p. 15; Riding The Merry-Go-Round, p. 15; The Menagerie, p. 16; Counting At The Zoo, p. 17; The Elephant, p. 17; Animals, p. 16; Monkey See, Monkey Do, p. 18.

GAMES

Review: Pop Goes The Weasel; Hickory, Dickory, Dock; Willowbee; Bird Catcher; Squirrel In The Trees.

Introduce: Carrousel, p. 13, Rhythmic Activities, Frances R. Stuart, Burgess Publ. Co.

Twenty-sixth Week

CONVERSATION TIME

Talk about the circus tent. How it is made, who puts it up, what it looks like, etc.

Have children tell what they like about the clowns. Let them tell about clowns they have seen at the circus. Talk about what they look like, their make-up, what they do in the circus, etc.

Relate something about the circus rings. Talk about what goes on in the center ring and the two side ones.

Let children tell about dog acts they have seen at a circus. Talk about the different kinds of dogs and the costumes they wear. Let children tell of dog acts they have seen and why they enjoyed them.

Talk about the kangaroo: what he looks like, characteristics, etc.

WORK PERIOD

Give tickets to children so they can attend the Shrine Circus.

Let them draw a picture of an act they enjoyed at the Circus.

Make a circus tent from two large pieces of unprinted newsprint. Paste papers together at the top. Cut an opening in the center of the paper. Let children decorate these with flags.

Draw and paint pictures of clowns. Make just the heads. Stress facial expressions: the sad clown, the happy clown, etc.

Draw a circus ring. Cut it out. Make performers to go into the ring. Use this for a bulletin board.

Paint pictures of dogs with their circus costumes.

SONGS & RHYTHMS

Review: Squeaker At The Zoo, pp. 129-135, Music For Young Americans, ABC Music Series.
Bear, p. 122; Elephant, p. 121; Lion, p. 120; Monkey, p. 120, The Kindergarten Book, Ginn & Co.

Introduce: My Broom Pony, p. 17, More Happy Songs For Happy Children by Meta Siebold, G. Schirmer, Inc.

STORIES

Homer And The Circus Train	Hardie Gramatky	Putnam's Sons
The Circus Comes To Town	Veronica Hutchinson	E. M. Hale & Co.
Hassan Boy Of The Desert	Dominique Darbois	Follet Publ. Co.
Katy No-Pocket	Emmy Payne	E. M. Hale & Co.
Let's Go To The Circus	Tony Palazzo	Doubleday & Co.
Gergely's Golden Circus	Peter Archer	Simon & Schuster
Whoever Heard Of Kangaroo Eggs	Sam Vaughn	Doubleday & Co.
Bad Eye The Clown	Nils Hogner	E. M. Hale & Co.
Animals In The Zoo	Feodor Rojankovsky	Alfred A. Knopf
Breakfast With The Clowns	Rosalie Slocum	E. M. Hale & Co.

FINGERPLAYS AND POEMS

Rhymes For Fingers And Flannelboards, Louise Scott & J. J. Thompson, Webster Publishing Co.

Ten Circus Wagons, p. 14; This Little Clown, p. 15; Riding The Merry-Go-Round, p. 15; The Menagerie, p. 16; Counting At The Zoo, p. 17; The Elephant, p. 17.

GAMES

Review: Willowbee; High Windows; Pop Goes The Weasel; Carrousel.
Introduce: Clap Dance, p. 19, Rhythmic Activities, Frances R. Stuart, Burgess Publ. Co.

Twenty-seventh Week

CONVERSATION TIME

Talk about our new month: Mention April Fool's Day.
Discuss the springtime: Signs of spring; What happens in the spring.
Talk about the grass: Let children go for a walk and look for signs of spring.
Talk about what is happening to the trees in spring.
Talk about pussy willows: where they grow: what they look like, etc.
Talk about the crocus: where it grows, when it comes up, what it looks like.

WORK PERIOD

Use dark paper and chalk to color large pussy willows. Mount and use as a bulletin board motif.
Cut kites from colored construction paper. Decorate the kites using scraps of colored paper to make a face. Make the tails by using cut paper straws and colored squares of paper strung together.
Color a spring picture showing the trees, grass, etc.
Go on an excursion to gather the crocus.

SONGS & RHYTHMS

Review: I Have A Little Sister, p. 46; What Are Babies Made of?, p. 47; Bed Time, p. 55; Pinky Winky Baby, p. 47, The Kindergarten Book, Ginn & Co.
Introduce: In The Merry Springtime, p. 3; Spring, p. 4; Good News, p. 5; Little Bluebird, p. 6; Nests, p. 6, More Happy Songs For Happy Children, Meta Siebold, G. Schirmer, Inc.
Review Bears' Walking and Dancing, p. 11, More Happy Songs For Happy Children, Meta Siebold, G. Schirmer.

STORIES

Pussy Willow	Margaret Wise Brown	Big Golden Book
Around The Year	Tasha Tudor	Oxford Univ. Press
Rain	Virginia Parsons	Doubleday & Co.
The Little Duck Who Loved The Rain	Peter Mabie	Follett Publ. Co.

The Round Robin   Joyce Holland   T. S. Denison &
                                                Co. Inc.

FINGERPLAYS AND POEMS

The Seasons, p. 306; Directions, p. 306; Daffodils, p. 306; How The
Flowers Grow, p. 307; Little Gray Pussy, 308; City Rain, 309; In Time
Of Silver Rain, p. 310; It Is Raining, p. 311; Rain, p. 312; Down The
Rain Falls, p. 314; Rain, Rain, Go Away, p. 315; The Rainbow, p. 316;
The Coming Of Spring, p. 318; April, p. 319.

GAMES

Review: Looby Loo; The Farmer In The Dell; Musical Chairs; Hickory,
   Dickory, Dock; Dog And Bone.
Introduce: Hi, Little Lassie, p. 33, Rhythmic Activities, Frances R.
   Stuart, Burgess Publ. Co.

Twenty-eighth Week

CONVERSATION TIME

Talk about the rain in the spring: what it does, why we need it.
Discuss planting a garden: what we must do to the soil, what seeds we
   will use, how we will take care of it.
Have children talk about some of our spring flowers. Go for a walk to
   see violets, tulips, daffodils, etc.
Talk about what is needed to make things grow in the spring.
Talk about the sun: what it is: what it does for us, etc.
Talk about the wind: what it does for us, etc.

WORK PERIOD

Take a walk to notice signs of spring: flowers peeking through, etc.
Make a picture of trees in the spring.
Go to the store and buy a kite. Fly a kite.
Draw spring pictures of activities in the spring.
Paint spring flowers.
Make pin wheels. Go outside and use them. Mount them on sticks.

SONGS & RHYTHMS

Review: In The Merry Springtime, p. 3; Spring, p. 4; Good News, p. 5;
   Little Bluebird, p. 5; Nests, p. 6, More Happy Songs For Happy
   Children, Meta Siebold, G. Schirmer, Inc.
Introduce: Peggy, p. 7; Mary And Joan, p. 8; Merry Sunshine, p. 9;
   Roller Skates, p. 12; My Scooter, p. 12; My Little New Kite, p. 13,
   More Happy Songs For Happy Children, Meta Siebold
Introduce: The Boy Scout March, p. 14-15, More Happy Songs For Happy
   Children, Meta Siebold, G. Schirmer, Inc.

STORIES

The Good Rain	Alice Goudey	Alladin Books
Seven Diving Ducks	Margaret Friskey	E. M. Hale & Co.
The Duck	Margaret Wise Brown	Harper & Bros.
Please Pass The Grass	Leone Adelson	David McKay Co. Inc.
Willie Waddle	Katherine Carter	The Steck Co.
I Like Butterflies	Gladys Conklin	Holiday House

FINGERPLAYS AND POEMS

Rhymes For Fingers And Flannelboards, Louise Scott & J. J. Thompson, Webster Publ. Co.

Making Kites, p. 124; Raindrops, p. 125; The Rain, 1. 125; The Wind, p. 125; Yellow Daffodil, p. 126; The Flower, p. 126; Relaxing Flowers, p. 126; Purple Violets, p. 127; Five Little May Baskets, p. 128; Pretending, p. 128.

GAMES

Review: Hickory, Dickory, Dock; Bird Catcher; Looby Loo; Pop Goes The Weasel; Clap Dance.

Introduce: Hippity Hop, p. 34, Rhythmic Activities, Frances R. Stuart, Burgess Publ. Co.

Twenty-ninth Week

CONVERSATION TIME

Talk about Easter. Why we have it; what it means to us; what we do on it.
Talk about rabbits. Let children tell what they know about rabbits: where they live, what they eat, what they do, etc.
Talk about easter eggs: kinds of eggs, colored eggs, etc.
Talk about easter chickens: color, size, habits, etc.
Talk about easter ducks: size, characteristics, etc.
Let children tell about going on an Easter Egg Hunt.

WORK PERIOD

Color eggs. Hard boil the eggs at school and let each child dye an egg. Write his name on it with wax crayon.
Make an Easter basket. Put grass in it and put the eggs the children dyed into the baskets.
Cut large Easter eggs and decorate them.
Color Easter chickens. Make up a story about them.
Color and paint yellow ducks.
Cut an Easter rabbit. Use for the bulletin board.
Make decorations for an Easter party: place mats, napkins, etc.

SONGS & RHYTHMS

Review: In The Merry Springtime, p. 3; Spring, p. 4; Good News, p. 5; Little Bluebird, p. 5; Nests, p. 6; Peggy, p. 7; Mary And Joan, p. 8; Merry Sunshine, p. 9; Roller Skates, p. 12, More Happy Songs For Happy Children, Meta Siebold, G. Schirmer.

Introduce: A Little Seed, p. 130; Little Johnny-Jump-Up, p. 103; A Blue Bird Sings, p. 105, The Kindergarten Book, Ginn & Co.

Children roll up in balls, pretending to be seeds. They unfold gradually. First one arm, then the other, reaches out and pushes up. Then the head is lifted. Nature's Dream (Arabesque) Kindergarten Book, Ginn & Co., p. 104.

STORIES

Home For A Bunny	Margaret Wise Brown	Simon & Schuster
My Bunny Book	Genevieve Cross	Cross Publications
A Trip To The Yard	Genevieve Cross	Cross Publications
The Easter Bunny That Overslept	Priscilla Friedrich	Lothrop, Lee, Shepard
Bunny's Easter Gift	Bill Martin	Tell-Well Press, Inc.
The Golden Egg Book	Margaret Wise Brown	Simon Schuster
Naughty Bunny	Richard Scarry	Golden Press
The Color Kittens	Margaret Wise Brown	Golden Press
The Golden Bunny	Margaret Wise Brown	Simon Schuster
Peter Rabbit And Reddy Fox	Thornton Burgess	Wonder Books
Mystery Of The Gatesign	Margaret Frisky	Childrens Press
My Red Umbrella	Robert Bright	Morrow Junior Books

FINGERPLAYS AND POEMS

Rhymes For Fingers And Flannelboards, Louise Scott & J. J. Thompson, Webster Publishing Co.

Five Little Rabbits, p. 76; Once There Was A Bunny, p. 76; This Little Bunny, p. 76; The Rabbits, p. 75; Twelve Little Rabbits, p. 75; Easter Bunny, p. 74; Five Little Easter Eggs, p. 73; On Easter Day, p. 73.

GAMES

Review: Hippity Hop; Clap Dance; Looby Loo; Hickory, Dickory, Dock; Bird Catcher.

Introduce: How D'ye Do My Partner?, p. 36, Rhythmic Activities, Frances R. Stuart, Burgess Publ. Co.

Thirtieth Week

CONVERSATION TIME

Talk about the new month of May: how many days in it; days of the week, special days, etc.

Discuss observing May Day: hanging baskets, making baskets, etc.
Talk about the Maypole and what we can use it for.
Discuss plans for Mother's Day: making a card, entertaining them.
Talk about plum blossoms and apple blossoms.

WORK PERIOD

Make a May basket. Cut it out and decorate it.
Make a large Maypole. Use it in the center of the room.
Learn a dance to use around the Maypole.
Make a Mother's Day card.
Plant some nasturtiums in a wooden box. Watch them grow.
Take care of the flowers by watering them and placing them in the sun.

SONGS & RHYTHMS

Review: A Little Seed, p. 103; Little Johnny-Jump-Up, p. 103; A Blue
Bird Sings, p. 105, The Kindergarten Book, Ginn & Co.
Introduce: Hopping, p. 28; Mother Dear, p. 23; The Rainbow, p. 21;
On The Grass, p. 21, More Happy Songs For Happy Children, Meta
Siebold, G. Schirmer, Inc.
Children can fly and flutter like butterflies. Let the music tell when
wings are folded, when they flutter and when they spread in flight.
Papillons No. 8, p. 108, The Kindergarten Book, Ginn & Co.

STORIES

Johnny And The Monarch	Margaret Friskey	E. M. Hale & Co.
All Ready For Summer	Leone Adelson	David McKay & Co., Inc.
The Good Rain	Alice Goudey	Alladin Books
Mother's Day	Reck & Fichter	Melmont Publishers
The Wonder Book Of Birds	Cynthia Koehler	Wonder Books
Johnny And The Birds	Ian Munn	Rand McNally & Co.
The Runaway Baby Bird	Marguerite Walters	Wonder Books
I See The Sky	Ann Peters	Wonder Books
Little Duckling	Helen Wing	Rand McNally
The Littlest Rabbit	Robert Kraus	Harper Bros.
Becky, The Rabbit	Gene Darby	Benefic Press

FINGERPLAYS AND POEMS

One Thousand Poems for Children, Sechrist, Macrae-Smith Co.
My Garden, p. 67; Happy Thought, p. 67; The Secrets Of Our Garden,
p. 68; The Gardner, p. 68; The Swing, p. 73; The Robin, p. 107; Sir
Robin, p. 107; The Brown Thrush, p. 109; Bob White, p. 108; Song Of
The Chickadee, p. 109; The Bluebird, p. 111; The Swallow, p. 112.

GAMES

Review: Two In The Middle; Hippity Hop; Clap Dance; Pop Goes The
Weasel; Hickory, Dickory, Dock.

Introduce: Shoo Fly, p. 91, <u>Rhythmic</u> <u>Activities</u>, Frances R. Stuart, Burgess Publ. Co.

Thirty-first Week

CONVERSATION TIME

Talk about spring flowers. Name some of the common ones. Discuss where they grow, what is needed to care for them.

Discuss spring activities. Let children tell about some of the things they like to do in the spring: roller skate, skip rope, teeter-totter, bicycle, etc.

Relate how we can tell the different birds: woodpecker, robin, bluebird, brown thrush, etc.

Talk about what birds do for us.

WORK PERIOD

Make spring flowers from egg cartons. Paint them and put them on paper stems.

Draw pictures of spring birds.

Paint bird houses.

Paint a frieze depicting a spring flower garden.

SONGS & RHYTHMS

Review: A Little Seed, p. 103; Little Johnny-Jump-Up, p. 103; A Blue Bird Sings, p. 105, <u>The Kindergarten Book</u>, Ginn & Co.

Review: Hopping, p. 28; Mother Dear, p. 23; The Rainbow, p. 21; On The Grass, p. 21, <u>More Happy Songs For Happy Children</u>, Meta Siebold, G. Schirmer, Inc.

Introduce: My Pretty Butterfly, p. 108; Little Bug, p. 109; Cricket, p. 109; A Bird In A Pear Tree, p. 105, <u>The Kindergarten Book</u>, Ginn & Co.

Flying Birds, p. 106, <u>Kindergarten Book</u>, Ginn & Co.

STORIES

Joe The Bluejay And Carl		
The Cardinal	Andre Dugo	E. M. Hale & Co.
Casper The Caterpillar	Celeste Foster	T. S. Denison & Co.
Johnny And The Monarch	Margaret Friskey	E. M. Hale & Co.
The Flower	Mary Downer	Young Scott
Night And Day	Margaret Wise Brown	E. M. Hale & Co.
The Carrot Seed	Ruth Krauss	Harper & Bros.
It Is Night	Phyllis Rowand	E. M. Hale & Co.
Fast Is Not A Ladybug	Miriam Schlein	E. M. Hale & Co.
Wake Up, Farm	Alvin Tresselt	Lothrop, Lee & Shepard
The True Book Of Birds	Margaret Friskey	Childrens Press

FINGERPLAYS AND POEMS

Let's Say Poetry Together, Carrie Rasmussen, Burgess Publishing Co.

Five Little Chickens, p. 11; Dandelion, p. 31; The Little Rose Tree, p. 32; A Comparison, p. 34; Catkin, p. 35; An Open Secret, p. 35; A Conversation, p. 36 Dandelions, p. 37; In My Garden, p. 38; The Swing, p. 47; Return Of Birds, p. 99; Winds, p. 99; May Day, p. 101.

GAMES

Review: Shoo Fly; Two In The Middle; The Farmer In The Dell; Dog And Bone; Hickory, Dickory, Dock; Pop Goes The Weasel.
Introduce: London Bridge, p. 49, Rhythmic Activities, Frances R. Stuart, Burgess Publ. Co.

Thirty-second Week

CONVERSATION TIME

Talk about the things children are going to do this summer.
Let children tell where they plan to spend their vacation.
Talk about the seasons of the year.
Discuss what we do in the summer that is different from any other time of the year.
Go to the park for a picnic.

WORK PERIOD

Draw a picture of something you do in the summer time.
Make pictures of summer flowers.
Paint a picture of a tree in the summer time.
Use finger paints. Let children cut out a flower from the finger painting they did.
Make folders. Put a flower on the outside of the folder.
Put things into the folders that were made during the year.
Help get the room ready for summer.

SONGS & RHYTHMS

Review: A Little Seed, p. 103; Little Johnny-Jump-Up, p. 103; A Blue Bird Sings, p. 105, The Kindergarten Book, Ginn & Co.
Review: Hopping, p. 28; Mother Dear, p. 23; The Rainbow, p. 21; On The Grass, p. 21, More Happy Songs For Happy Children, Meta Siebold, G. Schirmer, Inc.
Review: My Pretty Butterfly, p. 108; Little Bug, p. 109; Cricket, p. 109; A Bird In A Pear Tree, p. 105, The Kindergarten Book, Ginn & Co.
Review: Birds flying and flying a kite.

STORIES

Sounds Of A Summer Night	May Garelick	William R. Scott, Inc.
Maui's Summer	Arnold Bare	E. M. Hale & Co.
The Tadpole	Marjorie Flack	Doubleday & Co.
I Like Butterflies	Gladys Conklin	Holiday House
Willie Waddle	Katherine Carter	The Steck Co.
Good Bye Thunderstorm	Dorothy Marino	J. B. Lippincott Co.

FINGERPLAYS AND POEMS

A Summer Morning, p. 319; I'm Glad The Sky Is Painted Blue, p. 320; Little Rain, p. 321; Color, p. 322; The Crocus, p. 347; Watching Clouds, p. 351, Clouds, p. 352; I Heard A Bird Sing, p. 352; A Bird Came Down The Walk, p. 65; The Bird's Nest, p. 66; Sing Little Bird, p. 67; Be Like The Bird, p. 68; The Caterpillar, p. 73; Little Busy Bee, p. 76, The Sound of Poetry, Mary Austin, Allyn & Bacon, Inc.

GAMES

Review: London Bridge; Shoo Fly; How D'ye Do My Partner; Two In The Middle; Bird Catcher.

Introduce: Maypole Dance, p. 57; Rhythmic Activities, Frances R. Stuart, Burgess Publ. Co.

Chapter 15

EXCURSIONS

Going places and seeing things are an important part of the kindergarten program. Trips to the grocery store, a train ride, a trip to the fire department, or just a neighborhood jaunt, all help to broaden the experiences of the children and to give them a much clearer picture of the world about them. The reason some educators recommend field trips so highly is that children are helped to discover what some things mean by responding actively to them.

Excursions should be planned by the kindergarten teacher well in advance unless it is to be one in the immediate building. No well trained teacher would on a moments notice think of starting on a trip away from the building without some planning. As these trips usually take time from school, they should be worthwhile ventures.

In order to help in the planning of a trip, the teacher should make a study of the places in the immediate community that would lend themselves to excursions. It is fortunate that many excursions can be made on foot. Because of the safety measures involved, it is better not to go too far on the first trip. After the children have learned how to walk and stay together, how to cross streets effectively, longer excursions can be undertaken. Many teachers appoint leaders at the head of the group and at the back, and impress upon the children the need of staying together.

If this trip is to be of any distance, it may be advisable to charter a bus or to ask some of the parents to volunteer their time and transportation.

The teacher and children will want to plan the excursion together. There should be a real need for taking the trip. It may be that someone has a new baby brother, or has a litter of puppies and they would like to have the group see them.

It is always necessary for the teacher to notify the principal or superintendent of her plans, and then arrange for the transportation either by foot, bus, or car. When the child enters in the fall, many schools ask the parent to sign a permission slip giving their permission for the child to leave the school grounds on planned excursions or walks. If such is not the case in your school you would want to send home notes asking the parent to give this permission. Children are welcomed when arrangements have been made in advance with the place of business where they are to visit. If possible it is wise for you to visit ahead of time so you will feel acquainted and will be better able to motivate the questions that will be asked on the excursion.

On any excursion there should be something to look for. Before you leave the room you will want to discuss these things together so the children will have some idea of what they are going to see.

During the trip you will want to remind the kindergarteners of things they had wanted to look for. Maybe they had a real need to visit a grocery store in order to see how shelves were built and you will want to remind them of their reasons for coming. Also let the children ask questions about the things they see.

After the excursion or field trip be sure and give children an opportunity to express themselves freely. Children will want to talk about what they saw and they may wish to dramatize it.

You will guide the children's discussion of what they saw on the trip. As their ideas are organized you will help the children formulate them into experience charts. You may also wish to follow it through with pictures.

You will be able to judge your success by what the children do in their work period as well as other periods throughout the day. They will indicate at this time what they have learned. As you become the guide their experiences begin to take on meaning.

Day by day they will relive their experiences in various ways.

Many kindergarten teachers want to know some of the possibilities open to them for excursions. The following suggested list may be of help.

COMMUNITY

- Home
- School
- Church
- Public Service
    - Fire Department
    - Police Department
    - Children's Library
    - Safety
- Public Utilities
    - Water Department
    - Light Department
    - Gas Department

Stores
- Grocery
- Department
- Book

Amusements
- Parks
- Zoo
- Playgrounds
- Museum
- Theaters

Walks in the school neighborhood

COMMUNICATION

- Post Office
- Radio Station
- Television Station
- Telephone
- Telegraph
- Airport

CIRCUS

- Equipment
- People
- Animals

INDUSTRIES

- Lumber Yard
- Farms
- Oil Stations
- Packing Plant
- Biscuit Company
- Ice Cream Factory
- Artificial Ice Company
- Bakery
- Woolen Mills
- Hatchery
- Falls
- Dairy

Chapter 16

NUMBER CONCEPTS

As a kindergarten teacher you will be very interested in building number concepts. Although arithmetic is not taught as such at this grade level the child's interest in counting should be directed into meaningful experiences.

Number and measure enter into many of the play experiences of the five-year-old. Size discrimination, comparative concepts of more, less, tall, short, thin, narrow, all pave the way to easier understanding of number concepts. Many concrete suggestions come about in each day's teaching that offer the opportunity to build the basis for success in numbers.

The girls sitting in the <u>third</u> <u>row</u> of chairs may sing alone today.
You may choose <u>ten</u> boys to play <u>Ten</u> Little Indians.
Jerry may <u>count</u> the <u>number</u> of boys taking milk today.
Whose chain is the <u>longest</u>?
Which one of you lives the <u>farthest</u> from school?

Place three sizes of chairs in the circle. All the boys stand in the circle. One boy chooses a <u>tall</u> boy, <u>middle-sized</u> boy, and <u>short</u> boy, placing the tallest boy by the <u>tallest</u> chair, the middle-sized boy by the <u>middle-sized</u> chair, and the smallest boy by the <u>smallest</u> chair. When the children play the "Three Bears," this experience is enriched for them also.

Excursions or planned walks in or out of the school building offer excellent opportunity for learning numbers. "Let's <u>count</u> the number of blocks we have walked this morning." "<u>How</u> <u>many</u> robins did you see on our walk?" "I saw <u>two</u> churches this morning." Trips to the grocery store offer the children a chance to acquire concepts of buying and selling and of using money. "We will need <u>twenty-five</u> cents to buy this pumpkin." "<u>How</u> <u>much</u> will it cost to buy a Christmas Tree?"

The five-year-old likes to count. He will count the number of boys present, or the number of girls absent this morning. He may count the number of bottles of milk or the places to be set at the milk lunch time. Unless there is a felt need many kindergarten children have no real understanding of numbers over ten.

Most kindergarten teachers feel that it is too advanced to talk about arithmetic in the kindergarten, but when you realize how much our lives are governed by time and number concepts perhaps these children are not too young to enjoy beginning experiences that enrich their learning through their kindergarten games and experiences.

Children like to learn through play activities and when they are given a task in the form of a game, it does not seem difficult and they quickly learn and have a pleasant experience in doing that which builds the basis for success and happiness in numbers.

There is a new record available to kindergarten teachers called: "Professor Tubbs' School - Number Fun". It may be purchased from the Listen 'N Learn Record Co. , 2002 4th Ave. South, Minneapolis, Minnesota.

- Bouncing a ball a certain number of times while the children count silently and then choosing a child to bounce the ball the same number of times makes a game of counting.

- Different shapes can be drawn on the floor or on black-top playground area such as a circle, diamond, square, oblong. The child bounces the ball once in the circle, twice in the square, three times in the oblong, and four times in the diamond. Then the ball is given to another who attempts to do this also.

- Three circles can be drawn on the floor. In each one a number is placed. The child with the ball chooses a circle and bounces his ball according to the number in that circle. He chooses another child to take his place and points out to him the circle or circles the child is to use.

- The entire group of children enjoy counting together while a child jumps with his jumping rope, or while several children jump with their rope.

- One child may be chosen to bounce the ball. The others close their eyes and listen. He chooses someone to tell how many times the ball was bounced.

Chapter 17

DESIRED DEVELOPMENT DURING THE KINDERGARTEN YEAR

Since we make no attempt to teach any of the 3 R's in the kindergarten, we are doubly concerned with the formation of desirable habits and skills.

These goals are suggestions made by experienced teachers working with children during the various periods of the kindergarten day. *

Although no one child will likely attain all these goals and some may attain only a very few this list includes what teachers felt could be expected, at least in varying degrees before the child enters first grade.

CONVERSATION PERIOD - TELLING TIME

Can tell experiences in detail.
Repeats five to six word sentences.
Has outgrown his baby talk.
Has increased his vocabulary.
Enjoys listening while others take a turn.
Is willing to take his turn and has overcome his shyness.
Is becoming conscious of good organization of ideas when re-telling
    his experiences.
Speaks distinctly, plainly, and correctly.
Does not interrupt others.

ACTIVITY PERIOD - WORK TIME

Knows the location of materials and is able to get them.
Is persistent in finishing a task.
Is neat in his work.
Can work independently.
Is able to do creative work.
Can follow directions well.
Shows increasing skill in the use of scissors, paint, and other mani-
    pulative materials.
Is able to work well with others as well as alone.
Does not waste materials.
Finds something to do when work is finished.
Makes his hands and eyes work together well in cutting.
Learns to value and find joy in his achievements.
Is happy in his work.

MUSIC PERIOD - SONGS

Enjoys singing with group as well as alone.
Can sing a simple song alone.

*These growths are taken from a survey made by the author in her class at Augustana College in 1954.

Has begun to appreciate good music.
Has built up a selection of songs he can sing.
Can match tones fairly well.

RHYTHM PERIOD

Has learned to delight in rhythms and has developed a feeling for them.
Is able to interpret and express the moods of the music.
Knows and feels the difference between loud and soft music, and be-
    tween fast and slow.
Enjoys responding to the music.
Is willing to take this turn and play fair.
Can control the movements of his body as in skipping, running, jump-
    ing, etc.

STORY PERIOD

Is interested in books.
Knows how to care for and handle books.
Asks the meaning of words.
Can anticipate what may happen in a story or poem.
Has learned to listen to a story and not interrupt.
Can retell a story with enjoyment.
Can dramatize a story with imagination.
Likes to and is able to recite at least ten nursery rhymes.
Can remember and retell the events in a story in proper order.

GAME PERIOD

Has developed habits of fair play and sharing.
Joins in active play.
Is able to control his large muscles.
Waits for his turn.
Plays fair.
Is willing to take his turn and likes to see everyone have a chance to
    play.
Is friendly to other children.
Knows how to play several games and can tell the group how to play
    them.
Is willing to obey the rules of the game.

Chapter 18

A TEACHER'S ATTITUDES TOWARD HER PUPILS

1. Be absolutely fair in all your dealing with your children. Do not favor some at the expense of others.

2. Be yourself. Children are quick to sense your real personality.

3. Recognize that each child is different and that each is intelligent and has ability to reason. Do not pump him or ask him foolish questions.

4. Help the child to develop a calm, reasonable manner. This often prevents over-stimulation.

5. Move and speak quietly. Mean what you say.

6. Meet the child on his own level, by understanding of his problems, and not domineering.

7. The child will be better able to help himself if you act as his guide and not as his director.

8. Give the child time to solve his own problems, rather than to step in too often. Avoid unnecessary interference with his work where no physical danger is involved.

9. Try to make the school room a child's world.

Chapter 19

RESOURCES
AND GUIDES

Audio Visual Materials Portfolio. Washington, D.C. Association for Childhood Education International, 1200 Fifteenth St. N.W., 1951.

California Journal of Elementary Education. Kindergarten Issue. Sacramento, California State Department of Education, August 1955.

Kindergarten Teachers Portfolio. Washington, D.C., Association for Childhood Education International, 1200 Fifteenth St. N.W., 1951.

Lewis, Gertrude M. and Babbard, Hazel. Reporting Pupil Progress to
   Parents. Education Brief, Number 34. Washington, D.C., U.S. Office
   of Education, 1956.

Maine State Department of Education. Early Childhood Education Objectives
   and Goals. Augusta, State Department of Education, 1955.

More and Better Schools for Children Under Six Portfolio. Washington, D.C.,
   Association for Childhood Education International, 1200 Fifteenth Street,
   N.W., 1950.

National Council of State Consultants in Elementary Education. Planning
   for America's Children: Education for Children Below Six. Washington,
   D.C.

New Hampshire State Board of Education. What Should the Kindergarten Do
   for the Children? Concord, State Board of Education, Pamphlet No. 178,
   1949.

Bergamini, Yolanda and Swanson, Walter. "Does Kindergarten Make A
   Difference? School Executive, 74:54-5, December 1954.

East, J. K. "Kindergarten Is A Good Investment." School Executive,
   72:52-3, May 1953.

Hooper, Laura. "The Child-The Curriculum-The World of Materials."
   Childhood Education, 51:443-5, May 1955.

Seeds, Corrine. "Dramatic Play As A Means to Dramatic Social Living."
   Childhood Education, 19:218-22, January 1943.

Smith, Hyrum Mack. "Studying the Child in the Kindergarten." National
   Education Association Journal, 45:80-81, February 1956.

Taylor, R. R. "Is The Kindergarten A Learning Situation?" American
   Childhood, 38:23-5, April 1953.

Baltimore, Public Schools. Living and Learning in the Kindergarten. A
   Curriculum Guide for the Baltimore Public Schools, Baltimore, Mary-
   land. Bureau of Publication, Schools Administration Building, September
   1954.

Long Beach Public Schools. A Teacher's Guide for Kindergarten Education.
   Long Beach, California. Office of the County Superintendent of Schools,
   1955.

204

Selected References

BOOKS

Brogan, Peggy and Fox, Lorene K. Helping Children Learn. New York, World Book Company, 1955.

Culkin, Mabel Louise. Teaching the Youngest. New York, The Macmillan Company, 1949.

Gans, Roma, Stendler, Celia Burns and Almy, Millie. Teaching Young Children. New York, World Book Company, 1952.

Havighurst, Robert J. Human Development and Education. New York, Longrans, Green and Company, 19s53.

Gesell, Arnold. Child Development, An Introduction to the Study of Human Growth. New York, Harper and Brothers, 1949.

Hanna, Lavone A., Potter, Gladys L. and Hagaman, Neva. Unit Teaching in the Elementary School. New York, Rinehart and Company, 1956.

Hildredth, Gertrude. Readiness for School Beginners. New York, World Book Company, 1950.

Jenkins, Gladys, Shacter, Helen and Bauer, William W. These are Your Children. Chicago, Scott, Foresman and Company, 1953.

Jersild, Arthur. Child Development and the Curriculum. New York, Bureau of Publications, Teachers College, Columbia University, 1956.

Leonard, Edith M., Van Deman, Dorothy D. and Miles, Lillian E. Couseling with Parents in Early Childhood Education. New York, The Macmillan Company, 1954.

Lowenfield, Viktor. Creative and Mental Growth. New York, The Macmillan Company, 1952.

Monroe, Marion. Growing into Reading. Chicago, Scott, Foresman and Company, 1951.

National Society for the Study of Education. Early Childhood Education. The Forty-Sixth Yearbook of the National Society for the Study of Education. Chicago, University of Chicago Press, 1947.

Sheehy, Emma. The Fives and Sixes Go To School. New York, Henry Holt and Company, 1954.

Stephans, Ada Dawson. Providing Developmental Experiences for Young Children. New York, Bureau of Publications, Teachers College, Columbia University, 1952.

Wills, Clarice and Stegeman, William. Living in the Kindergarten. Chicago, Follett Publishing Company, Revised 1957.

FILMS

Brandon Films, Inc., 105 East 106th Street, New York 29, New York.
    Passion for Life.

California State Department of Education, Sacramento, California, with recording film strip.
    A Good Day in the Kindergarten.

McGraw Hill Book Company, Text Films Department, 330 West 42nd Street, New York 36, New York.

  The Terrible Two's and Trusting Three's.
  The Frustrating Fours and Fascinating Fives.
  From Sociable Six to Noisy Nine.
  Curriculum Based on Child Development.
  Child Growth and Development Series.
      Principles of Development
      Children's Emotions
      Social Development
      Play
  He Acts His Age.

National Education Association, 1201 Sixteenth Street N. W. , Washington, D. C.

  Skippy and the Three R's.

New York University Film Library, 26 Washington Place, New York 3, New York.

  Studies of Normal Personality Development.
  Understanding Children's Play.

State University of Iowa, Bureau of Visual Instruction, Iowa City, Iowa.

  Bulletin Boards for Effective Teaching.

Teachers College, Columbia University, 525 West 120th Street, New York 27, New York.

  A Day in the Life of a Five-Year-Old.

MAGAZINES

American Childhood Magazine is the only educational journal published exclusively for Primary Teachers .... Kindergarten through Grade 4. It offers a wealth of practical information and projects covering all phases of primary education.

1 Year --- $4. 00   2 Years --- $7. 00   3 Years --- $10. 00

Springfield 2, Massachusetts